The Modern Nations in
Historical Perspective

ROBIN W. WINKS, *General Editor*

The volumes in this series deal with individual nations or groups of closely related nations throughout the world, summarizing the chief historical trends and influences that have contributed to each nation's present-day character, problems, and behavior. Recent data are incorporated with established historical background to achieve a fresh synthesis and original interpretation.

YAHYA ARMAJANI, *author of this volume, is Professor of History at Macalester College and a past president of the Midwest Conference on Asian Affairs and of the Upper Midwest History Society. Persian-born and fluent in Persian, Turkish, and Arabic, Dr. Armajani has traveled extensively throughout the Middle East; he is the author of* Middle East Past and Present (*Prentice-Hall*), Adult Guide to the Middle East, *a* Descriptive Catalogue of Persian and Turkish Mss., *and numerous articles on Iran and the Middle East for English and Persian publications.*

ALSO IN THE AFRICAN–NEAR EASTERN SUBSERIES

Central Africa: The Former British States *by Lewis H. Gann*
Egypt & the Sudan *by Robert O. Collins & Robert L. Tignor*
Morocco, Algeria, Tunisia *by Richard M. Brace*
Nigeria & Ghana *by John E. Flint*
Portuguese Africa *by Ronald H. Chilcote*
Turkey *by Roderic H. Davison*
West Africa: The Former French States
by John D. Hargreaves

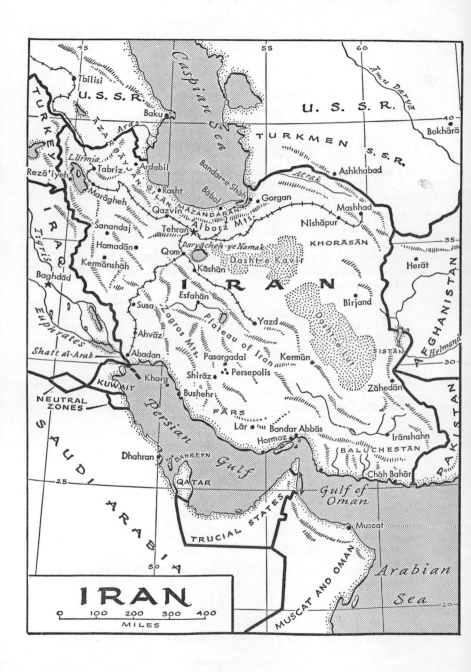

IRAN

0   100   200   300   400

MILES

The Modern Nations in Historical Perspective

IRAN

Yahya Armajani

PRENTICE-HALL, INC.   A SPECTRUM BOOK   *Englewood Cliffs, New Jersey*

10   9   8   7   6   5   4   3   2   1

PRENTICE-HALL INTERNATIONAL, INC. (*London*)
PRENTICE-HALL OF AUSTRALIA, PTY. LTD. (*Sydney*)
PRENTICE-HALL OF CANADA, LTD. (*Toronto*)
PRENTICE-HALL OF INDIA PRIVATE LIMITED (*New Delhi*)
PRENTICE-HALL OF JAPAN, INC. (*Tokyo*)

Contents

Preface

Anyone who has had experience in public speaking knows that it is much harder to make a fifteen-minute speech in a quarter of an hour than it is to make it in an hour. By the same token, it is almost impossible to make a one-hour speech in five minutes. To write the history of Iran, with such a rich and varied past from the beginning until present, in a small volume is like asking a man to compress a one-hour speech into five minutes. In order to do this I have tried to deal with the problems of Persian history rather than bother with strict chronology and to be interpretive rather than merely detailed. In the attempt to compress so much I have had to be very selective and to make generalizations. In all this I have opened myself to criticism, but I hope that I have been able to give the reader a fair picture of Iran.

In addition to my indebtedness to those acknowledged in the footnotes, I am especially indebted to the reader of the manuscript chosen by Prentice-Hall, but unknown to me, for his many useful criticisms. My thanks also to Dr. Mohamad Moghadam, Assistant Minister of Higher Education in Iran, for reading sections of the book and especially for the insight I gained in our extended discussions on the problems of Persian history and culture. My genial host in Tehran, Mr. Mahmud Divsheli, a student of Islamic law, was kind enough to discuss with me all points in this book pertaining to Islam.

For obvious reasons, writing the first chapter on contemporary Iran was the hardest. In addition to the persons named above, Dr. Mahmud Ziyāyi, a member of Iranian Parliament, and Dr. Richard Arndt, until recently the American Cultural Attaché in Iran, as well as Mr. Khosrow Riggi of the University of Minnesota and Mr. Gholam Vatandoost, a graduate student at the University of Washington, were kind enough to read the first chapter and share with me their knowledge and opinions of contemporary Iran from their very different vantage points. The contents of this book have been modified as a result of my recent visit to Iran. Needless to say I assume full responsibility for all mistakes as well as for interpretations and conclusions.

The system of transliteration in this book is based on the simple premise that Persian is an independent language and, like other languages, adapts borrowed words to fit its peculiar needs. Unfortunately, it is necessary to make this very obvious statement because there are many scholars who ignore this fact. Because Persians have adopted the Arabic alphabet and have borrowed many Arabic words, these scholars, who should know better, insist that the Persians should change the pronunciation of their own language to conform to particular qualities of the Arabic letters. This is pointless. When Persians adopted the Arabic alphabet they added four new signs that do not exist in Arabic: *p*, *ch* (as in chain), *zh* (as in measure), and *g*. They also changed the qualities of other letters, especially the vowels, to represent special sounds in Persian. If the reader studies the simple table below he will have no difficulty in pronouncing words and names as the Persians do.

i is always long, as in "cheer"
u is always long, as in "shoot"
ā is always long, as in "all"
a is always short, as in "hat"
e is pronounced, even at the end, as in "pet"
o is pronounced as in "for," except in two names, *Ferdosi* and *Dolat*, where it is pronounced as in "boat"
ey (or sometimes *ay*) is pronounced as in "may"
For the Arabic *hamza* and *ayn* I have used an apostrophe.

My special thanks to my secretary, Nancy Nielsen Benish, for the typing of the manuscript, which was made harder by my absence. I have come to admire the industry and patience of Mrs. Marjorie Streeter, production editor at Prentice-Hall, and her staff and the important part they have had in the publication of this book. My gratitude to my wife, who not only created the atmosphere in which writing was pleasant but also read the whole book and offered criticism.

YAHYA ARMAJANI

St. Paul, Minnesota

FOR NURENE AND BABAK

May Ahura Mazda protect this
country from a [hostile] army,
from famine, from the Lie!
Upon this country may there not
come an army, nor famine, nor
the Lie.   —*Darius I*

1

Contemporary Iran

On October 26, 1967, His Imperial Majesty Mohammad Reza Shah Pahlavi *Aryamehr*[1] was crowned *Shahanshah* of Iran. This impressive ceremony was unique in one aspect and unusual in another. It was unique because an empress was crowned for the first time in many centuries (the last queen to be crowned in Iran was Azarmidokht in A.D. 632, a few years before the Arab conquest). It was unusual in that the coronation ceremony was long overdue. The Shah took the oath of office as king on September 25, 1941, and was crowned twenty-six years later. Indeed many observers assumed that in an age when the institution of monarchy had been shaken to its foundations and king after king had fallen in the twentieth century, the kingdom of Iran would also disappear. With succeeding crises the prophecy of doom seemed more plausible.

In 1941 the country was occupied, after a brief skirmish, by British and Russian troops. That these two powers divided the country into two spheres of influence in much the same way as they had done in 1907 did not bode well. The fact that the ambassadors of the occupying powers did not even attend the swearing-in ceremony of the young Shah looked ominous.

Before the end of the Second World War it became apparent that the Soviet Union would not keep its promise of withdrawing its troops. Under the protection of the Red Army, Āzarbāyjān, one of the richest provinces of Iran, started a separatist movement and organized an

---

1. It means "sun of the Aryans." This title was bestowed upon him by the Persian parliament.

autonomous government. The nearby Kurds, probably encouraged by the Red Army, announced their independence. Iran had the dubious honor of being the first "problem" on the agenda of the then fledgling United Nations.

No sooner had the Soviet troops withdrawn and the separatist leaders scattered throughout the communist world than the oil nationalization issue under the leadership of Dr. Mohammad Mosaddeq plunged the country into a bitter civil strife. The climax came when tanks of the opposing sides were rumbling in the streets of Tehran. The Shah and the Queen left the country on August 19, 1953 in the twin-engined private plane piloted by the Shah himself. They flew to Baghdad and then to Rome. "It had been decided weeks before," writes His Majesty, "that if Mossadegh should use force to resist his deposition, we would temporarily leave the country. I had decided upon this move because I believed that it would force Mossadegh and his henchmen to show their real allegiances, and that thereby it would help crystallize Persian public opinion. Thus, while I was absent from the scene we would in effect have a real referendum—one in which dead people would not vote." [2]

But world opinion at the time, unaware of the prearranged plan, believed (and some still believe) that the Shah had been forced to flee and the monarchy had come to an end. The day he left, organized mobs in Tehran were yelling "down with the Shah" and destroying the royal monuments in the city. Indeed, the Persian ambassador in Iraq tried to have the Shah arrested in Baghdad and the Persian chargé d'affaires in Rome refused to give the Shah the latter's own car keys.[3] But the Shah returned in triumph only three days after his departure. In its long and tumultuous history, Iran had weathered many a storm and had survived. Once again Iran showed that it had not lost its resilience. It had bounced back and the Shah had bounced back with it.

No sovereign had been so deeply and personally involved in the crisis of a country as had Mohammad Reza Shah in the struggle for survival. As in 1967 he crowned himself Shahanshah of Iran, he and many of the onlookers must have thought of the fact that, during the twenty-six years since his ascension to the throne, at least five attempts had been made against his life. Each time he had miraculously escaped assassination. It is easy for a disinterested outsider to dismiss these incidents as routine for any head of state. But it can never be routine for the object of those attempts.

These incidents have created in the Shah a feeling of resignation in facing danger; he has said, "I never know whether the next glass of water I drink will be my last." It has also strengthened a sense of mis-

---

2. H.I.M. Mohammad Reza Shah Pahlavi, *Mission for My Country* (New York: McGraw-Hill, 1961), p. 104.

3. Ibid., p. 105.

sion in him. He has dwelt on the proposition that "I must be here for something." [4] No doubt he must feel that as heir to the throne of Cyrus he too is the beneficiary of the blessings of God who had taken Cyrus "His anointed by the hand to subdue nations before him and undo the might of kings; before whom gates shall be opened and no doors be shut: I will go before you and level the swelling hills; I will break down gates of bronze and hack through iron bars. . . ." [5] This mystical relationship between the king and the people on the one hand and between the king and his job on the other is constantly present in the mind of the Shah and is therefore an important key to the understanding of Iran today.

The coronation which almost failed to materialize took place long after the Shah took the oath of office. The delay had many causes, among them the numerous national and personal crises which have been mentioned and perhaps also the fact that there was no male heir to the throne. But in addition to these reasons there may perhaps have been a psychological reason for postponing the coronation all those years. The Shah has been reported to have said repeatedly that he did not find any glory in being king over millions of poverty-stricken and disease-ridden people. At the age of twenty-two, when he was being driven to the Persian parliament, or the Majles as it is known, to take the oath of office as Shah, he recalled feeling "enthusiasm for the Crown among the people in the streets, and it gave me not only personal courage, but a determination to resist and to continue the kingship." [6] He has considered himself a "revolutionary operating from the throne," and has set for himself the goal of building a "government that is based on democratic practice at the bottom." His purpose was to break up "the old system—anything that had a feudalistic character." [7]

In 1941 the young Shah inherited the throne. For twelve years he reigned as a constitutional monarch, but he discovered that democracy could not work without democrats. There was no willingness to compromise and those who demanded democracy often wanted their own forms of autocracy. In 1953 he returned to Iran with a resolve to rule. It is reasonable to assume that with this new resolve he had also developed a program. He probably decided that he would not seek the crown until such a time as he had a viable program under way and had earned it. Whether by 1967 he had earned the crown is a question that will be answered by future historians. Contemporary Iran, however, has taken its direction from the attempt of the Shah to earn his crown.

Every aspect of the life of Iran has been influenced by the guiding policies of the Shah. To be sure, he is not alone either in conceiving

4. E. A. Bayne, *Persian Kingship in Transition* (New York: American University Field Staff, 1968), p. 38.
5. Isaiah, 45:1,2.
6. *Mission for My Country*, p. 123.
7. Ibid., p. 133.

them or in working them out. A new class of able and educated young men and women has emerged who give reality to the hopes and policies of the Shah. Nor could all the achievements of the second half of the twentieth century have been possible without the foundations prepared by almost a century of effort by reformers before him. But, on the whole, it has been his responsibility and his show.

What is going on in contemporary Iran has been named the "White Revolution," in contrast to the past and present revolutions in other parts of the world and also in Iran, which have usually been bloody. This is not to say the way has always been lined with white roses, but by comparison it has been bloodless, a revolution by decree, a real attempt to turn an ancient despotism and its subjects into a modern country and a socially just nation. It has been a genuine revolution, if more social and economic than political, for it has penetrated every fibre of the life of the people and has made response to the challenges facing the country. These challenges include man versus the land; modernization versus traditionalism; secularism versus religion; the settled versus the nomad; and the village versus the city.

Man versus the Land

The geography of Iran has always presented its inhabitants with two realities, one is in the topography of the land itself and the other is in its location. A traveler approaching Iran either by air or by land is impressed by massive surrounding mountains and border deserts. It is not necessary here to go into a detailed description of the land and climate of Iran, but suffice it to say that the one characteristic that fits the 628,-000 square miles that constitute the country is aridity. The Caspian littoral with its annual rainfall of sixty inches is the obvious exception, but the rest of the country is high and dry. Indeed between the two massive mountain ranges, the Alborz from the northwest continuing along the north and the Zagros also from the northwest extending south and southeast, lies the plateau of Iran, which has within it two uninhabitable deserts, the Kavir and the Lut.

Throughout the centuries, the Persians have responded to this natural challenge. The response has not been merely to eke out a bare subsistence from an inhospitable land but rather to build empires and to develop a culture which transcended Iran's boundaries. They built dams on the few rivers in the country and constructed cisterns and viaducts. A unique Persian method, however, has been the construction of *qanāts*, underground conduits which bring water for scores of miles from the mountains to the plains. It goes without saying that whenever the Persians have failed to respond to this constant challenge and have allowed the dams to be neglected and the *qanāts* to be clogged, it has invariably meant economic as well as cultural and political stagnation.

Flying over Iran one can readily see the countryside dotted with thousands of what look like ant hills that show that the *qanāt* system is still operative. But the face of the land has been changed most by the modern dams, which provide water for irrigation, which in turn has changed the barren desert into a productive farm. They also generate electric power for industry and private use. Dams already completed or under construction, such as Dez, Kārun, Karaj, Aras, Sefidrud, Kuhrang, and others, and the six more under consideration will put one million hectares of land under cultivation.[8]

In addition to the dams the face of the land has been cut by a network of highways, railroads, oil and gas pipe lines, all of which help raise the standard of living and, hopefully, the quality of life and culture of the people. Only can one hope that the planners and engineers will not emulate the reckless destruction wrought by the people of Europe and the United States and instead will conserve the health and beauty of the land. The extensive forestation program being carried out at present is a large step in the right direction.

Another geographical reality is the location of Iran athwart the line of communication between Asia and Europe. Culturally speaking, the West ends in Iran, and the East begins there. This is a privileged position, but has its disadvantages also. Iran shares indirectly in the problems of East Asia and Europe and more directly in the vicissitudes of the Middle East, Russia, Central Asia, and the Indian subcontinent. The religion and social values of Iran are a merging of East and West into a new culture which in turn has influenced both the East and the West.

The three main routes of the ancient world passed through Iran. The northern route, commonly known as the silk road, connected China and Central Asia with Asia Minor and Europe by passing through Ray (ancient Rhages) and Tabriz. The central route passed through Ray and the Levant, and the southern route used the waterways of the Persian Gulf and the Arabian Sea. Over these routes flowed commerce and wealth. But conquerors also have used these routes and have attacked Iran from east, west, north, and south. As late as the Second World War, Iran was called the "bridge of victory," over which lend-lease material went to the Soviet Union. Though Iran is part of the Middle East, it cannot be separated from the life and destiny of the rest of Asia, or even of Europe.

MODERNIZATION VERSUS TRADITIONALISM

Among developing countries economic advance is considered a cardinal point in the process of modernization and industrial development is believed to be the backbone of economic growth. Reza Shah paid

8. *Statistical Yearbook*, Plan Organization, no. 287, Tehran, June, 1971, p. 43.

more attention to industrialization than to any other sector of the economy. In contemporary Iran, however, all aspects of life, as well as the economy, are emphasized. We have discussed the human element in the agricultural life of the country. Hand in hand with land reform there have been significant attempts to enable the farmer to become economically independent.[9] By 1968 the Shahpur plant produced 130,000 tons of chemical fertilizer annually, and there were upward of 18,000 tractors in operation. There were more than 7,500 cooperatives serving 1,130,000 families in 18,800 villages. These cooperatives engage in production as well as marketing and purchasing. The establishment of agricultural banks has freed the peasant from the clutches of the money lender.

The economic life of the country has been projected in development plans. Dr. Issawi reports that as a result of the Third Plan (1965–1968), "Iran now has an infrastructure capable of carrying a modern economy." In 1967 the rate of growth was over 10 percent and by 1970 a growth of 12 percent was reported.[10] The Fourth Plan, which started in 1968, will eventually invest $11 billion in agriculture, industry, and construction and other sectors of national life. By 1969 annual income per capita had grown from less than $100 before the Second World War to over $300.

Railways and roads have been extended, ports have been expanded, and airports have been built. By 1967 the annual per capita use of electricity had risen to 150 kilowatt-hours from only 12 in 1948. During this time there was upwards of $693 million of investment in housing, transport, and trade. Food processing, textiles, assembly plants for radios, cars, buses, and many other products are part of the developing industries of the country.

Capital for this vast development has come from two main sources. One of them is through loans and commercial agreements with foreign countries. The main contributor in loans and investments has been the United States. But in recent years Iran has had commercial agreements with other countries, including the countries of the Soviet bloc. The Soviet Union, for example, is building a steel mill outside Esfahan in return for natural gas from Iran.

The other source of capital is, of course, oil. In cooperation with different oil companies of the world, the National Iranian Oil Company has expanded the oil fields on the mainland as well as opening offshore fields in the Persian Gulf. The island of Kharg has become an important center from whose modern docks supertankers load crude oil for the markets of the world. The *Etela'at* (air edition) of July 16, 1970, reported that "during the previous two months period, in produc-

9. In this discussion of economic growth, I draw heavily on Charles Issawi, "Iran's Economic Upsurge," *Middle East Journal*, Vol. 21, no. 4 (Autumn, 1967), pp. 447–61.

10. *Etela'at* (air edition), April 22, 1970.

tion and export of crude oil, Iran has attained third place in the world and has gone ahead of Venezuela which for many years occupied the third place."

Anyone visiting Iran is impressed by its economic prosperity. Nevertheless, there is still poverty in the land and occasional beggars are still seen in the streets of cities, which fact shows that it will take some time before the general increase in gross national product reaches all the segments of society. The rich are getting richer, and enterprising young men returning from the West are creating wealth for themselves. But it would seem that the poor are not getting poorer and neither are they standing still. There is every indication that they are also benefiting and it is hoped that, with the general health, social security, education, and other programs which have been inaugurated, a degree of equality in the distribution of national wealth will be achieved. The danger, however, is the pressure of centralization, which has the tendency to channel economic power into a small circle and thereby prevent the benefits from reaching others.

The process of modernization and the encounter with the West has a human element even more important than its economic or industrial counterparts. The person who has given up the camel for the car, or the oxen for the tractor, or the kerosene lamp for the electric light has already changed his mode of living and sooner or later is bound to change his attitude. This kind of change has been going on in Iran for the past fifty years at an accelerating rate.

The foremost means of implementation for a meaningful program of modernization is education. Quantitatively there has been amazing progress. The preuniversity school population has more than doubled since 1960. In 1971 there were 72,000 students in institutions of higher learning in Iran, more than 15,000 of them women. There were 40,000 Persian students in thirty-six countries. Forty-one percent were in the United States; only eleven students were in the Soviet Union.[11] There has been, of course, the tremendous problem of the "brain drain," but there is also a steady returnee flow. Among those who do return, however, there is a "piling up of professional man power in the one or two largest cities, with consequent underemployment of some skills (notably medicine) and chronic difficulty in getting educated people to live and work in the provinces." [12]

Mostly because of education, and especially as a result of the conscious attempt by the government, women have been given an important share in the social, economic, and political life of the country. The crowning of the empress was the culmination of one of the most important and drastic changes in the social structure of Iran. Reza Shah (1925–1941) had ordered the unveiling of women in 1936; but at his

11. Ibid., January 4, 1970.
12. George Baldwin, "Brain Drain or Overflow?" *Foreign Affairs*, Vol. 48, no. 2 (January, 1970), p. 366.

abdication in 1941 things had reverted to the old pattern, and the new Shah had to start all over again. As late as June, 1963, there were bloody riots in Tehran, Esfahan, Shiraz and other cities over the freedom of women and other reforms. The combination of reactionary clergy and landlords could not stem the tide nor withstand the pressure exerted by the Shah and his government. Lest anyone think that the coronation of the empress was only a hollow ceremony, a few weeks before (September, 1967) the constitution was amended to make the queen the official regent in case of the demise of the king and the minority of the crown prince.

There are women senators, deputies of the Majles, lawyers, educators, and heads of administrative departments. There is one woman in the cabinet. Literacy and health corps, which were originally devised for men as an alternative to military service, have been extended to include women. The services of these young people and the presence of educated young women serving in the villages has a tremendous effect on the life and attitude of the villagers.

Modernization has affected literature, art, and music. In any process of modernization the first steps are almost always imitative. In literature and art, in which Iran has had a distinguished past, the imitative phase seems to have been short. The reform of Persian literature that started during the turn of the twentieth century has continued to the present.[13] After the Second World War the brightest luminary of Persian letters was Sādeq Hedāyat, whose tragic death by suicide in 1951 put an end to a young and promising life. From 1930 until his death he produced over thirty volumes on fiction, drama, social criticism, travel, folklore, ancient Persian culture, and other topics. Throughout, he shows a sensitivity, depth, vitality, and ecumenicity seldom seen anywhere.[14] Part of this tradition is being carried on by a number of young contemporary writers such as Sādeq Chubak, Jalāl Āl-e Ahmad, and others.

The "new poetry" and the "new art" of Iran show both originality and specific Persian characteristics. Art and music are under the direct patronage of Her Majesty the Empress Farah. The Art Festivals of Shiraz are becoming world famous. In the beautiful Rudaki Hall in Tehran, western opera is performed by Persian singers, and once in a while purely Persian music and folk dances are presented. In music, however, which remained practically dormant during the Islamic period, the imitative phase seems to be at its height. Cinema is still in its infancy and most of the programs on the increasing number of television stations in Iran are imports from the United States. Now and then, however, imaginative pictures and programs are presented on both the screen and television.

13. See below, chapters 7 and 8.
14. For a detailed discussion of Hedayat, see H. Kamshad, *Modern Persian Prose Literature* (Cambridge University Press, 1966), pp. 137–208.

One of the most curious aspects of modernization concerns the Persian language. During Reza Shah's time an academy was established for the express purpose of replacing Arabic and other foreign words with Persian and devising new Persian words for objects and concepts imported from Europe. Many Persian words in common use today are from this period. Between 1960 and 1970 the Persian language was swamped with foreign words, especially from the United States. Every summer, when hundreds of students go home from abroad for visits, the general complaint is that these young people have forgotten their mother tongue and mix in foreign words in their speech. But this practice is not the monopoly of young people educated abroad. In one four-page newspaper alone I found no fewer than fifteen foreign words, for at least eight of which there are Persian words that were in common use a decade ago. The amazing phenomenon, which is a paradox of nationalism, is the fact that stores, restaurants, cinemas, and so forth with foreign names attract more customers at higher prices than do those with Persian names. Indeed, a first-class guest house is called a *hotel,* while a third-class one goes by the Persian word, *mehmānkhāneh.*

A number of Persians and most of the foreign observers of Iran believe that unless there is social and institutional change there cannot be real development and modernization. In other words they seem to be saying that unless the Persians adopt the cultural, social, and spiritual foundations of the West they will not be able to use the physical and economic aspects of Western civilization to good advantage. One of the most recent observers, Professor Norman Jacobs, believes that since Persians have not accepted, understood, or absorbed the social and cultural foundations of the West that they therefore interpret economic development as "A scheme to get rich quick . . . ," "A proliferation of Western gadgets . . . ," "A system synonymous with political prestige . . . ," "A system synonymous with social prestige . . . ," "A means to insure political control over the population." [15]

Aside from the fact that such a cynical interpretation can also be found in the West, the crucial question is how can a nation, especially with the modern means of communication, wait to change culturally or spiritually before it adopts the fruits of Western civilization? This becomes especially confusing because the West is also hopelessly confused. The narrow empiricism of the West which measures development and modernization by statistical studies and the rate of growth of the gross national product is often misleading because it does not stress the importance of social and human criteria.

Another keen observer of Iran, this time a Persian, Professor Amin Banani,[16] in examining the moral and humanitarian idealism of the

15. Norman Jacobs, *The Sociology of Development, Iran as an Asian Case Study* (New York: Praeger, 1966), chapters 3 and 12, passim.
16. *The Modernization of Iran, 1921–1941* (Stanford University Press, 1961), pp. 147 ff.

West states that it is either based on Christianity or on the "foundations of anthropocentric thought in the West, be they eighteenth-century nationalism, nineteenth-century positivism, Marxist socialism, or twentieth-century scientism." If it is Christianity, then Islam belongs to the same tree and has always dreamed of establishing a "City of God," as has Christianity. But if the source is the materialistic trends of the West, then one cannot "resist the allure of one form or another of Marxist socialism, combining as it does the pseudo-scientific, rationalistic approach, the humane message of justice and equality, and the massive sanction of half the world."

Professor Banani rejects the secularism of the latter and opts for the spiritual values of the former but "sees both Christianity and Islam powerless to combat the evil and iniquity that he finds on every side." Putting Christianity and Islam in the same boat, as it were, he states that "What is needed is nothing short of a rebirth of the spiritual values that once animated both the East and the West."

RELIGION VERSUS SECULARISM

It is almost impossible to define religion in terms satisfactory to those who are religious; this is also true in defining secularism. There are varieties of religious beliefs and expressions, and there are numerous patterns of secularism. There are secularists who are antireligion; there are those who are religious but are anticlerical; and there are secularists who are neither antireligion nor anticlerical: they just do not think that religion is relevant and worth bothering about. When such a discussion is held in the context of Islam, the religion of 98 percent of the people of Iran, it is rather confusing because Islam as a religion does not distinguish between the "religious" and the "secular," and does not separate the mosque from the state. The first mosque in Islam was not only the place of worship but also the seat of government, the court of law, and the headquarters for the armed forces. Correspondingly, the Prophet and the early caliphs were not only the leaders in worship but they were heads of state, justices in court, and commanders in the armed forces.

With such a background the world of Islam should not have the problem of secularism versus religion. But in modern times at least one country, Turkey, has officially separated religion from the state; and while most of the others, including Iran, have not been so drastic as to announce it publicly, they have nevertheless discarded the Islamic *Shari'a* (law) just as effectively as Turkey. It is perhaps a truism to state that vis-à-vis the modern nationalistic state and the scientific civilization, Islam is going through the same type of struggle that Christianity went through in the eighteenth and nineteenth centuries. Very likely the fact that the religiosecular laws of Islam drawn up in the seventh and eighth centuries are binding in the twentieth century makes the problem of adjustment more difficult. Furthermore, hundreds of Persian students returning after some years of study in Europe and America have been influenced by the anti-institutional sentiments of youth and especially the opposition to organized religion.

If one accepts the statement that Islam is basically theocratic, then certainly the Shi'a branch of Islam, which is the state religion of Iran, is even more theocratic. In Shi'ism the Imams, the direct descendants of the Prophet through his daughter Fātemeh and Ali, and especially the twelfth Imam, Mehdi, who is hidden but shall reappear, are the true rulers of the world. All heads of state must rule in the name of the hidden Imam or else they are "usurpers."

The early rulers of the Safavid dynasty (1580–1736) which was responsible for establishing Shi'ism in Iran, claimed to be the "supreme guide" and themselves the spokesmen for the hidden Imam. When their power waned the leaders of the Shi'a clergy posed as spokesmen and issued authoritative pronouncements, *fatva*, on religious, political, social, and moral subjects. The history of Iran in the past two hundred years has been partially the story of the increasing influence of the clergy. A number of these, especially during the constitutional struggle at the turn of the twentieth century, were liberal; but on the whole they have been rigidly reactionary and have withstood change.

There are certain beliefs and practices, however, which make Shi'ism somewhat more flexible than it seems. One of these is the belief in *ejtehād*, that is, the ability of certain leaders of the clergy to interpret and pronounce independent judgment in the name of Imam. Such a person is called *mojtahed*. Inasmuch as there is no hierarchy, a mojtahed reaches this high office not by a system of appointment but by unofficial common consent and by virtue of his piety and learning. Consequently there may be four or five mojtaheds at any given time. It is possible in such a situation, as has happened many times, that these mojtaheds do not agree in their interpretation of the law and issue contradicting opinions. For example, the mojtaheds were on both sides of the constitutional struggle and the chief mojtahed who was against the constitution was executed when the liberals came to power. The same division occurred in 1963 with the freedom of women and land reform. One of the mojtaheds who was against these reforms was forced into exile and a second one into retirement. It is possible for a shrewd leader or political party to carry out drastic change with the help of some of the mojtaheds and still be within the religious laws.

Another reason why change is possible within the framework of religion in Iran is because Shi'ism itself is speculative, given to mysticism, and believes in saviors and saints. Even though Islamic mysticism, Sufism, has not by any means been a monopoly of Persians or Shi'is, nevertheless it has been called the "supreme manifestation of the Persian mind in the religious sphere." [17] Most Persian poetry is full of mystic allusions that suggest that the inner light is more important than the law, which is described as the "shell." Once the shell is broken and the kernel is taken out, one is apt to become somewhat careless about the care of the shell.[18] At best, the shell is kept around for the sake of appearances very much like the Bible in the United States, which has been described as the "least read best seller."

In the context of this brief discussion it is safe to say that the "secularists" in contemporary Iran are divided into two large categories. One group, for various reasons, is content to keep the appearances whenever necessary. They may be avowed atheists who do not care to express their views; they may be persons who do not find any kind of religion relevant in the modern world but are not against it either; or they may be religious mystics who believe the essence of religion is not the law, Shari'a, but the inner light. Perhaps the vast majority in this group is with those who, though not antireligious, believe that Islam has proven impotent in the face of modern problems and do not expect eighth-century laws to be applicable to twentieth-century conditions. Consequently they ignore religion and, more often, substitute nationalism and loyalty to the state as the cohesive force. If, however, religion could be brought to serve nationalism they would avail themselves of it. Perhaps Reza Shah belonged to this group.

The second category of secularists are basically anticlerical. They believe that a moral and spiritual foundation is necessary for every society. They are convinced that the moral and spiritual degeneration of Iran began with the disintegration of the Safavid dynasty "when inept monarchs chose to share their power with the assembly of Shi'a divines, the stranglehold of the clergy has paralyzed every source of cultural vitality and intellectual vigor in Iran." [19] They feel that it is possible to reinterpret the laws of the Koran to fit modern conditions, and to revive the social spirit of Islam. The Shah of Iran, who may belong to this group, has said that he wants "to rebuild the faith in the way the Prophet really meant the religion to be." [20] Conservative Islam is a constant threat from the right, and the government has no inclination to let it rear its ugly head. Perhaps this is the reason for the Shah's statement that "Iran *needs* religion, but we should modernize it with more schools and regularized salaries," [21] that is, for the clergy.

A word must also be said about the vast majority of the Persians, namely the peasants, who follow the folk religion of Islam, which is

17. G. M. Wickens, "Religion," in A. J. Arberry, ed., *The Legacy of Persia* (Oxford University Press, 1953), p. 158.
18. Rumi, a famous Sufi poet, has said, "We have taken the kernel out of the Koran and have left the shell for the asses."
19. Banani, *Modernization of Iran*, p. 156.
20. Bayne, *Persian Kingship*, p. 50.
21. Ibid., p. 53.

only beginning to be affected by development and modernization. As they sit on the tractor rather than walk behind a plow; as they learn to read; as they discuss their problems in cooperatives; and as they listen to corpsmen and -women rather than to the mollahs, there is no telling what kind of folk religion will evolve. The Shi'i villager has not been so much concerned about the Shari'a. He has been more interested in the lives and deeds of the saints than in the laws of the Prophet. The Shi'i villager, like his Roman Catholic counterpart, invokes the names of the saints more than he does of God or the Prophet. In time, as has happened in the history of religion, there will be new saints with modern ideas together with the old saints who have changed their practices to fit modern times.

THE SETTLED VERSUS THE NOMADS

"The life in Iran is dominated above all by the disparity between the nomadic peoples and those who are settled—between the shifting habitat of the former and the permanent homes of the latter." [22]

"Throughout history the steppe and the sown have existed side by side in Iran, with little understanding or appreciation of one by the other." [23]

The above statements explain the problem faced by the leaders of Persian society especially in the twentieth century. Interestingly enough, nomadism is comparatively recent in the long history of Iran. In ancient times there were more settled areas than in more recent years. Apparently there were very few nomads when Herodotus was writing his history. They made up only one-tenth of the army of Xerxes. Present nomadic life goes back to the advance of the Arab bedouins from the southwest and of the Turks and Mongols from the northeast. These invaders not only destroyed most of the settled areas of the country but continued their way of life in the isolated mountains of Iran. Among today's nomads, for example, the Qashqā'i tribe came into being in 1415 and the Bakhtyari tribe was formed in the seventeenth century. The Khamseh was a confederation created by the merchants of Shiraz in the nineteenth century to protect the caravan route.[24]

The tribes probably form about one-sixth of the population, and they migrate between the mountains and the lowlands every year in search of grass for their flocks. They are governed by a leader, usually hereditary, who is called "khan." They are almost self-sufficient; and

22. X. DePlanhol, "Geography of Settlement," in W. B. Fisher, ed., *The Land of Iran* (Cambridge University Press, 1968), p. 409.
23. Richard N. Frye, *The Heritage of Persia* (New York: World Publishing Company, 1963), p. 14.
24. For information on the population of Iran, this account draws heavily on W. B. Fisher, ed., *The Land of Iran*.

to acquire the few necessities they cannot produce, they sell or barter sheep, milk, butter, cheese, and wool to or with the townsmen. Whenever the central government has not been strong enough, the tribes have looted the towns and villages in their path and have destroyed farms and orchards. The tribesmen's loyalty is to the tribe rather than to the central government. Naturally they do not want to understand such modern concepts as income tax, parliaments, military service, or national frontiers. In the past the tribes were allowed to have their own organization and in return pay tribute and supply the ruler with troops when needed. But in these days of national budgets, national armies, and national education, the tribes are fighting a losing battle.

Reza Shah's program of nationalism and centralized government could not allow the separatist proclivities of the tribes. He tried to force them to settle and transported each tribe to a different region of the country. Their leaders were imprisoned and their sons were kept as hostages in the capital city. Reza Shah's program was not altogether successful. What little success his program did enjoy was not brought about by force but by the building of the trans-Persian railroad, which opened the tribal preserves to the public; by military conscription, which made the tribal youths mingle with the youth of the rest of the country; and by education, which helped give the tribal youth a new vision and opened their eyes to new opportunities.

During the Second World War when Reza Shah had to abdicate the throne, most of the tribes reverted to their old ways and some of them, such as the Qashqā'is rose in open rebellion. But now the government does not have to force the settlement of the tribes. It is depending rather on the efficacy of roads, dams, and education. The men and women of education and health corps, whose job it is to organize schools and health centers in the rural districts, hold their classes in the open air and travel with the tribes. Perhaps the tribes will not disappear in their entirety, for neither the habit of annual migration nor tribal values are against citizenship in a modern state. But given modern developments, two things are bound to occur. The first is that the tribal organization will no longer be able to satisfy the increasing expectations of life that modernization will create. The second is that even though values may not change, certainly priorities will, and the inevitable result will be the disappearance of the nomadic way of life. The extensive system of elementary education among the tribes, headed by Mr. Mohammad Bahmanbegi, himself a Qashqā'i, and especially the tribal high school in Shiraz, which he has founded, shows a quality of education that might be a model for the whole country.

The Village versus the City

One of the important facts to remember about Iran is that there has always been mobility not only across the country but within the social structure. Nomads have settled in villages and villagers have gone to dwell in cities. Commoners have sometimes become kings; more frequently they have been made ministers and dignitaries of state. Nevertheless, villagers and city dwellers have been separate with different interests and values.

Iran has had cities from ancient times. Some of them have been on international routes. They have been destroyed and rebuilt on the same site over and over again. But the basic pattern of society in Iran has always been rural. Even with the rapid urbanization of the country in the past decades, the 1966 census shows that out of a population of 25 million, 61 percent lived in rural areas. This is a decrease of 7 percent in ten years.[25] Athough the peasants have always been in the majority they have not been aware of their power as a class and have remained inactive. Insofar as the educated Persian liberals were concerned, the peasants of Iran were reactionaries. They always voted for the landlord and were guided by the village mollah (clergyman), who was often in the pay of the landlord or in league with the "bailiff," who was usually worse than the landlord.

Before the massive land reforms, 56 percent of all cultivated land belonged to 1 percent of the population. The religious endowments (owqaf) owned about 15 percent of the cultivated land and the rest belonged to smaller landlords which included a few peasants.[26] With some exceptions, mainly in the fertile Caspian littoral, the peasants were sharecroppers. Usually, with variations as to size of shares and distribution based on locality, the produce at harvest time was divided roughly into fifths. The first fifth went to the owner of the land. The second fifth went to the person who provided the seed, who was the landlord. The third fifth went to the supplier of the water, who was also the landlord. The fourth fifth went to the person who provided the oxen, who in 75 percent of the cases was either the landlord or the local gāvdār, who in turn was either the bailiff or a rich peasant. The last fifth belonged to the peasant himself; from it he had to pay his taxes and support both his family and the local mollah, who, in some cases, demanded the haqq-e Imam, or the "portion of the Imam." Consequently the peasant was perpetually in debt to the landlord, and in cases of a wedding or a funeral, to the ever-present money lender.[27]

Ever since the 1906 revolution, governments and reformers had been talking about land reform but without doing anything. Even Reza

25. Ferydoon Firoozi, "Iranian Census 1956 and 1966: A Comparative Analysis," *Middle East Journal*, Vol. 24, no. 2 (Spring, 1970), p. 221.

26. K. S. McLachlan, "Land Reform in Iran," in *The Land of Iran*, pp. 685 ff.

27. For an authoritative analysis of the agricultural system, see A. K. S. Lambton, *The Persian Land Reform, 1962–1966* (Oxford: Clarendon Press, 1969), and her *Landlord and Peasant in Persia* (Oxford: Royal Institute of International Affairs, 1953).

Shah was too interested in industrialization to do anything about land reform. The first real step in what, years later, came to be known as the White Revolution was a *farman*, issued by the Shah on the 7th of Bahman A.H. 1329 (1951). In this decree he transferred the vast lands which he had inherited from his father to the peasants who were working the land. The peasants had to pay the price of the land, reduced by 20 percent, in long-term installments; these payments were, in turn, to be used to establish cooperatives and other programs which would help the farmer. From 1951 to 1963 some 517 villages had been distributed among the peasants.

"My programme of land distribution," according to the Shah, "was intended not only to benefit the peasants on the Crown lands, but also to set an example for the big private landlords. . . . But I am under no illusion that they will be moved merely by the power of example. We shall use stronger measures." [28] The stronger measures came on May 6, 1962, when the Shah dissolved the Majles and delayed calling for new elections. In the meantime a new liberal cabinet implemented the royal decree for land reform in which no person was allowed to have more than 400 irrigated and 800 unirrigated hectares. The program was carried out in three phases, and by 1970 over two million peasant families had been favorably affected. Even though this was less than the total number of peasants in the country it was a far reaching reform and aroused the wrath of both landlords and reactionary clerics. There were uprisings and bloodshed, but the Shah did not hesitate to send the opposition leaders, including some important clerics, to jail or into exile.

All reforms in history have been accompanied by social, economic, and political problems, and this one is no exception. But with the other phases of the program such as the establishment of cooperatives, development banks, literacy programs, education, village houses of justice, social security, health centers, and so forth, this might be more successful than most. An experienced observer, Miss Lambton, visiting the rural areas after the land reform states that "the changes brought about by the land reform in the four years between 1962 and 1966 were considerable whether measured in social, political, or economic terms." [29]

The changes land reform has wrought upon the majority of the population of Iran are basic and have far-reaching potentialities. For example, the cities have also changed glaringly in their size. Of the 9.7 million inhabitants of urban areas, according to the 1966 census, 5.6 million live in fourteen large cities and 235 small towns. Among the larger cities, Tehran and Ahvaz have grown by over seven times and Abadan by ten times in twenty years.[30] Tehran with a population of about three million is the largest. Indeed no other city in the country has reached a million population, but all cities have grown considerably.

28. *Mission for My Country*, p. 204.
29. Lambton, *The Persian Land Reform*, p. 347.
30. Firoozi, "Iranian Census," p. 225.

Industry, better roads, economic opportunities, better education and health facilities, and the presence of modern conveniences of life have attracted people from the rural areas and towns to the large cities.

Walking in the streets of large cities, one can still see the characteristics of a quarter of a century ago, in sharp social contrasts. Modern apartment buildings stand next to old mosques and houses built of sun-dried bricks. The rich and the best educated persons rub shoulders with the poor and the illiterate. Women with the latest minis, midis, and maxis dance to tunes recently imported from Europe and America, while a few blocks away their sisters lead secluded lives. Nevertheless the character of the city has changed.

In the past the government of the country was a city government, usually operated in the interest of the city dwellers. Today, however, cities share the annual budget to meet the increasing needs of the peasants. A good example is education. More and more the kindergarten, primary, and secondary education in the cities is being turned over to the private sector, while the Ministry of Education spends its time and energy for education in towns and villages. Consequently education is a booming business in the large cities. Qualified individuals with subsidy from the government and high tuition charges to parents provide education for the children of the cities and make money in the process.

It used to be that the Iranian city dweller was the individual in transition between the established patterns of the past and the unaccomplished hopes of the future. He was caught between the placid villagers who did not want to go anywhere and the satisfied Europeans who acted as though they had already arrived. At best he carried the burden of the whole country on his shoulders, and at worst he was the shrewd opportunist who profited by the confusion of his fellow countrymen. All this has changed or is changing rapidly. The city dweller of twenty-five years ago now has to share his concerns and power with the peasants, who have acquired a goal and awareness, and with a new class of Persians, which has replaced the Europeans as engineers, technicians, and heads of industry.

The craftsmen who made up the bulk of the city are no longer important and have lost their power to the leaders of industry. The bazaar, which was the center of political power until the late 1950s has been largely replaced by the *khiyābān*, the "avenues." The clergymen and the absentee landlords who influenced and used the bazaars have lost their power to the intellectuals and technocrats. The bazaar will always be there, and it is hoped that the craftsmen will not disappear; but they are already on the fringes and no longer at the center. They are mostly used by the rising new class as showpieces for cultural relics and the tourist trade.

With these changes have also come the din and confusion of traffic, smog, and pollution by industry. Tehran is a modern city with the same problems of pollution, congestion, smog, and slums as Tokyo, New York, Los Angeles, and London. There are those who wish that modernity had not exacted such a high price, but the devotees of modernism delight in every puff of black smoke that comes out of the factory chimneys and lull themselves with the Persian saying "there is no rose without a thorn."

Conclusion

In the long and complicated process of development and in the many challenges facing contemporary Iran, whether they be social, political, economic, educational, religious, or whatever, the Shah is an active participant. He presides over the cabinet and councils. He has presided over the four national conferences held in three years for the improvement of higher education. He sends messages to various planning or evaluation gatherings he cannot attend. According to the Constitution, he is Commander-in-chief of the armed forces; he declares war, concludes peace, makes treaties, can dissolve the Majles and call for new elections, appoints half the members of the Senate, suggests legislation but may not delay the execution of laws passed by the Majles; he may veto bills, but the Majles has the power to overrule him.

He appoints the members of the cabinet; and probably no other sovereign in history, certainly none in Persian history, has traveled as much as he has in the interest of the state. He holds press conferences for national and world reporters and defends his views on national and international problems. He makes speeches to groups as though he were running for public office. Indeed in these speeches his purpose is to "sell" his platform, which he describes as a "national revolution for the social, political, and economic equality for the masses of Iran." [31] He has the power, prerogatives, and the role of the President of the United States with the difference that he is in office for life and is above criticism. Like the President of the United States, he finds it necessary to "push" for the implementation of his programs.[32] He does this pushing through persuasion, through inspection, through the power of the army and SAVAK (the bureau of security and counterintelligence), and through the prestige of the monarchy in the history of Iran.

In a country where so much is going on at a rapid pace; where modern education, with all its implications, is being developed and accelerated; where a managerial class is being trained and given freedom to make decisions, it is obvious that political development will accompany or follow social and economic development. What form of government Iran will have half a century from now is hard to predict. It is signifi-

31. Bayne, *Persian Kingship*, p. 53.
32. Ibid., p. 233.

cant, however, that the Shah thinks it will be democratic, but "whatever parliamentary democracy we have must adapt itself to the nature of Iran." [33] He believes that it is part of the "nature of Iran" to continue the institution of monarchy. There is a mystical relationship, he is convinced, between every Persian and his king. He thinks that if the king is wise enough to keep this relationship open and to work for and with the people, the Persians will go on following their king.

In the long and tumultuous history of Iran, Persians have killed or rejected their kings and have accepted new dynasties, but they have always had the institution of monarchy. Persians have been very reluctant to destroy their traditions; quite often rather than getting rid of them they have superimposed the new over the old. It is significant to note that the Constitution of Iran, adopted in 1906, is the oldest constitution in all of Asia. Other nations have written new constitutions whenever new regimes have come to power. The Persians, however, have amended rather than changed theirs. Even during Reza Shah's period, when the constitution was ignored, the Persians, including the Shah, celebrated the anniversary of its adoption.

It is important to note that Pre-Islamic names such as Cyrus, Darius, Bahrām, Hushang, and a hundred others have been used in Iran all along and are being used today, while in neighboring countries, which have had as glorious pasts as Iran, names such as Amenhotep, Ramses, Sargon, or Assurbanapal are all but forgotten. The kings of Iran, even the ones who were Turks or Mongols, have claimed to be wearing the *tāj-e kiyāni*, or the Crown of the Kiyan, the first dynasty to rule Iran. A few years ago, when the Iranian Student Association in the United States wanted to choose an emblem, they quite naturally chose —Moslems though they were—the symbol of Ahura Mazda superimposed by the trinity of Zoroastrian ethics, "good thought, good speech, good deed." As this is being written, the Persians are busy preparing for an imposing celebration of the "2,500th anniversary of the founding of the Persian empire by Cyrus." The hearts of the Persians are still in the ruins of Persepolis, and the past is quite present in their thinking. To understand contemporary Iran we must go to the time when Persepolis was still standing.

33. Ibid., p. 61.

2

Ancient Iran

Practically everyone knows that Persians have a long history, but not everyone is aware that the Persians are very conscious of it. For over a thousand years Persians in many walks of life have chanted their history in the matchless poetry of Ferdosi, very much as the Greeks used to recite the exquisite poems of Homer. It was after the Islamic conquest of Iran that Abol Qāsem Ferdosi of Tus in the northeast spent thirty-five years in research and writing and completed sixty thousand couplets depicting the history of Iran from mythological times to the coming of Islam. The book is called *Shahnāmeh* 'Book of Kings'. It is not only a great literary masterpiece, but it has been an inspiration to generations of Persians.

The *Shahnāmeh* mentions four dynasties in pre-Islamic Iran, namely the Pishdādian, the Kiyānian, the Ashkānian, and the Sasanian. The first two are semimythological, ending with the fall of the Achaemenian Empire. The third is the Persian name for the Parthian dynasty, and the fourth is the Sasanids, who ruled Iran immediately before the advent of Islam.

The first king of the Pishdādi dynasty, named Keyumars, is the same as the first man in the Avesta Gayomareta. He subjugated the beasts of the field and the demons, who eventually killed his son Siyāmak. The next king was Hushang, who separated iron from the rock and accidentally discovered fire. To celebrate the discovery, he established the festival of Sedeh, still celebrated in some parts of Iran. His son Tahmures domesticated animals, taught people the carding of wool and spinning. He conquered the demons but spared their lives, and in return they taught him the art of writing.

By far the most famous king in this dynasty was Jamshid, the same as the Yama of the Upanishads and Yima of the Avesta. He had a cup in which he could see everywhere in the world. He ruled seven hundred years over men and beasts and divided society into four divisions of clergy, military, farmer, and artisan. He also inaugurated the festival of Noruz, or New Year, at the vernal equinox. This has always remained the national festival of the Persians.

Jamshid's kingdom was usurped by Zahāk or Azhi Dahaka (modern Persian *ezhdaha* 'dragon') of the Avesta, who had two snakes growing out of his shoulders which had to be fed fresh human victims.[1] After a thousand years of tyranny, a certain blacksmith, Kāveh, raised his leather apron as a banner of revolt and brought Faridun, a scion of the dynasty of Kiyān, out of hiding and proclaimed him king. The young shah imprisoned Zahāk on the summit of Mount Damavand, about sixty miles northeast of Tehran. After that he divided his kingdom among his three sons. Salm, the eldest, got "Rome" and the West; Tur got Turān (central Asia) and China; and Iraj, the youngest, got Iran. The older brothers were jealous of Iraj, and a good portion of *Shahnāmeh* is taken up with the rivalry and exploits of the descendants of these brothers.

One is tempted to continue the recital and interpretation of the mythology, especially when one faces such a dearth of material describing the historical events of ancient Iran. Unlike its ancient neighbors, especially Greece and Rome, Iran seems a barren desert insofar as historical information is concerned. Almost all we have are architectural monuments, works of art, pottery, and coins uncovered by archeologists. With the exception of some inscriptions and tablets, the mostly silent evidences have been interpreted by scholars already influenced by the detailed accounts of Iran written by Greek historians such as Herodotus, Xenophon, Polybius, and others.

The fact that the Greeks were not impartial toward the Persians has not only affected their writings but perhaps also the way European scholars have interpreted archeological finds in Iran. Fortunately, however, new discoveries and the accounts of early Moslem historians about pre-Islamic Iran have tended to change former interpretations, and our present idea of ancient Iran is quite different from that of a half century ago.

It is hard to imagine that an empire as expansive and a civilization as advanced as ancient Iran, which produced religious leaders, architects, artists, and administrators, failed to produce men of letters, historians, or even chroniclers to set down the daily events of the vast empire. Generally, however, the Persian scholars take it for granted that there must have been plenty of records but that these were destroyed by the

---

1. No doubt because the Arab conquest was still fresh, Ferdosi makes it appear that Zahāk was an Arab!

invading Greeks or by the Arabs, who invaded Iran about a thousand years later. The philhellene scholars of the West and the Arabophiles of both the East and the West, however, strenuously object to this accusation and take it for granted that "before Islam, chronological history as we know it from the Greeks or the Muslims did not exist in Iran." As evidence, the same author states that "many Oriental peoples, the Iranians and Indians among them were more concerned with religion than with history." [2]

This juxtaposition of religion and history as an either-or proposition is difficult to accept. The Hebrews, who were most certainly concerned with religion, were also concerned with history, while the Hindus, who were equally religious, were not so much concerned with history. The difference obviously is not concern or lack of concern for religion but rather the fact that Judaism, Christianity, and Islam, all of which are concerned with history, are "revealed" religions, that is, they claim personal revelation from God, while Hinduism, which has not shown too much interest in history is "nonrevealed." [3] God reveals himself to a certain person at a certain time, place, and condition. Such an event forms the stuff of history, and knowledge of such an event is most important for the claims of a religion.

Zoroastrianism is also a revealed religion. The ancient Aryan religion that in India developed the concept of Brahma, Vishnu, and Shiva in Iran was transformed by Zoroaster after he received revelation from Ahura Mazda. Brahma is a concept that does not depend upon time or space. Zoroaster, on the other hand, is a person; and whether he lived or not, and where or when he lived, are most important. In the same way that most of the Hebrew kings and Moslem caliphs considered themselves to be under the command of God, doing His will, the inscriptions of Cyrus, Darius, and other Persian kings attribute their deeds to the will and command of Ahura Mazda. Furthermore, Zoroastrianism, like Christianity and Islam, believes in the "end of days" and a beginning and an end of the history of man. Consequently, it seems too superficial a solution to say simply that "chronological history . . . did not exist in Iran."

This is a very important and complex point and the purpose is not to argue it here. It is mentioned only to illustrate the fact that not only is the reason for the scarcity of written history in Iran controversial, but the very paucity of information has made practically everything about ancient Iran a controversial issue. Obviously this short survey of Iran is not the place to argue each point. The best that can be done is to raise the questions and leave the resolution, insofar as any historical

2. Richard N. Frye, *The Heritage of Persia* (New York: World Publishing Company, 1963), pp. 4–5.
3. "Revealed" and "nonrevealed" are not adequate terms. I am aware that the Vedas are "revealed." Here the term is used in the sense of a disclosure from a personal god.

question can be resolved, to the time when more evidence may come to light.

For many centuries the words *Iran* and *Persia* have been used interchangeably to identify the same country. The peoples of the land have always called it Iran, while westerners, influenced principally by the Greeks, have referred to it as Persia. In about 1935 Reza Shah Pahlavi, believing that the name *Persia* denoted a backward country to the peoples of the West, ordered that henceforth it should be called Iran, a new name to the westerner, to demonstrate the modernity of the country under his rule. Unfortunately the courtiers did not dare to inform the Shah that the name *Persia* reminded the westerners of beauty and things exotic rather than ideas of backwardness. Time proved that no one in the West wanted to own an Iranian rug, nor wanted to exchange his Persian cat for the Iranian variety! Ever since the Second World War both terms have come back into vogue.[4]

In any case, Fars is a province of Iran, and Persians belong to a people called Aryans, and their country was referred to as *Iran*, sometimes *Iranshahr* "the polis of Iran" or *Iranzamin* "the land of Iran." *Aryan* is a term used to denote a family of languages and only secondarily refers to the people who speak those languages. In other words it is not meant to denote a race. "The use of modern substitutes for Aryan, such as the term *Indo-European*, is motivated by political and social rather than scientific reasons, as also witnessed by the German preference for *Indo-Germanic* as against *Indo-European* favored by the French and British scholars. If the argument is the geographic extent of these languages, with the Indian languages in the easternmost and the European or Germanic languages prevailing in the westernmost territories of the Aryan-speaking people, one need only be reminded that the Indians called themselves and their ancient language Aryan (Indian being a relatively modern term, and for that matter dubious in its application) and that the westernmost Aryan nation is Eirinn (Ireland being the semantic equivalent of Iran and cognate with it)."[5]

Much has been written on the original homeland of the Aryans. The region north of the Black Sea, Eurasia, the Oxus region, and the plateau of Iran have been mentioned. It was first believed that the Aryans came to Iran about the first millennium B.C., but thanks to recent archeological discoveries in Siyalk in central Iran, Hasanlu in Azarbāyjān and other places, it is presumed that the Aryans were in the region long before then. This would seem to support some Persian scholars who believe that the Aryans were there to begin with and from there migrated eastward to India and westward to Europe. The excavator

4. In this book *Iran* has been used as the noun form, and *Persian* has been used as the adjective form.
5. M. Moghadam, "Persian and English," *Iran Review*, no. 5 (August-September, 1960).

of Siyalk,[6] however, believes that there were different invasions of Iran by the Aryans. The Persian and some other tribes were relative new-comers, invading the country through the Caucasus and from Trans-oxiana, thus from both sides of the Caspian Sea. While the previous Aryan invaders, such as the Hurrians, the Mitanni, and the Kassites had been absorbed by the "natives," the new Aryan tribes, the Persians and the Medes, who settled in the Zagros valley, were not absorbed but became one of the three principal rivals for the supremacy of the region. These three rivals were Assyria, the dominant power at the time, the kingdom of Urartu, which later became Armenia, and the Iranians, who comprised two groups known as Medes and Persians. The Iranians, during their sojourn in the Zagros region developed the use of iron which had been known to the Hittites centuries before.

Whether the Medes and the Persians invaded the country or whether they were dwellers of the land, they had become fairly prominent during the first half of the first millennium before Christ. The first re-corded reference to the Persians (Parsua) and the Medes (Madai) is found in the records of Shalmaneser III, king of Assyria in 844 and 836 B.C. respectively. These two were by no means the only Aryan tribes. The Zikirtu were scattered in Āzarbāyjān, the Parthava (Parthians) in the Caspian region, and the Haraiva in Khorāsān. Perhaps during the eighth century B.C., when the power of Assyria declined, the Persians broke out of the Zagros valley and went eastward to the mountainous region north of the Persian Gulf. There they settled and gave their name *Parsa* (modern *Fars*) to the region, which eventually became Persia. The Medes, however, seem to have stayed in western Iran in the region of Ecbatana (modern Hamadan) and continued the struggle against Assyria. Cayaxares, the king of the Medes, in alliance with Nabopolassar of Babylon put an end to the Assyrian empire in 612 B.C. by capturing Ninevah. Western Asia, thus divided between the Baby-lonians and the Medes, did not remain tranquil for long. Soon these two powers began to fight each other for supremacy.

THE ACHAEMENIDS

While these two adversaries were busy fighting each other, the Persians took advantage of the confusion and strengthened themselves without hindrance. The founder of the ruling house of the Persians was Hakhāmanesh, whom the Greeks called Achaemenes, and the dynasty he established is called the Achaemenid. The earliest text in existence is a gold tablet written in old Persian by Aryaramnes a grandson of Hakhāmanesh, and son of Chishpish (Teispes to the Greeks). He refers to his father as the "Great King, King of Anshān," and to his brother Kurosh (Cyrus I) as "King of Anshān," and to himself as "King of Kings,

6. R. Ghirshman, *Iran* (Baltimore, Md.: Penguin Books, 1965), p. 73 ff.

King of Parsa." He lived about 640–590 B.C. and wrote, "This land of the Persians which I possess, provided with fine horses and good men, it is the great God Ahura Mazda who has given it to me. I am the king of this land." This rare document found in Hamadān is important in at least two points: First, it is written in a very advanced alphabet; and second, it contains this reference to Ahura Mazda as the supreme giver of power. These points will be discussed later, but it should be pointed out here that even though the Persians were supposed to be vassals of the Medes, they had achieved enough organization and power to call themselves "King of the land of Parsa."

It was not the direct descendants of Aryaramnes, however, who were the first to make the name of Hakhāmanesh world famous, but his brother's grandson, Kurosh II, known to the Persians also as Kuros (or Cyrus) the Great. Cyrus, whose mother was a Median princess, established his capital at Pasargadai and eventually was able to unite the Medes and the Persians under his own rule in about 559 B.C. He chose Ecbatana to be the administrative center of his forthcoming empire. From there he marched against Lydia in Asia Minor, and after capturing Sardis, the capital, went against the rich Greek cities. These cities held the key to the commerce with the West, and it was important for the new empire to be able to use this key at will. The fact that Cyrus did not meet with too much resistance was perhaps in part because of the willingness of the Greek merchants to enhance their business by being part of a young and aggressive empire. If they considered such a possibility they certainly had reason to be pleased with their decision.

After securing Asia Minor, Cyrus went eastward and established his suzerainty over the Aryan tribes and built fortifications beyond the Āmu Daryā (Oxus) river. Only then was he ready to deal with Babylon, which was the strongest power challenging the ambitions of the young monarch. Babylon, under Nabonidus in 539 B.C. was not at the zenith of its power, and there was enough discontent among the leaders for the city to fall into the hands of Cyrus without too much resistance. By this time the Persians had introduced a new idea of conquest. After each victory they tried to win the confidence and friendship of the enemy rather than to destroy him. Cyrus treated Nabonidus kindly; when Nabonidus died the following year (538 B.C.), Cyrus arranged for a state funeral and personally participated in it. He not only liberated the Jews, which is well known, but also other groups that had been taken captive.

He left his son Cambyses in Babylon to prepare for the conquest of Egypt and he went east to subdue the restless nomads. He was killed in battle, and his body was brought back to Pasargadai and placed in a tomb which stands to this day. In the appraisal of the life of this noble builder of an empire one cannot do better than Professor Ghirshman, who speaks of him thus: "A great captain and leader of men, he was favoured by the fate that befell him. Generous, benevolent, he had no thought of forcing conquered countries into a single mould, but had the wisdom to leave unchanged the institutions of each kingdom he attached to his crown . . . We never see Cyrus, like the Romans, ally himself to a rival people, treat it as an equal, and then, turning upon it in a moment of weakness, subject and oppress it. The Persians called him 'father,' the Hellenes whom he conquered regarded him as 'master' and 'lawgiver,' and the Jews as 'the anointed of the Lord.' " [7]

Cambyses (530–522 B.C.) continued the program of his father and took Egypt. It seems that he followed the conciliating policy of Cyrus, but scandalous events together with his probably impulsive nature have not left him with a good name. He is accused of the mysterious death of his brother Bardiya (called Smerdis by Herodotus). When Cambyses was in Egypt he heard that a man had ascended the throne of Iran who claimed to be the slain Bardiya. Cambyses rushed for Iran but died on the way. Whether he died in an epileptic fit or committed suicide is not known. In the meantime the false Bardiya, whose real name was Gaumatu the Magian, was accepted as the new ruler. Darius, son of Hystaspes the Achaemenian, however, with the help of the army which had remained loyal, overthrew the pretender and proclaimed himself king. The whole affair had taken only a few months in the year 522 B.C. On a high rocky bluff overlooking the road between Kermānshah and Hamadān known as Behistun, one can still see Darius under the protection of the winged Ahura Mazda, stepping on the body of the pretender. The inscription relates the story of the revolt very much as was described above and the part of Darius in restoring the throne of Hakhāmanesh.

After spending some time in quelling the rebellion that had sprouted in many parts of the country, Darius continued the expansion of the empire and got deeply involved with the Greeks of Europe. The difficulty was that the European Greeks were enticing the Greeks of Asia Minor, who were under the Persians, to revolt. In 512 Darius crossed the Bosporus and advanced through Thrace to beyond the Danube. In the end, however, Darius felt obliged to stop the trouble at the source. The campaigns of Darius against Greece ended in the famous battle of Marathon (490 B.C.) in which the Persians were defeated; thereafter they withdrew to Asia Minor.

At the death of Darius in 486 B.C., his son Xerxes I (Khshāyārshā) continued the campaign and succeeded in taking Athens in 480 B.C. and burning parts of the city. The victory, however, was short-lived, for the Persian fleet was defeated at the battle of Salamis and the Persians, once again, were forced to withdraw to Asia Minor. Although the Greeks were justly proud of their victories, the defeats did not destroy the Persians. All the Persians had to give up was their ambitions in Europe, if they had any. On the other hand, the Persians were successful in

7. Ibid., p. 133.

stopping Greek interference in the affairs of Asia Minor. The Persians were able to work out friendly relations with the Ionians and continued unhampered until the rise of Alexander in 330 B.C.

ADMINISTRATION AND ECONOMY

The Achaemenid dynasty, which lasted some 230 years, created not only the first great empire of recorded history but the first world civilization. It was not one culture imposed on others but a bringing together of diverse nations under one canopy. It was the first commonwealth of nations in which the king was the symbol of unity as well as the center of power. The Achaemenians were tolerant, conciliatory, and appreciative of the contributions and talents of other cultures. In contrast to the rigidity of empires before and after them, they were flexible and changed with the requirements of the times and the needs of each nationality. Each group had the freedom of its own culture and language. The Persians did not impose either their religion or customs upon the conquered people. Perhaps the only exception was the celebration of Noruz (New Year) when representatives of all the nationalities of the empire were required to present themselves before the king. The magnificent relief of the walls of the grand stairway of Persepolis depicts these representatives, each in his national costume bringing his gifts.

Their tolerance and flexibility was implemented through a superb system of administration. Herodotus relates that the empire was divided into twenty provinces. Each was headed by a satrap, who was usually a Persian appointed by the king. In addition to the satrap each province had a military commander and a tax collector. Periodically a special inspector, called the "ears and eyes of the king," would visit the provinces unannounced to examine the conduct of affairs. All the provinces were connected with each other and with the center by a system of roads which can be traced even to this day. To facilitate communications within the empire, post stations were built along all routes to provide rest stations for the caravans and fresh horses for couriers on government business. As part of this wide network of roads and communications for commerce and government, mention should be made of the fact that Darius dug the canal connecting the Red Sea with the Mediterranean, which has been called Suez in modern times.[8]

The unity and stability of the empire encouraged the flow of commerce, and merchants were able to travel all over the empire. There is evidence that Khārazmians from eastern Iran were plying their goods

8. The canal was originally dug by the Egyptian pharaohs, but it had been destroyed. Apparently Darius erected stelae along the course of the canal, one of which was discovered by de Lesseps when he was supervising the digging of the modern canal in 1866.

in upper Egypt.[9] To help the flow of commerce the empire adopted uniform weights, measures, and coinage. The Persians established private banks and businessmen were able to float loans, make deposits, invest in land and other ventures, and transact their business by writing checks. Banking houses such as the House of Murashu and Egibi not only carried out the normal activities of banking but were tax collectors as well.

Even though there was industry to take care of the basic needs of the empire such as clothing, shoes, furniture, and the like, the main source of wealth in the empire was agricultural and pastoral. In an arid country like Iran, water was (and is) a precious commodity, and the government built underground canals (*qanat*), a method still used in Iran, and regulated the use of water. The government also transplanted fruit trees, carried out a program of forestation for economic purposes, and established mines, quarries, and fisheries.[10]

One of the most interesting discoveries about ancient Iran is the system of wages established for laborers throughout the empire. The numerous tablets found in the treasury at Persepolis, and translated by Professor George G. Cameron,[11] reveal an amazing array of regulations concerning wages, work, modes of payment, labor exchange, and the like. In these treasury tablets, which are really pay sheets for the building of Persepolis, it is quite evident that payment for different classes of workers such as unskilled and skilled labor, women and children, are strictly regulated. From these detailed accounts one can deduce not only that Persepolis was not built by slave labor but that Persian society was hardly a slave society. At least one can safely say that Persian economy was not based on slavery as the Roman empire was or even Athenian society, whose democracy was limited to the free citizens and excluded the slaves. The slaves of the Achaemenid empire were "juridical persons" and were sometimes better paid than free men.[12]

ART AND ARCHITECTURE

The same tolerance and flexibility which characterized the Achaemenid empire, administration, and commerce permeated its art, architecture, and religion. It was not a question of the conqueror's religion, art, and culture imposing themselves on all others, but a blending of the civilizations of the ancient world—Mesopotamia, Egypt, Syria, Asia Minor, the Greek cities, and even India—into one distinctive and original whole. The inscription by Darius describing the building of the palace in Susa depicts the cosmopolitan and cooperative nature of

9. Frye, *Heritage of Persia*, p. 120.
10. Ghirshman, *Iran*, p. 182.
11. George G. Cameron, ed., *Persepolis Treasury Tablets* (Chicago: University of Chicago Press, 1948).
12. Frye, *Heritage of Persia*, p. 109.

the empire. Skilled workers were brought from Sind, Egypt, Bactria, the Greek cities of Asia Minor and other localities.

Generally the style of art and architecture of the Persians differs from other Middle Eastern peoples. There is a greater plasticity and roundness of figures, and there is a more realistic relationship of clothing to the contours of the body. On the whole the Persians have not used large canvases. Professor Ghirshman, however, believes that the Persians did not show much interest in scenes from real life and considers the row of figures on the royal stairway at Persepolis as only partially an "attempt at realism." Nevertheless, it must be noted that in Persian art and sculpture, in stark contrast to those of Assyria and Babylonia, there is no savagery and war. On the whole, a person strolling through the ruins of ancient Achaemenid palaces, be it Susa, Pasargadai, or Persepolis, finds the art and architecture more contemplative and the conflicts more spiritual, such as struggle between good and evil, rather than crude.[13]

The flexibility of the empire was further evidenced by the fact that the court was not fixed in one place. Cyrus used Ecbatana (Hamadān), which was the ancient capital of the Medes. Darius used Babylon for a while, but later he built Susa as the winter capital and the administrative center of the empire. He built a strong citadel separated by a wide avenue from the houses and villas reserved for officials and merchants. It was indeed the capital of the world to which kings, ambassadors, artists, and scientists came.

The palaces that represented the inner spirit of the Persians rather than the necessary outer trappings of the empire were located deep inside Parsa, the native homeland of Hakhāmanesh. One of these was Pasargadai and the other Persepolis. Pasargadai was something of a national shrine. The name, which is the Greek form of the original, is almost certainly misspelled. It probably should have been *Pārsa* rather than *Pasar*, and perhaps the original name was *Pārsāgerd*, 'fortress of Persia' or *Pārsāgadae*, 'throne of Persia' or *Pārsākadeh*, 'house of Persia.' [14] It was located on the plain of Morghāb between the Morghāb and Polvār rivers on the Shirāz-to-Esfahān road. This was the ancient capital of the Achaemenid princes. Their temple was erected there, and Cyrus the Great built his palace there. The art and architecture is original Persian. The Achaemenid kings were crowned in Pasargadai, where they would don the robe of Cyrus and eat a peasant's meal as part of the ceremony. Several of the kings were also buried on the outskirts of the city in a place now called Naqsh-e Rostam. About the only buildings which are relatively intact are the Ka'ba of Zoroaster, a temple in

13. William Cullican, *The Medes and the Persians* (New York: Praeger, 1965), p. 104 ff.

14. For this and a detailed description of Pasargadai, see Ali Sami, *Pasargadai*, trans. R. N. Sharp (Shiraz: Musavi Press, 1956).

the proximity of the royal tombs in Naqsh-e Rostam, and the tomb of Cyrus the Great, which dominates what used to be the royal gardens. Since the time of the Islamic conquest, the tomb of Cyrus has been called the "Tomb of the Mother of Solomon," Pasargadai the "Martyrdom of the Mother of Solomon," and one of the palaces as the "Throne of Solomon." It is quite likely that the Persians invented these names to prevent the desecration of the tomb and other buildings by the intolerant Moslems—the latter being convinced of the holiness of Solomon and in awe of his exploits.[15]

If Pasargadai was the spiritual shrine of the ancient Persians, Persepolis was the Portal of all Nations, symbolizing the internationalism of its builders. It was begun by Darius and completed by Xerxes. Its style was generally that of Pasargadai but more developed and suited for its cosmopolitan use. It is built on a raised platform overlooking the plain of Marv and consists of living quarters, treasury, and audience hall (apadana) of a hundred columns. All of this is built on a terrace approached by a double flight of stairs which leads to the "Portals of all Lands" and then to the audience hall. Its most important ceremonial use was at Noruz (New Year) when the representatives of the commonwealths in the empire would present themselves before the king of kings with gifts. In the midst of cosmopolitanism and diversity of cultures, the Noruz ceremony was the symbol of the unity of the empire in which all participated.

ALPHABET AND WRITING

It has already been stated that the gold tablet of Aryaramnes, great grandfather of Darius, was important in two points. The first is that it is written in a very advanced alphabet, and the second that it contains reference to Ahura Mazda.[16] The discovery of this tablet has made Professor Ghirshman state that the "invention of cuneiform writing to express Old Persian probably goes back to Teispes (c. 700 B.C.)." [17] "Inasmuch as this tablet is written in a "very advanced" alphabet, it indicates that alphabet was known to the Persians long enough for them to experiment with it. Indeed the most recent discovery (1970) at Tappeh Yahya of a similar alphabet written around 3500 B.C. shows that alphabet was prevalent in Iran and India before Assyrian or Babylonian times. Notwithstanding this fact, European scholars believe that the Achaemenids wrote their decrees and kept their books and archives in an alphabet which is commonly called Aramaic.[18] Pre-

---

15. Ibid., p. 22 ff.
16. The most recent discovery of a cuneiform tablet dated about 3500 B.C., by Professor Lamberg-Karlovsky of Harvard, at Tappeh Yahya in southeastern Iran, may modify the presently held theories.
17. Ghirshman, Iran, p. 163.
18. Ibid., p. 163 ff., and Frye, Heritage of Persia, pp. 127 ff. and 173 ff.

sumably, because this form of alphabet was better known than the Persian, the Aramaic alphabet was used for writing Persian. The word *Aramaic*, however, is a late nineteenth-century discovery or invention. Formerly what is now known as Aramaic was called Syriac; and no grammar has yet been written for Aramaic because there are not enough samples for the purpose. In any case the discussion of language and alphabet is beyond the specialty of this author, but it is of interest to note that European scholars, in tracing the origin of alphabet and especially of writing in ancient Iran, have not used the Pahlavi or the Arabic and Persian sources written in early Islamic times about pre-Islamic Iran. These writers are Mas'udi, ibn-Moqaffa', Hamzeh Esfahāni, ibn-Nadim, Abu Reyhān Biruni, Mohammad Khārazmi and others who have written extensively on this subject. Even Avicenna has an important monograph on the alphabet and writing.

According to these sources, the pre-Islamic Persians had seven different sets of alphabets and each was used for a special purpose.[19] These were:

1. *Ām Dabireh.* The common alphabet, which had twenty eight styles but only seven are recorded. These deal with legal papers, city, treasury, national accounting, and so on.

2. *Gashteh Dabireh.* This alphabet had twenty-eight letters and was used for treaties and royal decrees.

3. *Nim-gashteh Dabireh.* This also had twenty-eight letters and was used in medicine and philosophy.

4. *Farvardeh Dabireh.* This had thirty-three letters and was used in keeping royal records.

5. *Rāz Dabireh.* This had forty letters and was used for codes and classified documents.

6. *Din Dabireh.* This unique alphabet had sixty letters and was used for writing religious hymns and prayers to be chanted in worship. With this alphabet all the peculiarities such as intonation and length of vowels of a word could be designated so that the reader would not mispronounce the holy word.

7. *Visp Dabireh.* This was an international alphabet by which all languages and all sounds, even the "sound of falling water" could be written. This alphabet had 160 letters for all languages and 205 letters for all sounds.

19. For all of this I am indebted to Zabih Behruz, *Khat va Farhang* (*Alphabet and Education*), *Iran-Kudeh* no. 8, ed. Mohamad Moghadam (Tehran, 1950). More than half of this interesting volume deals with the origin of the alphabet; a complete alphabet is introduced; the rest of the volume deals with the history of writing in ancient Iran and India. Why such works by Behruz and others by Moghadam and Kiya, both of the Department of Linguistics and Ancient Languages at the University of Tehran, are ignored by contemporary European scholars is a puzzle to this author.

It is neither within the scope of this volume to dwell on this important matter much longer, nor is it within the competency of the author to draw any conclusions. These are recorded here for the first time in English so that those experts who do not have access to Persian and Arabic may be able to pursue the problem.

RELIGION

The other point in the inscription of Aryaramnes is that he was king by the grace of Ahura Mazda. This provides the opportunity to discuss the religion of ancient Iran, founded by Zoroaster, which without doubt is the most significant contribution of the Persians to the world. Indeed, the tolerance, flexibility, devotion to truth, and all other lofty attributes heaped upon the ancient Persians by friend and foe, are all rooted in Zoroastrianism. Unfortunately, Zoroastrianism, more so than any other subject in ancient Iran, because it is a religion, has been a subject of controversy. Where Zoroaster was born, whether in northeastern or northwestern Iran, is not the subject of so much heated controversy as is when he was born. European scholars used to claim that Zoroaster was born in the middle of the sixth century B.C. In direct contrast is the claim of Zabih Behruz,[20] who believes that Zoroaster was born on the 21st of March 1767 B.C. In recent years, however, European scholars have come to believe that for the birth of the Persian Prophet 1000 B.C. is "a shade more reasonable," to quote Professor Frye.[21]

The controversy involves the message of Zoroaster also. As it has been mentioned in the beginning of this chapter, European scholars, steeped in the Greco-Roman civilization and influenced by the Judeo-Christian tradition, are loath to accept any lofty philosophical or ethical concepts which antedate the Greeks or the Old Testament. It is only recently that western scholars have come to the conclusion that "Zoroaster is, in fact, in the full sense of the word, *the first theologian*," [22] or that the Gathas, which are the most ancient hymns of Zoroaster, should receive the "same attention as the Psalms in Hebrew literature." [23] One might add that the Gathas are as lofty as the Psalms and lack the vengeance and nationalism which permeates the latter. As late as 1894, J. Darmesteter said about Zoroaster: "How is one to accept that a man who lived at least six centuries before our era, far away

20. Zabih Behruz, *Taqvim va Tārikh dar Iran* (*Calendar and History in Iran*), *Iran-Kudeh* no. 15 (Tehran, 1952).
21. Perhaps another century of scholarship will bring the date closer to that set by Behruz.
22. Jacques Duchesne-Guillemin, *The Hymns of Zarathustra* (Boston: Beacon Press, 1952), p. 2.
23. Richard Frye, quoted in the preface to Duchesne-Guillemin, *The Hymns of Zarathustra*, p. viii.

from Greece, could have expressed his views on God and the world in philosophical language . . . ," and he concludes that "These discourses must, therefore, be forgeries composed seven or eight centuries after the time of the prophet to whom they are attributed." [24] Even more recently, in 1937, Professor Nyberg of Sweden, in an attempt to minimize the spiritual and ethical message of Zoroaster, pictures him "as a kind of shaman, or Mongol sorcerer who intoxicated himself with hemp fumes." [25]

The purpose here is not to refute such statements or build up an argument contrary to such allegations, but it is enough to show what Greek orientation has done to the interpretation of Persian culture. Zoroastrianism developed during the course of the Achaemenid through the Sasanian periods. It will obviously be beyond the scope of this volume to trace such a development. What is undertaken here is a very brief account of the religion of Zoroaster as it became prevalent in later years.

Zoroaster, which is the Greek form of the original *Zaratushtra* and modern Persian *Zardosht*, was a prophet who claimed to have a special revelation from Ahura Mazda. He preached the coming of a new kingdom and, like many prophets, he was ignored and sometimes ridiculed. After many years of struggle and disappointment, he at last won over Prince Vistaspa who ruled in a principality in eastern Iran, to his views. From then on until the end of his life he preached the Kingdom of Goodness, Life and Light. The way of Zoroaster revolutionized the old religious practices of the Aryans who accepted him.

If it were not for Zoroaster, perhaps the religion of the Iranians would have developed along lines similar to those followed by the religion of their kinsmen, the Aryans of India. The revolution of Zoroaster reversed the process so that the gods (*daiva*) whom they shared with the Hindus became devils (*div*) to the Iranians.[26] Professor Frye is correct when he says that the old Aryan religions were "rite-centered" while the reforms of Zoroaster were "belief-centered." The belief proclaimed by Zoroaster was trust in the goodness and justice of Ahura Mazda and faith that in the end only He would be victorious. Zoroastrianism is based on what later became known as Dualism. In the Gathas, Zoroaster proclaimed:

"I will speak of the two spirits
Of whom the holier said unto the destroyer at the
       beginning of existence:

24. Ibid., p. 3.
25. Ibid., p. 3.
26. It is interesting to note that the words for God and Satan in the West come from the same root, one from Sanskrit *daiva*, Greek *theos*, and Latin *deus*, and the other from Old Persian *div*, and English *devil*.

Neither our thoughts nor our doctrines nor our
    minds' forces,
Neither our choices nor our words nor our deeds,
Neither our consciences nor our souls agree."

The "holier" person in the hymn is Ahura Mazda and the "destroyer" is Ahriman. Ahura Mazda is the creator of life, light, and goodness while Ahriman is the lord of death, darkness, and evil. The greatest difficulty in all theistic religions has been to explain how an all-powerful and all-loving God can conceive of evil, let alone allow it. Either He is all powerful and not all good or He is all good and not all powerful. In Zoroastrianism power is sacrificed in favor of love and goodness. Ahura Mazda and Ahriman are always at war with each other for supremacy in the world at large, in every community, and in the heart of each person. Each wages war with the aid of his "hosts," which are called angels and demons,[27] but the most important soldier in each army is man. Inasmuch as man joins the hosts of Ahriman, then death, darkness, and evil will dominate the world, or society, or a person's life. And to the degree that man joins Ahura Mazda, the forces of life, light, and goodness will conquer in the world, in the community, and in the individual. Man, therefore, stands between the primordial goodness and evil and by his choice can help in the expiration of falsehood and death, and the establishment of truth and life. The essence of the revelation of Zoroaster is to encourage man to choose Ahura Mazda. It is a secret revealed only to Zoroaster and may be accepted by all who would believe. The revelation in this is that the war between Ahura Mazda and Ahriman is going to be won by the former. Ahriman may win battles here and there, but in the end goodness shall defeat evil, light shall vanquish darkness, and life shall overcome death.[28]

Both Ahura Mazda and Ahriman help and guide men who volunteer in their service with their "spirit"—Ahura Mazda with the "Holy Spirit," *Spenta Mainyu*, and Ahriman with the "Evil Spirit," *Angra Mainyu*.[29] Those who give their allegiance to Ahura Mazda are enjoined to struggle against the foe with the weapons of pure thought, pure speech, and pure deed.[30] Of course very few men are able to be always

27. Among the hosts of Ahriman, the chief of staff, as it were, is "Druj," the Lie, hence the prayer of Darius is to protect his people from him.

28. Job, which is very likely a Judaized Zoroastrian story, illustrates this truth in that Job with the unreplenished power of God overcame the replenished power of Satan.

29. This concept borrowed by the Hebrews and Arabs is expressed in both languages by the word *wind* ('*ruwah*,' '*ruh*') but does not approach the fullness of the meaning of *Mainyu*.

30. Fire as light and also as the best purifier has been the symbol of Ahura Mazda. Even to this day on the last Wednesday of the old year Persians in general and Zoroastrians in particular make small bonfires and jump over them purifying themselves for the new year. Water, which is the second purifier, also has a place in Zoroastrian symbolism. John the Baptist baptized with water and promised the coming of a greater One who would baptize with fire.

on the side of Ahura Mazda or even of Ahriman. No matter how good a man is, he has done some evil; and no matter how evil a man is, he has done some good. There is a well-developed system of rewards and punishments as well as eschatology and apocalypse in Zoroastrianism. Every person's thoughts, words, and deeds are recorded. On the Day of Judgment, if evil outweighs good, then the person is destined to go to hell, but if the good outweighs evil he is destined to go to paradise (Persian *perdows* or *ferdows*). There is no forgiveness in Zoroastrianism, and each person is rewarded and punished in an intermediary state called *hamestagan*, a prototype of the Roman Catholic purgatory. Unlike purgatory, however, *hamestagan* is not controlled from the earth. The Last Judgment will take place at the *Chinvat* Bridge, where the victorious Lord Ahura Mazda himself will separate the good from the bad and the soul, *urvān* (modern Persian *ravān*) of the good will live in the abode of light.

It is hoped that in this very brief and telescoped description of Zoroastrianism, the reader, whether he be of Jewish, Christian, or Muslim background, has come upon familiar terms and concepts such as angels, hosts, heaven, hell, purgatory, last judgment, evil spirit, holy spirit, prince of light, prince of darkness, kingdom of God, life overcoming death, baptism by fire, and the *Chinvat* Bridge (*Sarat* Bridge in Islam). These concepts, and others that are part of Zoroastrianism, developed in diverse ways in the theistic religions that followed it.

3

Ancient Iran—Parthians
and Sāsānians

The bright star of the Achaemenians began to fade after the death of Xerxes II in 423 B.C. Even though Artaxerxes I followed the tolerant policy of his fathers, he was a man of weak character and did not lead his troops in person. Nevertheless, the old stability continued. There was a period of peace with Greece and peaceful acts, such as allowing Ezra to return to Jerusalem with a number of Jewish families who were living in exile, and travel and interchange of knowledge became possible.

During the reigns of Darius II and Artaxerxes II, however, the momentum of stability slackened and the era witnessed intrigue and corruption within the empire. Insofar as relations with the outside world were concerned, gold replaced personal valor and intrigue took the place of rational policy. The result was uprisings at home and rebellion abroad. At the end of the Peloponnesian wars many Greek soldiers were unemployed; they became mercenaries of the Persian empire and, in time, formed the bulk of the Persian army. This in itself was a great blow to the prestige of the empire but even a greater one was the revolt of Cyrus, a nephew of the king. He was defeated, and it must have been during this turmoil that Xenophon wrote about the escape of ten thousand Greeks from Iran. Athens had lost its power and Sparta was not able to control the destiny of the Greeks. A new power was emerging in Macedonia under Philip. On the other hand, it appeared that Artaxerxes III (359–338 B.C.) was destined to save the Persian empire. He was harsh and cruel but had an iron will and started to quell rebellions with a strong hand. He reconquered Egypt and restored the empire established by Darius I. But this was short-lived, for the same year (338 B.C.) that Philip of Macedonia put an end to the independence of Greek states, Artaxerxes was murdered by poison.

Philip had become master of a united Greece while on the throne of Persia sat a young man, Darius III (336–330 B.C.), brave but inexperienced, facing for the first time the combined power of the Greeks. Philip had been murdered; his son Alexander faced Darius III of Persia.

ALEXANDER

The conquest of Alexander has been emotionally described as a crusade for the "liberation" of Greek cities from the Persian yoke and the dissemination of Greek democracy and culture. Indeed, the life of Alexander himself has been surrounded by so much legend that it is extremely difficult to sift fact from fiction. The records of the conquest of Persia by Alexander are exclusively from Greek sources and, quite understandably, exaggerated in favor of the Greeks. The fact that Persia was defeated is uncontestable, but the motives of Alexander and his Greek allies were not as lofty as they sometimes are portrayed. If Alexander took scholars and scientists with him on the expedition, it was not altogether for the lofty purpose of dissemination of knowledge but also to be able to choose the best and bring it back as war booty. To be sure, there was the idea of liberating the Greek cities from the Persian yoke—even though, to his surprise, Alexander found that some of the cities did not want to be liberated simply because there was no yoke. There was also, like the Crusades of the Middle Ages, desire for loot, commerce, adventure, and expansion of territory and power. At the battle of Issus, among the people taken prisoner in the Persian camp were ambassadors of Sparta, Athens, and Thebes, who no doubt were sent to make a deal with the Persian king, which shows that the most important members of the "Panhellenic movement" were playing on both sides of the fence.[1]

In any case, there were three main battles between Alexander and Darius. The first was on the banks of the River Granicus in 334 B.C. in which the Persians were defeated and Alexander almost lost his life, and where Greek mercenaries in the Persian army were massacred even though they had surrendered. The second and the more decisive battle took place a year later at Issus in which, at the advice of a Greek deserter, Darius was persuaded to advance to meet Alexander. The result was disastrous for the Persians. Darius fled, but his mother, wife, and children fell into the hands of Alexander. Rather than pursuing the Persians, the young conqueror spent nearly three years subduing

1. Ghirshman, *Iran*, p. 210.

Egypt in order to secure his flank. During this short interval Darius is said to have offered to divide his empire with Alexander, to leave his son as hostage, and to pay ransom for the liberation of his family. All this Alexander refused, and the two armies met for the last time on October 1, 331 B.C. at Gaugamela, some seventy-five miles from Arbela in Assyria. The result was the same as the previous two battles, and the scholars believe that the main reason for these defeats was the fact that the Persians, who had been so flexible in other things, had remained rigid in their military tactics and were oblivious to new methods and weaponry of war employed by Alexander. Darius escaped to Ecbatana; but the power of the Persian empire was spent, and a few months later Darius was murdered by one of his own men and the rule of the House of Hakhamanesh came to an end.

From then on the conquest of Iran by Alexander was practically uncontested. He took Susa and marched against Persepolis. The conqueror had, by now, forgotten about the "crusade." Fusion of culture and blood between Greeks and Persians had become more important than the "liberation" of Greece from Persia. He himself donned Persian attire, married Roxana, a Persian princess, and ordered or encouraged the mass marriage of his men with Persian women. He posed as the legitimate successor of the Achaemenids, retained the Persian satraps at their posts, and adopted the Persian method of administration. At Persepolis, however, whether by accident or design, the spirit of crusade and vengeance took the upper hand. Persepolis, which had become "the richest city under the sun" was handed over to the soldiers for plunder. Men were slain, women were enslaved and the "Macedonians fought one another for the plunder." "So thorough was the search for loot that only a handful of coins have been unearthed by the excavators." The climax of these barbarities was reached when, at the order of Alexander, the magnificent edifice was burned to the ground.[2]

Exalted and world encompassing as the ideas of Alexander may have been—ideas such as the fusion of races and civilizations under one authority, the founding of intercultural colonies, freeing the world from economic divisions, and establishing a peace which was both Eastern and Western—all came to naught with his premature death in 323 B.C. a mere seven years after his conquest of Persia. His death relegated all those ideas to the realm of the "might have been." What really did occur is so vastly different from what might have occurred if he had not died that all the luster of "Hellenism" and its "contributions" fades as the subject is studied more carefully.

2. For a detailed description of the destruction of Persepolis and its consequences see A. T. Olmstead, *History of the Persian Empire* (University of Chicago Press, 1948), pp. 519 ff.

HELLENISM

Professor Frye expresses the opinion, which other western authorities have expressed in diverse forms, namely, that "the conquest of the Achaemenid empire by Alexander . . . marks the end of that ancient history and the beginning of a new era, an era of oecumenical culture generally called Hellenism." [3] In the light of the fact that all these authors, without exception, have devoted the greater portion of their books praising the oecumenicity, open-mindedness, tolerance, and internationalism of the Persians and how under the Achaemenids all nationalities were allowed to develop their talents freely, one is amazed to read that Hellenism *started* an oecumenical culture in the East rather than, at least, continued the tradition already started by the House of Hakhāmanesh.

But did the heirs of Alexander continue such a spirit? It is commonly accepted by all historians that, following the death of Alexander, his fledgling empire was plunged into a bloody struggle between his generals. The bloodshed and destruction continued for forty years until, at long last, the situation was stabilized by the formation of three kingdoms: European Greece under a Macedonian monarchy, Egypt under Ptolemy, and western Iran under Seleucus. The Seleucid kingdom, which controlled the western part of the Achaemenian empire, was highly centralized and autocratic. It had to be because it was not a national dynasty and could not trust the Iranian majority. The Seleucids did not "attempt to continue the policy of the fusion of races." [4] They established Greek centers in different cities in the empire, and the most they could do was to preserve Greek supremacy for a while.[5] The fact that some Greek inscriptions have been found in these centers is not an indication of a new wave of Greek influence. After all, part of the Greek culture was developed under the Achaemenid rule, and its Golden Age was at a time when, thanks to the open door policy of the Achaemenids, there was a great deal of interchange between the two peoples. It was not as though the Persians had built a dam waiting to be destroyed by Alexander in order to let the waters of Greek culture overrun the land of Iran. Scholars from Theodor Noldeke until the present have agreed that "Hellenism never touched nearer than the surface of Persian life." [6] It seems that inasmuch as it did, if one has to judge the Seleucids as the chief missionaries of Hellenism, then it

3. Frye, *Heritage of Persia,* p. 124.
4. Ghirshman, *Iran,* p. 225.
5. It is doubtful whether they were actually cities; they were more likely quarters in the cities or cantonments outside of established cities.
6. Theodor Noldeke, *Aufsätze zur Persichen Geschichte* (Leipzig, 1884), p. 134.

destroyed the spirit of tolerance, good will, and dialogue that the Achaemenids had started. Never again do we see in that part of the world, or anywhere else for that matter, another empire based on tolerance as was that of the Achaemenids. At the time of the Achaemenids the boundary of political struggle between the rulers of the major portion of Europe and Persia was the Straits of Bosporus and Dardanelles, while after Alexander it was pushed eastward to include Asia Minor within the western orbit. The Parthians and the Sasanids fought against the Romans and the Byzantines respectively. To show that it was not really the *West* against the *East* as Professor Ghirshman would have us believe when he talks about "the *conscience Européenne* of the fourth century B.C. that led to the campaign of Alexander," [7] the Ottoman Turks who occupied the same territory as the Byzantines before them and who most certainly were not led by "*conscience Européenne*," fought the Safavids, the Afshārs, and the Qājārs who occupied the same territory as the Sasanids and Parthians before them, along the same borders and heaven knows for what reasons.

To be sure, the Seleucids, who ruled Iran proper for about a century, were not without influence in art and architecture as well as in commerce and social life. This is especially so because the Persians have been able to adapt themselves to new situations and to adopt new ways. This is true now as it was in the days of Herodotus who wrote: "There is no nation which so readily adopts foreign customs as the Persians. As soon as they hear of any luxury they instantly make it their own." But whether the normal influences of an occupying power, which admittedly was itself influenced by the occupied people, should be magnified to such exaggerated proportions as Hellenism has been in the history of Iran and the Middle East is a question that should be scrutinized.

THE PARTHIANS

By the time the grandson of Seleucus, Antiochus II (261–246 B.C.) succeeded to the throne, the Parthians had become a serious menace in eastern Iran. In 246 B.C. Arsaces I, known to the Persians as Ashk, established a kingdom. The Seleucids were caught between the growing power of Rome on the west and the Parthians on the east. The Roman encroachments, at the expense of the Seleucids, enabled Mithridates I (171–138 B.C.) to extend his power over Bactria, Parsa, Susa, Media, and Babylonia. The destruction of the Greek empire was assured; but the Parthians were not accepted by the bulk of Iranians as liberators, and there were many uprisings and attempts to establish new kingdoms in different parts of Iran. But these were of no avail. The star of the Parthian fortune was on the rise and the successors of Mithridates

7. Ghirshman, *Iran*, p. 352.

strengthened their hold on their gains and expanded the empire. By the time of Mithridates II (127–87 B.C.) the Parthians had a bona fide empire extending from India to Armenia, and the ruler took upon himself the title of "king of kings."

The Romans, in the meantime, were gradually advancing eastward. The inevitable conflict between the two advancing empires, who did not know very much about each other, began under the reign of Phraates III (69–57 B.C.) and continued off and on until the end of the Parthian dynasty in A.D. 227. The world of west Asia and Europe was virtually divided between the Romans and the Parthians. Romans, such as Mark Anthony, Octavian, Tiberius, Nero, Trajan, and others well-known in the West, were engaged in wars with the Parthians, to the Romans a name synonymous with *Persians*. These wars were not just for the advancement of prestige and power. Iran was astride the trade route between East and West. The Romans wanted the silk, spices, ivory, perfume, and precious stones of India and China, while the manufactured goods of Rome such as bronze, glassware, wines, oils, and gold especially had customers in the East. Iran, in the main, was the entrepreneur and the specialist in transportation, both on land and water.[8]

Out of the ruins of the empire that Alexander wanted to establish, two new world empires had emerged. One was Rome, which had a Greek heritage, was conscious of it, and built upon it. The other was Parthia, which also, albeit to a lesser degree, had a Greek heritage that it allowed to fade away. In the beginning the Parthians tried to steer a middle course between the Greeks and the Persians. While they considered themselves restorers of the Achaemenid empire, at the same time they introduced themselves on their coins as philhellene to the Greeks. Their records were kept in Greek and their diplomatic language, during the early years, was Greek. As time passed, however, they forsook the Greek and became the Iranians that they were, adopting consciously many things from the old Persian empire. In time they spoke Middle Persian, wrote in Pahlavi script, and their bards sang about the heroes, *pahlavāns,* which songs in part became the source of the epic of *Shāhnāmeh.*[9]

Even though the Parthian kings were mostly involved in the affairs of Mesopotamia and their struggle with Rome, they did not neglect their contacts with the East. As early as 115 B.C. an embassy from China visited Iran and concluded a treaty with Mithridates on the

8. The fact that empires in Iran did not build strong navies has led scholars to the mistaken conclusion that Iranians were not seafarers. Linguistic evidence alone refutes this because words such as *anchor, helm, barge, captain, lateen,* and others prevalent in Arabic (and some in English) are derived from Persian. Furthermore, place names on the shores of the Indian Ocean from Zanzibar to Malabar are Persian. See George F. Hourani, *Arab Seafaring in the Indian Ocean,* trans. into Persian by M. Moghadam (Tehran: Franklin Publications, 1959), pp. 173 ff., under "Comments by the Translator."

9. Frye, *Heritage of Persia,* p. 170.

movement of caravans through Iran. These contacts are recorded in the Chinese sources as well. Furthermore, Parthian coins found on the Volga attest to the relationship.

MITHRAISM

Practically all scholars believe that during the Parthian period great changes occurred in Iran in religion, art, and literature. It is difficult to know what these changes were and from what source they arose. Usually western scholars consider Hellenism to be the source of these great changes which occurred during the second century B.C. and on into the middle of the Parthian period. This may well be, but it is useful for us to consider, in bare outline, the new theory advanced by Zabih Behruz[10] and Mohamad Moghadam,[11] both of whom have been mentioned before. The great event, according to these scholars, was the birth of Mehr (Mithra) or the Christ, on Saturday night, December 25, 272 B.C. He died at the age of sixty-four by natural causes, but his message was accepted by many, and the missionaries of the faith took the message to all parts of the world from China to Ireland. The Parthians adopted Mithraism as their official religion; and up to the fourth century A.D., not only was it prevalent in Rome, but it was the official religion of the Roman empire. Inasmuch as this person Mehr was born of a virgin named Nāhid Anahita ("immaculate"), and inasmuch as the worship of Mithra, and Anahita, the virgin mother of Mithra, was well-known in the Achaemenian period, it is as yet not clear to this writer whether the religion adopted by the Parthians and accepted in many parts of the world was a revival of the old Mithra worship, or was caused by a religious leader named Mithra.

Not much is known about the life and works of Mithra, but what little information is available is strangely similar to the life and works of Jesus of Nazareth; about the only differences are the location of birth and the fact that Mithra of Iran died a natural death while Jesus was crucified.[12] While Christianity was based on prophetic Judaism, Mithraism was based on Zoroastrianism, which would probably account for the idea that "The Parthians in a sense rescued the Zoroastrian religion, giving it the basis of a canon which passed to the Sāsānians and down to the present day."[13]

These problems, however, are not within the scope of this survey; but it must be noted that there is a great mass of archeological and lin-

10. See his *Taqvim va Tārikh dar Iran* (*Iran-Kudeh* no. 15).

11. See his *Mehrābeh yā Paresteshgāh-e Din-e Mehr* (*Mithraeum or the Temple of the Religion of Mithra*) (Tehran: Iran-e Bāstān, 1965).

12. One wonders whether the statement in the Koran concerning Jesus, "They did not kill him, they did not crucify him," refers to Christ Mithra rather than Christ Jesus.

13. Frye, *Heritage of Persia*, p. 170.

guistic evidence that shows the tremendous influence of Mithraism in Europe, Iran, and as far east as China and Japan. Later it became the rival of orthodox Zoroastrianism in the Sasanian empire and of Christianity in Europe. In Christian church history it is known as one of the "mystery religions." In the gradual disappearance of Mithraism, its temples were destroyed and churches, Zoroastrian fire temples, and even mosques were built over them. The Churches of St. Prisca and St. Clemente in Rome are good examples of this fact. Temples of Mithra have also been found in London, Austria, Hungary, Ireland, and other locations in Europe.[14] The ideas and rituals of Mithraism, however, are so mixed with the ideas and rituals of the religions which supplanted it that "even though on the surface they destroyed the religion of Mithra, in reality the religion of the person whom the Iranians called 'Victorious' and the Romans named the 'Undefeatable Lord' is alive within other religions and actually has remained undefeatable." [15]

In Mithraism, the bull, Persian *gāv* or *go*, was the symbol of the passion of man, which is also alluded to in Persian Sufi poetry. Since Mithra killed the bull in a cave, Mithraic temples were usually built in caves, examples of which are to be found in the mountains of the Italian Alps and the Balkans. In localities where there are no mountains, the "holy of holies" of the Mithraic temples was given a cave-like appearance by building special domes over it. The Persian word for dome is *āveh* (English abbey) and *Mehrābeh* found its way into Arabic as *Mehrāb*, which is the holiest place in the mosque. Since the shedding of the bull's blood was for the remission of sins, this fact was ritualized in Mithraic worship. A holy table (Persian *miz*, Latin *mass*) was set on which wine and bread and sometimes meat were placed symbolizing the blood and body of the bull. This was called the *hu khoresht*, good food (Greek *eucharist*) which was partaken of by the worshippers. Reliefs or drawings of this and other Mithraic rituals are found wherever Mithraic temples have been found. In Iran evidences of Mithra worship may be seen in Sāveh, Tāq-e Bostān, Susa, Bishāpur, Sistān, Khorāsān and other places. Professor Ghirshman, the excavator of Bishāpur, believes it to be the ruins of a Zorastrian fire temple. He and other western scholars believe the other relics in Iran mentioned above to be types of Sasanian art forms. Professors Behruz and Moghadam, however, disagree with these findings.

Of course part of this is not new. It has been recorded that the cult of Anahita was very popular in the Parthian period, and it was exported beyond the western frontiers of Iran. Anahita, exalted as the "Mother of the Lord," probably gave rise to the exaltation of Mary as "the Mother of God" and the naming of many churches after her. Professor

---

14. See Vermaseren, *Mithras, the Secret God*. My information, however, is taken from Moghadam, who has used the above-named work extensively.

15. Moghadam, *Mehrābeh*, p. 48.

Ghirshman[16] believes that pirates took Mithraism to Rome. It is curious that pirates, of all people, would be interested in religion in general or in Mithraism in particular.[17]

Some thirty-five kings ascended the Parthian throne in about 464 years. It would be well beyond the scope of this brief survey to discuss any number of them. All that can be said is that the Parthians did try to restore the ancient Achaemenian culture and added significantly to it. They also tried to create a commonwealth of nations, as the Achaemenians had done, and had the custom of choosing their kings. This probably explains why they were not strong enough to create a viable central government. Neither did they impart a sense of belonging or nationhood to the diverse groups under them. This was left for the Sasanians to accomplish.

The Sasanians

The origin of the Sāsānians is obscure, but it is certain that they sprung from Fārs, the native land of the Achaemenians. Ferdosi relates that Sāsān was a shepherd whom Pāpak (or Bābak) the king of Estakhr (near Persepolis) liked very much and gave his daughter Dinak to him in marriage. They had a son named Ardeshir who founded the Sāsānian dynasty. The inscription of Shāpur I, found on the Ka'ba of Zoroaster in the outskirts of Pasargadai, leads historians to surmise that Ardeshir Bābakān, was the son of Bābak and the grandson of Sāsān. Sāsān and Bābak were probably priests in the temple of Anahita in Estakhr. In about A.D. 211, Ardeshir organized a revolt against the Parthians and by 224 was in control of a good portion of southern Iran.

The Sāsānians claimed to be the descendants of the Achaemenians whose name still carried a great deal of weight among the Iranians. The Parthians, who were also Iranians, never gained the prestigious position of the Achaemenids and were considered inferior. Whereas the Achaemenids had created a national empire based on tolerance and flexibility and had achieved a unity through diversity, something that the Parthians were not able to achieve, the Sāsānians created a national empire based on imperialism and achieved unity through forced conformity. In time Zoroastrianism was adopted as the state religion, and it was interpreted to voice and approve the policies of the state. It also adopted the rigidity and power of the state, became fat and corrupt with the state, and eventually died with it. Over four centuries of rule, sometimes brilliant and relaxed and often mediocre and cruel, the Sāsānians extended the frontiers of the empire and built a civilization which was basically Persian and which rivaled that of Rome.

16. Ghirshman, Iran, p. 270.
17. Moghadam thinks that piratos does not have anything to do with "pirate" but comes from Persian pir, the elder in the priestly hierarchy of Mithraism.

One of the great kings of the early Sāsānian period was Shāpur I (A.D. 240–272). In the Sāsānian period, Iran, was menaced from two sides, on the west by the Romans and on the east by the Kushāns, who dwelt around Peshāwar in modern Pakistan. The tribes in the Caucasus were also thorns in their flesh, but not as painful as the other two. The Parthians and the Achaemenians had also been pressed from both sides in a similar manner: recall that Cyrus the Great was killed in a battle against the tribes of the east. Shāpur I went against the Kushāns first, and after dealing them a severe blow he captured Bactria. He then crossed the Āmu Darya (Oxus) and came home via Tashkent and Samarkand. He was now ready for Rome. In a war which lasted intermittently for over fifteen years, Shāpur won his greatest victory against the Emperor Valerian in 260. The Roman emperor was captured along with some 70,000 Roman troops. Shāpur immortalized this victory on rock reliefs at Bishāpur and Naqsh-e-Rostam, both located in Fārs. The Roman soldiers were settled in communities in different parts of Iran.

CHURCH AND SOCIETY

Shāpur had great interest in peaceful pursuits as well as war. He completed the reorganization of the empire that had been started by his father. He also ordered the translation of scientific and philosophical works into Persian. He was tolerant enough to give his protection to Māni, the founder of Manichaeism. Māni was the promoter of one of the long line of syncretistic religions which found fertile ground in Iran, the most recent of which is Bahāism founded in 1844. Manichaeism, a blending of Zoroastrianism, Buddhism, and Christianity into a universal religion, found many adherents in Iran and in the West. But the Zoroastrian mobads (priests), who had become powerful as an arm of the state, could not allow such a heresy any more than could the Christian priests whose religion would soon become the official religion of Rome. Soon after the death of Shāpur, his son Bahrām I, goaded by the Mazdian priests, killed Māni in 272. This did not end Manichaeism, but Māni's followers were persecuted as heretics by the Zoroastrians and Christians alike.[18]

During the thirty-seven years between the death of Shāpur I in 272 and the accession of Shāpur II in 309, no less than six kings ascended the Sāsānian throne. During this period of confusion, Iran was not strong enough to curb the pressure of Rome or resist the raids of the Kushāns. It seems that Shāpur II (309–379) had to do the work of his namesake all over again. He subdued the Kushāns, annexing their territory, and expanded the boundaries of his empire to the borders of Chinese Turkestan. Then he faced Rome and recovered the territories they had overrun.

18. A famous Manichaean who turned Christian was St. Augustine. Later Mithraism replaced Manichaeism.

In the protracted wars between Iran and Rome, Armenia was caught in the middle and suffered the most, now being annexed by one or occupied by the other. During the Parthian period, one of the Arsacid (Parthian) princes had been appointed king of Armenia and the region enjoyed semi-independent and sometimes independent existence. During the Sāsānian times, however, and the wars with Rome, Armenia became a buffer state. Quite naturally two parties developed in the area, one inclined toward Iran and the other toward Rome. When Christianity became the official religion of Rome after the conversion of Constantine, and later when the Armenians became Christians, their situation altered. Christianity, which had been tolerated during the Parthian and early Sāsānian periods and was allowed to spread in the empire and to build churches and establish bishoprics, became suspect as the official religion of the arch enemy, Rome. During most of the long reign of Shāpur II, and intermittently afterwards, the Christians were persecuted and sometimes massacred in cold blood.

It has already been stated that the Sāsānians set about to establish a strong central empire in which unity was achieved through conformity. In such a society each segment that enjoys a certain amount of power and has developed a vested interest is in turn centralized and becomes very jealous of its power and privileges. Often these different segments cooperated with each other in the face of a common enemy, to keep their power, and sometimes they vied with each other to gain more power at each other's expense. In the early Sāsānian period, toward the top of the pyramid of power there were the king and his warriors, the priests, and the nobility. Later on the scribes, who served the ever increasing activities of the central government, and the lesser nobility (dehqān) joined in the power struggle. In the struggle for power between the king and the large landowning nobility, the priests were in the middle sometimes helping the king against the nobility and sometimes joining the nobility in deposing the king in favor of another member of the royal family. Apparently the tradition of legitimacy in the royal line was quite strong. Only once did a strong member of the nobility and a popular general, Bahrām Chubin, lead a coup d'état in about A.D. 590 and try to be king. But he failed, mostly because he was not a member of the Sāsānian family.

The established Zoroastrian Church, under the Sāsānians, developed a hierarchy as well as an orthodox theology. The Avesta was put into writing, and Zoroastrianism developed a rigid theology which matched the rigidity of the state it served. In this hierarchy the office of hirbad was in charge of the fire temples. Above this was the mobad, the priests who were headed by the mobadān mobad, the chief religious leader of the realm. At times we read about the "Mobad of Ahura Mazda," which must have been an honorary title bestowed upon an individual by the king. As a centralized organization, the church could not tolerate innovation. We have seen how it dealt with the Manichaeans. The

Zoroastrian priesthood was also very jealous of the spread of Christianity and encouraged the persecution of that group. They relegated the worship of Anahita and Mithra to the background and gradually destroyed it. The persecution of the Christians came to an end, insofar as the government was concerned, when during the reign of Bahrām V (421–439) the new Catholics summoned a synod which made the Christian Church of Iran independent of that of Byzantium. Since that time the Persian Church has been usually called "Nestorian."

The Communism of Mazdak

There were over thirty kings in the Sāsānian dynasty, and most of them did not accomplish much. Since the Byzantine empire was going through similar vicissitudes, it could not take advantage of the Sāsānian weakness. In the East, however, a new group from Central Asia had succeeded the Kushans. They were called Ephthalites and were probably members of an Iranian tribe or one greatly influenced by them. In the second half of the fifth century they defeated the Sāsānians and, for intermittent decades until about A.D. 531, they had the upper hand and the situation in Iran was confused. There were pretenders to the throne and rivalries among the nobility and the army generals for power. The greatest sufferers were the peasant masses, who had to provide soldiers for the civil and national wars and paid taxes to carry on the struggle for power among the nobles. Some of the vassal states revolted, and there were fresh raids from the Ephthalites, who demanded and received tribute. Economic depression and famine encouraged the masses to join the revolt of Mazdak.

The revolt of Mazdak was a socioreligious movement, partly based on abstinence and avoidance of hatred taught by Māni, and partly based upon the equal distribution or sharing of goods and also of women.[19] It was a kind of a "communist movement" which demanded the dispossessing of the rich in favor of the poor. King Qobād I (488–531), who was himself pressed by many problems, championed the cause of Mazdak, perhaps to free himself from the clutches of the nobility, and introduced new laws favoring the program of Mazdak. But the nobility and the Zoroastrian as well as the Christian clergy were against the Mazdaki movement and the king. He was deposed, but after two years he was reinstated to the throne with some help from the Ephthalites. In the meantime, the Mazdaki movement had become a full-fledged social revolution. Qobād, who had very likely compromised his support of the Mazdaki movement as a price for the crown, was

19. The reader should be cautioned that Moslem writers were in the habit of accusing any group they did not like of sharing their women. Since part of the Mazdaki program had to do with women, perhaps the king, princes, and the nobility kept so many women in the harems that there were not enough of them outside—hence the equal distribution of women.

cool toward the revolutionaries. He allowed the Mazdaki centers to be destroyed and the rebels massacred. This did not end the movement, for we hear about it well into the Islamic period.

SĀSĀNID ACHIEVEMENT AND DECLINE

The most popular of the Sāsānian kings in the folklore of Iran is Khosro I (531–579), whose very name became synonymous with "king," and whose title, *Anushiravān* "The Immortal Soul," shows the legend which has been built around him. He was called "The Just," a title he did not deserve because he instigated the massacre of Mazdak and his followers. He was a strong king, worthy of comparison with Shāpur, but because he was a bright star in the dark skies of Sāsānian fortune, his light has shone even brighter than it actually was. He restored the land taken from the landed gentry by the followers of Mazdak. He repaired roads, bridges, and canals which were destroyed in the civil strife and inaugurated extensive legislation in fiscal matters. He ordered a survey of the land and a census of population as well as livestock, date palms, and olive trees. He helped the peasants by changing the tax system from a fixed amount to one proportional to the yield. Even though he returned the property of the nobility, he did not allow them to regain their lost power. Instead, he created a new class of landed nobility called *dehqān*, who became the backbone of the local administration in Iran for centuries. He strengthened the bureaucracy so that the office of *Dabirān Dabir* (Chief of Administration) became very important in the empire. He also reformed the army by introducing compulsory military service and creating "peasant-soldiers." For the defense of the empire, he settled tribes at the frontiers and gave them the responsibility of securing the frontiers against foreign enemies. These *marzbāns*, "watchers of the border," also called *marzdārs*, "keepers of the border," became a permanent institution in Iran until the twentieth century. Khosro did not forget the traditional enemies of the Sāsānians. He crushed the power of the Ephthalites and dealt a severe blow at the Byzantines.

Notwithstanding all this, the attempt of Khosro was at best a rearguard action against annihilation. Decay had already started and the continuation of the senseless wars against Byzantium, heavy taxation on the population to carry on the wars, economic stagnation, and internal strife did not help the situation.

The Sāsānians, as heirs of the Achaemenids, built a national empire. They indeed nurtured the "conscience Iranienne," which they had inherited, by contributions of their own, and this consciousness has appeared and reappeared in Iran in times of stress as well as periods of glory. Sāsānian art, according to the experts in the field, was "the culmination of a millennium of development." [20] Typical of all periods

20. Frye, *Heritage of Persia*, p. 222.

of Persian art, "It was receptive to foreign influences, but it adapted them to the traditions of its native land, and as the art of a world empire it spread into far distant countries." [21] Strangely enough they did not rebuild the Achaemenian cities of Pasargadai and Persepolis, but built cities of their own. Chief among them were Bishāpur in Fārs, Ctesiphon, which the Parthians had started on the Tigris River, and Gondishāpur in Khuzestan. Works from Byzantium as well as India on literature, philosophy, and medicine were translated. Gondishāpur became "the greatest intellectual center of the time," and boasted a prominent medical college which lasted well into the Islamic times. Borzu, the famous minister and physician of Khosro Anushiravān, is reputed to have translated many books on medicine from India. His famous translation, however, is the fables of Bidpāy and he is also credited with bringing the game of chess from India and creating the game of backgammon (Persian, *nard*) to match it.

Since Iran and Byzantium were the two most civilized empires of West Asia and Europe, one should expect great interchange between them. There was trade in spices, precious stones, and silk. The most important commodity was silk, in which Iran had a monopoly. Although Iran and Byzantium had contiguous boundaries for over three hundred years, there was little cultural exchange. Constant wars and insecure peace, no doubt, contributed to this paucity. War had become a habit, most of it as senseless as it had been between the Romans and the Parthians before and was to be between the Ottomans and the Safavids centuries after them. The wars between these powers were very much like the trench warfare in Europe during the First World War. Attacks brought counterattacks, and neither side had anything to show for them except loss of life and property.

The two empires produced two more giants to continue the useless war: Khosro Parviz (591–628) in Iran and Heraclius (610–641) in Byzantium. For nineteen years the Persians under Parviz swept everything before them, took Damascus, Aleppo, and Antioch. In 614 the Persians sacked Jerusalem and carried away the "True Cross" of Jesus, a most cherished Christian possession. By 617, the Persian army was poised across the Bosporus from Constantinople. The inevitable counterattack was started by Heraclius in 622, and six years later it was the Byzantine army that stood at the gates of Ctesiphon, the Persian capital. The victories of both Parviz and Heraclius were empty. Even though Khosro Parviz was killed by his own sons and the country was, once more, plunged into chaos, Heraclius was too exhausted himself to pursue his victory. He satisfied himself with retrieving the "True Cross." The two empires had bled each other to death and the end for both came from an unexpected source—the desert of Arabia.

21. Ghirshman, *Iran*, p. 318.

4

Iran under Islam

The territory and climate of the Arabian peninsula were too inhospitable to arouse the greed of the Byzantine or the Persian empires. Furthermore, the roaming Bedouins, who constitute five-sixths of the population, proved uncontrollable. Trade with the people of the desert was not so great as to induce the empires to fight over it. There were periodic raids by the Bedouins; in order to protect themselves from such raids, the two empires had agreed to give autonomy to two strong tribes and had given them the responsibility for keeping the raiders in check. Thus, the Ghassanids and the Lakhmids of Hira had special arrangements with Byzantium and Iran respectively. The milder climate of south Arabia had allowed the creation of a settled culture. The Yamanites of the south traded with Iran and their caravans traveled north through Hejaz to Syria. Settled communities along the trade route such as Mecca and Yathrib (later called Medina) had a large south Arabian population.

It is generally presumed that many waves of raiders have emerged from the Arabian peninsula and have settled in the Fertile Crescent.[1] Assyrians, Babylonians, Chaldeans, and Hebrews are supposed to have come from the desert. The last large raid in known history occurred about the middle of the seventh century A.D.; it created an empire and also established a religion. The people who emerged from the desert are known as Arabs and the religion they preached is called Islam.

---

1. "Fertile Crescent" is used to define a territory that covers Iraq, Syria, Lebanon, Jordan, and Israel.

ISLAM

Islam is the religion of submission to the will of Allah, a deity who was vaguely familiar to the pre-Islamic Arabs and the same as *El-loh* or *Elohim*, the deity described in the Old Testament. Mohammad received his revelation from Allah toward the end of the month of Ramazān in A.D. 610. At the time he was forty years old, married, and a prominent member of the Qoraysh tribe in Mecca. The important members of the Qoraysh, Mohammad among them, did not only have the business monopoly in the city of Mecca but were also custodians of the holiest shrine in Arabia, the Ka'ba, which was located in the city and attracted thousands of Bedouins every year, who came for pilgrimage as well as trading.

The message of Mohammad was monotheistic and against the pantheon of gods and goddesses which surrounded the Ka'ba. Since Mohammad identified Allah with the God of the Jews and Christians, he considered his message to be in line with the Judeo-Christian tradition. Other religions, such as Zoroastrianism, Buddhism, and so on, were outside the tradition and, therefore, were not acceptable as authentic.

Like many a prophet before him, Mohammad clashed with his fellow businessmen of the tribe, who saw in his message the destruction of the Ka'ba and, with it, the business opportunities the pilgrims brought every year. For twelve years they opposed him and Mohammad did not have many converts for all his efforts. Fortunately for him, however, he was invited by the tribes of Medina, a commercial rival of Mecca, to become their leader. He accepted the invitation and with a number of his followers migrated to Medina in 622. This migration or *Hejra* marks the beginning of the year one of the Moslem calendar.

In Medina, Mohammad was both the new head of the state and at the same time the prophet of Allah. As head of the state he was the judge, legislator, organizer, and the man responsible for the welfare of the community. As a prophet he had to see that the will of Allah was proclaimed. In his mind and in the opinion of his followers the two roles were combined. In his person as prophet-king, religion and state became one and inseparable. Islam became a theocratic society and has remained so, at least in theory, to the present time. As prophet he revealed the will of Allah, and as head of the state he enforced it. Raiding and the search for booty was a time-honored practice among the inhabitants of Arabia, and Mohammad's position demanded that he lead them in battle. Mohammad, however, used these engagements to subdue the tribes and bring them under the rule of Allah, whose prophet he was. To recount the many battles in which Mohammad was engaged is not in the scope of this volume. But suffice it to say that by his death in 632, he had unified Arabia under the banner of

Islam. He subdued Mecca and ordered the destruction of the idols; but he preserved the Ka'ba, which embodied the holy black stone, and continued it as a shrine for Moslem pilgrimage in exactly the same manner as it had been in pagan times.

The religion that Mohammad preached was straightforward, simple, and extremely egalitarian. The philosophical ramifications and theological speculations that are part of Islam today are additions made later, when the simple faith came in contact with the more sophisticated ideas of the Greeks and Persians.

The death of the Prophet created one of the most thorny problems to disturb the body politic of Islam throughout the centuries to this day. The problem was that of the succession to his political office. Even before the interment of Mohammad's body, a bitter struggle arose over succession. On the whole there developed three different opinions. On the one side were the legitimists, who were later called *Shi'is*. They believed that succession belonged exclusively to the descendants of the Prophet. Since Mohammad did not have a male issue, the prize, they believed, should go to Ali, who was the first cousin, adopted son, and son-in-law of the Prophet, and one of the first to accept Islam. He would be followed by his two sons and their descendants.

The next group, whose opinion on the caliphate was accepted by the Sunni sect of Islam, believed that since the Prophet himself was a member of the Qoraysh tribe, that only a member of this tribe could succeed him. As we know, this group won the day for the first three caliphs, and the members of the Omayyad and Abbāsid dynasties belonged to the Qoraysh tribe.

The third group, a minority, believed that the caliphate should not be limited to a family or a tribe. They took Mohammad at his word that greatness was based on piety and not on blood. These people, who later became known as *Khārejites*, "Seceders," were puritans in their social ideals and personal life and loved the simplicity of the prophetic message. They claimed that even a slave could become a caliph. Unfortunately they did not have a large following but they were the self-appointed vigilantes for the purity of Islam and became thorns in the flesh of the established Moslem governments.

When Abu Bakr was chosen the first caliph, he had to spend his whole term of office, which was less than three years, in subduing the rebellious tribes. Their allegiance to Mohammad had been superficial and, with him gone, they severed their relations and reverted to their old ways. Some of them even claimed prophets of their own.

THE CONQUEST OF IRAN

After the death of Abu Bakr in 634, Omar was chosen caliph. It was under the inspired leadership of Omar that the Arabs of the desert erupted like a volcano and consumed everything before them. The ease with which the Arab armies defeated two of the largest empires of the time has baffled historians. We have already seen how the Byzantine and the Sāsānian empires had bled each other to death. The heavy taxes to finance the war and to enable the Sāsānian nobility and royalty, who were exempt from taxation, to live the life of luxury must have been unbearable for the masses. The Mazdaki revolt had not been able to break the stratification of society, which had closed the door of opportunity to others. Religion in Iran had become an arm of the state and an oppressor of the people. Under these circumstances it is not too surprising that the Arabs defeated the Persians. The Sāsānians did not expect attacks from the bedraggled Bedouins any more than the Romans expected the Huns, or the Chinese the Mongols.

It cannot be determined whether Mohammad had visions of a world empire. We know that Abu Bakr, who had his hands full with the rebellious tribes, was reluctant to order his brilliant general, Khāled ibn-Valid to go to Syria. Even Omar, who was certainly enthusiastic for conquest beyond the borders of Arabia, did not set out to conquer according to a studied plan. The whole thing started more like a raiding party, which the Arabs were used to, than a full-fledged military campaign. Also it must be considered that it had become necessary for Omar to send out the Bedouins to war. The new religion, imposed on the Arabs by Mohammad and again by Abu Bakr, had disrupted their mode of life. Among other things, they were asked to pay taxes, which they had never done before. Furthermore, they were forbidden from raiding, which had been a habit of generations and could not be abandoned so easily. So Omar encouraged them to fight non-Moslems outside of Arabia, thereby ridding himself of Bedouin intransigence at home and affording the new government the prospects of victory abroad. The Bedouins, who had heard of the fabulous wealth of Iran and Byzantium, were very eager to go, especially when they were exempt from paying taxes.

The adventure of raiding and the prospects of rich economic reward were strengthened by a new faith that what they were doing was for the cause of Allah. What was heretofore a raid was elevated into a *jehad*, holy war, which, in case of death, would assure them entry into paradise. Without Islam, the victories of the Arabs would not have been much more than raiding sorties, and without the military victories, Islam woud not have become much more than a tribal religion in Arabia. In the early days, the mosque in Medina, which Mohammad had built, was not only a place of worship, but also the court of law and headquarters for military command. Omar, like other caliphs, was the leader in time of prayer, the judge, and also the supreme military commander. It is futile to try to separate the religion of Islam from the military campaigns of the early Moslems. Moslem historians have not done so. "In the mind of every Arab from Omar down to the lowliest soldier, Allah, Mahammad, war booty, tribute, martyrdom, and paradise were all part of the same indivisible package." [2]

From the start of the raids against Iran in 634 until the death of Yazdgerd III (632–651), the Arabs and the Persians were engaged in no less than thirty-three battles, the most important of which were the battles of Qādesiyeh in 637, Ctesiphon shortly afterward, and Na-hāvand in 642.[3] In the *Tārikh* of Tabari, and also in *Kāmel al-Tavārikh*, corroborated by the historian Ya'qubi, we read a story which illustrates the attitude of the Persians toward their Arab foes. After the battle of Qādesiyeh, Sa'd ibn-Vaqqās, the commander of the Arabs, sent a delegation to Yazdgerd in Ctesiphon and asked him to accept Islam or pay tribute. When the delegation arrived, the Persian courtiers laughed at the bedraggled appearance of the Bedouins and compared their spears to women's distaffs. Yazdgerd looked down upon them in contempt and asked: "Aren't you the same people who eat lizards and bury your children alive?" They answered: "Yes, we were poor and hungry but Allah has willed that we become rich and satisfied. Now that you have chosen the sword, it shall judge between us." This con-temptuous feeling was a major cause in the defeat of the Persians. Judging by the writings of modern Persian historians, the Persian attitude has not changed very much.

Thus it was that in the course of a decade the Arabs of the desert had reduced the size of the Byzantine empire by half and had van-quished the Sāsānians altogether. Yazdgerd III was a fugitive after the battle of Nahāvand and was eventually murdered by his own people in eastern Iran. For an understanding of the history of Iran it is essential for the reader to realize that the defeat of Iran at the hands of the Arabs has always been considered by the Persians as a great calamity and has not been forgotten by them. Iran has been invaded by many nations in its long history, but the Persians have forgotten about prac-tically all of them except the Arab conquerors.

After the first victories over the Byzantine and the Persian empires, it became evident to the Arabs that these colossi were not invincible. Omar and most of the Omayyad caliphs were desirous of creating an empire ruled by the Arabs in which Islam was the dominant religion and Arabic was the official language. Of course, the early Arab Moslems were not the first people in the history of the world nor the last to dream such a dream, but they succeeded more than most. What is of interest in this study is to note that the Persians brought about the defeat of the Arab dream. It was the Persians who, after recovering from the shock of defeat, consciously tried to destroy the Arab he-gemony and were successful in A.D. 750. It was the Persians who, unlike

2. For a discussion of this subject, see my *Middle East Past and Present* (Prentice-Hall: Englewood Cliffs, N.J., 1970), p. 50 ff.

3. Abdol Rafi' Haqiqat (Rafi'), *Tārikh-e Nehzathā-ye Melli-ye Iran* (*History of the National Uprisings in Iran*) (Tehran: Sherekat-e Chāp, 1969), pp. 28–108.

the Egyptians, Syrians, Iraqis, and others who adopted Arabic as their mother tongue, refused to speak Arabic and, as soon as they could, stopped writing it. It was the Persians who changed Islam before accepting it; and since 1500 they have belonged to a sect which sets them apart from the majority of the Arabs.

The peoples of the Fertile Crescent, Egypt, and North Africa were under a foreign power, Byzantium. In the victory of the Arabs, all that happened to them was a change of masters, and they had every reason to welcome such a change. A vast majority of them became Moslems, and they all adopted the Arabic language. If they remember the surrender of Damascus, Jerusalem, Alexandria and other cities to the Arabs, they do so with pride for the victory of Islam. This was never so with the Persians. The lament of the Persian poet, Khāqāni Shirvāni, (1106–1185) when he visited the ruins of the palace of Ctesiphon, *Tāq-e Kasra,* is known by every Persian, and the story of the battle of Qādesiyeh in Ferdosi's *Shāhnāmeh,* has been memorized by most of the schoolchildren in Iran. On the eve of the battle, Rostam Farrokhzād, the commanding general of the Persian forces, has a premonition of defeat and writes a moving letter to his brother in Ctesiphon. Two lines there are indicative of the feelings of the Persians.

> Drinking camels' milk and eating lizards' meat
> Have caused these Arabs, bedraggled, with bare feet!
> To want the Crown of Kiyān upon their pate.
> A thousand curses be on thy head, O fate!

The Persians did not forget their defeat and neither did they forgive Omar, who was the main cause of their defeat. Perhaps it was no accident that the second caliph of Islam was assassinated by a Persian on November 23, 644.[4]

SHI'ISM

Inasmuch as about 95 percent of the people of Iran are Shi'is and Shi'ism is the official religion of Iran, a short description of its origins and tenets is essential to the understanding of the Persian scene.

It may be stated with some reservations that the first four caliphs of Islam were "elected" to the high office. Of these, the first three, namely Abu Bakr, Omar, and Osmān were members of the Qoraysh tribe but did not satisfy the requirements of the legitimists: they felt that Mohammad had actually left a will in which he had nominated Ali and that Abu Bakr and his friends had destroyed it. Be that as it may, when

---

4. Until the second decade of the twentieth century, the Persians used to observe the anniversary of the assassination of Omar as *Id-e Omar Koshān,* The Festival of Killing Omar, and as part of the ceremony burned him in effigy.

Osmān was assassinated in 656, Ali simply assumed the office, as the fourth caliph, to the satisfaction of all those who believed that he was the only legitimate successor. Times, however, had changed. The Arabs were masters of a large empire, and a new generation of sophisticated Arabs had come to power who did not think very much of the simplicity and egalitarianism of the Prophet, nor did they feel any awe or respect for those who had been close companions of the Prophet.

No sooner had Ali been proclaimed caliph than other claimants challenged his right. The most important of these was Mo'āviyeh, a relative of Osmān, who was governor of Syria with headquarters in Damascus. He accused Ali of the murder of Osmān and refused to pay allegiance to him. The dispute culminated in a battle at Seffin, on the Euphrates, in July 657.[5] In the heat of the battle when the soldiers of Ali held the upper hand, Mo'āviyeh asked for a truce and arbitration. Ali, whose valor and piety overshadowed his political acumen, accepted arbitration. The Khārejites, who preferred Ali to others and were fighting under his banner, were so disgusted that they left the scene with the cry: "There is no arbiter except Allah." Before any conclusive decision was issued by the arbitration board, however, one of the Khārejites assassinated Ali during January 661.[6]

Hasan, the oldest son of Ali, was proclaimed caliph, but Mo'āviyeh offered him protection and royal pension and asked him to withdraw. Hasan accepted, and Mo'āviyeh became the ruler of Islam with Damascus as his capital. This, however, did not end the claim of the partisans of Ali[7] that the caliphate should remain in the household of the Prophet. Now that Hasan had withdrawn, the only rallying point was Hosayn, his younger brother, who was indeed willing to press his claim and lead a revolt against the Omayyads. In 680, when Yazid became caliph, Hosayn did not acknowledge him and secretly left Medina to join his followers in Kufa on the Persian Gulf. The plot was discovered, however, by the agents of Yazid; and the small party, including women and children, was ambushed at Karbalā, south of modern Baghdad, on the 10th of Moharram. Hosayn was beheaded and the women and children were taken captive.

Under usual circumstances, the above story would have been recorded as an abortive coup d'état; but in this case, Ali and Hosayn dead became more formidable foes of the ruling caliphate than when they were alive. Hosayn came to be considered as the "Lord of all martyrs" for the cause of Allah, and his death became the rallying oc-

5. This was the second time Ali defended his office. The first was December 9, 656, in the Battle of the Camel, when he defeated two of his rivals, aided by Ayisha, the young widow of Mohammad.

6. Another person was supposed to do away with Mo'āviyeh but he was not successful in the attempt.

7. In Arabic it is "Shi'at Ali," hence Shi'a and Shi'ism.

casion for the opponents of the caliphate. With a cause and martyrs, the followers of Ali separated themselves from the main body of Islam and formed a religiopolitical community with a philosophy, theology, government, and ethics of their own.

"From the earliest times there can have been scarcely a belief or a dream, a cult or a hope, but was eventually either integrated into, or held in suspension in that potent elixir which is Persian culture." [8] If there is any truth in the above statement, then Islam went through this process and one of the results was Shi'ism and the other was Sufism, which will be discussed later. This is not to say that either of them were Persian creations. Both have their roots in Islam and the Koran, but there is no question that both have the stamp of Iran and show characteristics that are integral parts of the Persian culture. In the world of Islam *Shi'i* and *Sufi* have usually been connected with Iran.[9]

As a religion, Shi'ism is speculative with Zoroastrian and Christian overtones, and incorporates within itself mysteries, saints, intercessors, belief in atonement, and the spirit of high cult—all of which are repugnant to the majority of the Sunnis. In Sunni Islam, only the Koran is infallible, while in Shi'ism infallibility has been extended to include Ali and his eleven descendants who each are called *Imām*. The doctrine of the *Imāmate* in Shi'ism believes that Mohammad and the twelve Imams are sinless, and there are some who have elevated Ali to the position of man-God. The death of Hosayn has provided the Shi'is the opportunity to pour out their religious feelings in processions, self-mortifications, in passion plays and poems presenting this death as vicarious for the sin of the world.

In Sunni Islam, Mohammad is the last of God's prophets. The Shi'is confess this also, but they seem to qualify it by stating that Ali, as the "rightful heir," has received the "light of prophecy" from Mohammad and has passed it to his descendants, the twelve Imāms. This doctrine has two important ramifications. The first is that while in Sunni Islam, the Koran and the *Sunna*, the practices of Mohammad, form the sole bases of Islamic law, the Shi'is believe in *ejtehād*. This means that the Imāms and, in their absence, their spokesmen, have the right of interpretation. Second is the political theory that evolves from this doctrine. Since the spiritual and temporal powers of Mohammad have passed on to Ali and successively to the other Imāms, it follows that the only legitimate government belongs to the Imām. Consequently, governments which are not under the Imām or his agents, among them all the Sunni caliphs including the first three, are "usurpers." The summation of this important doctrine has been added to the

8. Arberry, *The Legacy of Persia*, p. 149.
9. There is a tradition that Hoseyn married a daughter of Yazdgerd and therefore the Shi'i Imams are legitimate rulers as descendants of both the Prophet and the Sasanian kings. See Rafi', *National Uprisings*, p. 136.

creed of Islam. To the "I believe that there is no God but Allah: I believe that Mohammad is the Messenger of Allah," the Shi'is add "I believe that Ali is the Regent (*vali*) of Allah."

The Shi'is also have a doctrine of the *Return*. This is similar to the return of the deliverer in Zoroastrianism, the coming of the Messiah in Judaism, and the "second coming" of Jesus in Christianity. The majority of the Shi'is believe that there were twelve Imams and that the twelfth, the Mehdi, "Messiah," disappeared in 878 and shall return at the end of time when he will bring the whole world under the jurisdiction of Shi'i Islam.[10]

Among the Shi'is there is an important sect who do not believe in twelve Imāms or the return of the Imām. The sixth Imām had two sons, Esmā'il and Musā. He first appointed Esmā'il, but because of the latter's alleged excessive drinking, habits, transferred the succession to Musā. This sect, however, considers Esmā'il as the seventh Imām. Their official name is Esmā'ili but they are also known as "seveners" as distinguished from the majority, the "twelvers." They organized a most extensive net of missionary activity in the world of Islam, and one of their number founded the Shi'i Fātemid dynasty in Egypt in 969. A well-known branch of the sect is the Assassins (Arabic, *hashishi'in*) founded by Hasan Sabbāh (d. 1124), who reputedly caused their volunteers to smoke hashish before going on their missions of political assassination. But this is doubted by modern scholarship. They have always had a living Imām who claims descent from Esmā'il. At present they are scattered in many parts of the Islamic world, principally in Iran, Pakistan, and East Africa. Their leader is Karim Āqā Khan, the living Imām, who guides the destinies of the group mainly from Europe.

IRAN UNDER THE OMAYYADS

The empire which the Omayyads wrested from Ali was already very large, but the momentum of conquest was in full force. In the West they conquered Spain and in the East they crossed the Āmu Daryā (Oxus) as the Sasanids had done and even went beyond Sir Daryā (Jaxartes) and exacted tribute from the Turkish and Buddhist strongholds. They also went south toward India and captured territory along the Sind River and the Punjab area.

The Omayyads tried to establish an empire that was Arab first and Moslem second. There were others who felt that the Prophet would have wanted an empire that was Moslem first and Arab second. Only a small minority believed that in Islam there should not be a "second" place to be given to the Arabs or any other nationality. The Omayyads, however, preached the superiority of the Arabs, and in this they were

10. In Iran the person who gives the call to prayer sometimes ends it with "*O Sahab al-Zaman*," "Owner of the Ages (Messiah), hasten thy appearance. The world is getting out of hand, put your foot in the stirrup."

following the policy set by Omar, who has sometimes been called the "second founder" of Islam. Islam believes in the brotherhood of all Moslems.[11] Omar interpreted Islam to be a brotherhood of Arabs who had become Moslems. The non-Arab converts could join this community but would not be part of its inner governing circle, a privilege reserved only for the Arabs. To this end Omar banished all non-Moslems from Arabia in order to keep the home base purely Arab and Moslem. He forbade Arabs from obtaining land in conquered territories in the hope that without land of their own, "home" would always be Arabia. He discouraged intermarriage, even with converts, in order to keep the blood pure and the Arab military aristocracy intact. In order to prevent the Arab warriors from mingling with the conquered peoples, he ordered the building of military cantonments where the conquerors and their families lived.[12]

In keeping with the above principles, the original egalitarian message of Islam had given way to the stratification of society into four groups, very much as the Sāsānian society had been stratified. At the bottom were the slaves. These were white, black, and yellow and were captured from all parts where Arab arms had been victorious. Judging by the number of slaves in both the Omayyad and Abbasid societies, one may safely conclude that early Moslem society was based, to some degree, on a slave economy.[13]

Above the slaves were the *zemmi* (Arabic, *dhimmi*), members of the tolerated religions, Judaism and Christianity, whom the Moslems called the "people of the book." Every zemmi had to pay a special head tax, called *jezye*, but he was free to practice his religion and was judged in his own religious courts. The Zoroastrians of Iran were not considered zemmi at first, but very early the Arabs realized that they could not kill all of those who did not belong to the "people of the book." Consequently they extended this status to the Zoroastrians also and taxed them accordingly. On the whole the zemmi was a third-class citizen and was restricted in his dress, hairdo, manner of riding, holding of public office, and so forth. In practice, however, many Jewish and Christian zemmis held important public offices, but such a privilege was denied a Zoroastrian, unless he had become a Moslem.

Above the zemmis were the non-Arab Moslems, *mavāli*, or clients. In theory every non-Arab convert to Islam had to have an Arab sponsor, whose client he became. This second-class status of the non-Arab Moslem became the bone of contention and the source of rebellion.

---

11. Islam does not preach the brotherhood of all peoples. This is not to say that it is against the idea.

12. Those familiar with British imperialism in India will recall military cantonments on the outskirts of main cities.

13. In Islam, no Moslem can become a slave. Non-Moslem slaves who accept Islam remain slaves but their children are free. Islam considers the liberation of slaves efficacious for gaining reward in heaven.

The primary burden was borne by the Persians because they constituted the most important single group among the mavāli. The Arabic word for non-Arab is *ajam*, and it has been customarily used by historians to denote a Persian. To this day the Arabs sometimes refer to Iran as "the land of the Ajam." The Persians who had become Moslems, either by conviction or for expediency, became very bitter when they were considered inferior to the Arabs. Quite naturally they espoused the egalitarian principles of the Koran, while the Arabs were inclined to interpret the Koran from a limited point of view.

At the top of the pyramid was the Arab Moslem, who not only did not pay any taxes but, as a soldier, received an annual stipend from the public treasury. All Arab Moslems were registered and classified according to length of their conversion to Islam, service to the Prophet, position in the tribe, and the like. It is reported that even the lowest Arab soldier collected an annual stipend of 600 derhams.[14] Before long many non-Arab Moslems, in order to escape degradation, to receive a stipend or to gain privilege, "passed" as Arabs and some went even farther and "passed" as descendants of Mohammad himself.[15]

The doctrine of Arab superiority was easier claimed than demonstrated. About the only thing that the early Arabs, who emerged from the desert, could do well was fight. They considered agriculture beneath their dignity and did not have the experience to administer the large empire they had acquired. They depended heavily on the Greeks and the Persians. They borrowed the satrap system from the Persians and adopted the tax laws of Khosro Anushiravān. In the Sasanid system, the nobles and the knights were exempt; all adult males paid a head tax, and cultivators and merchants paid a percentage of their income in kind or cash. The Omayyads copied the above except that in the new regime it was the Arabs who were exempt from taxation. Thus the condition of the cultivators and peasants in Iran remained virtually intact. The *dehqāns*, or country squires, created by Khosro remained on their jobs and collected taxes and managed the land as they had done before. Some of them, for expediency or out of conviction, became Moslems, but the peasants were hardly bothered.

The Omayyad caliph Abd al-Malek (685–705) inaugurated a program of Arabization. He ordered all government records that were kept either in Greek or Persian (*Pahlavi*) to be changed into Arabic. This caused havoc and bloodshed in Iran and was not fully implemented until 741. But once the Persians saw that it was inevitable, quite characteristically they accepted it. Persians like Sibveyh wrote the most authoritative grammars for the Arabic language which have been used

---

14. Evidence of this identification of Islam with Arabism is still seen in the requirement of reading the Koran, offering prayers, and giving the call to prayer in Arabic.

15. The number of these "descendants," *seyyeds*, in Iran alone is legion, let alone the rest of the Moslem world.

by generations of Arabs. One of the most hated agents of Abd al-Malek in the program of Arabization was the satrap of Iran, Hajjāj ibn-Yusof. In Persian history he is a bloodthirsty tyrant while to the Arabs he is the defender of the faith! According to Moslem historians, he beheaded thousands of Persians who had continued to write in Persian and tortured those who praised Iran. He forced the Persian Moslems to pray in Arabic. The author of the *History of Bokhārā* reports that those Persian Moslems who did not know Arabic were placed in rows and had to repeat the words of the prayer after an Arab. It is reported that in his inaugural speech as satrap of Iran, Hajjāj said: "By God . . . I see heads before me which are ripe for cutting and can see the streams of blood pouring out between the turbans and the shoulders. . . ." [16]

Abd al-Malek also issued the first coins in Arabic. Heretofore the Arab conquerors had been using Byzantine and Persian currency. Coins in the name of the caliphs written in Pahlavi were in use up until the reign of Abd al-Malek. Indeed the local princes in the region of Māzandarān and Tabarestān, along the Caspian littoral, used Pahlavi on their coins until the twelfth century.[17]

As it has been noted, during the Omayyad dynasty, mainly because of their policy of Arab superiority, the bulk of the Persians in the countryside and cities were not affected. The Omayyad policy, however, limited the power of the bureaucrats, nobles, and government officials in Iran, even those of them who had become Moslems. Ibn-Hazm reports: "Because of their vast empire and suzerainty over many nations, the Persians had reached a stage where they considered themselves free and others slaves. When they were conquered by the Arabs, whom they considered lowest of all, it was very hard for them and their sorrow was doubled." [18] Humiliated as they were, the Persians, especially those who had become Moslems, did everything in their power to destroy the Omayyads.

The Omayyads were not without their enemies among the Arabs. These were the Shi'is, the Khārejites, the religious Moslems who thought the Omayyads too worldly, and claimants for the caliphate from other branches of the Qoraysh tribe. The Persians encouraged them all and offered them hospitable location for conspiracy in Khorāsān, which was quite removed from the capital. The leader of this conspiracy was a young Persian by the name of Abu Moslem Khorāsāni. Not much is known about him except that his real name was Behzādān. Even though he was a Moslem, he is reputed to have had Zoroastrian tendencies. Around 740, the descendants of al-Abbās,

16. As quoted by Rafi', *National Uprisings*, p. 163.

17. Sa'id Nafisi, *Tārikh-e Ejtemā'i-e Iran az Enqerāz-e Sasanian tā Enqerāz-e Amaviyan* (*The Social History of Iran from the Downfall of the Sasanians to the Downfall of the Omayyads*) (Tehran: Bonyad, 1956), p. 147.

18. As quoted by Abdol Hoseyn Zarrinkub, *Do Qarn Sokut* (*Two Centuries of Silence*) (Tehran: Amir Kabir, 1956), p. 61.

the uncle of the Prophet, claimed their right to the caliphate, and they conspired with Abu Moslem, who was in Kufa at the time, to go to Khorāsān and lead the movement.[19] Apparently the claim of the Abbāsids, who were members of the clan of the Prophet, satisfied the Shi'is for it is reported that the fifth Imām, Mohammad, sent a delegation to Khorāsān and encouraged his followers to help the Abbāsids.[20]

In any case, the pro-Abbāsid forces that finally emerged were commanded by Abu Moslem, who unfurled the Abbāsid flag and marched against the Omayyad strongholds. After nearly two years of warfare, the "Black Shirts" of Abu Moslem faced the main Omayyad forces on the banks of the Greater Zāb River, in January of 750, and defeated them. In April of the same year Damascus was captured, and the unity of the Arab empire was shattered never to be revived again.

IRAN UNDER THE ABBĀSIDS

The victory of the Abbāsids was not simply a transfer of power from one Arab group to another. It rather ushered in a new era. The center of cultural emphasis shifted from Syria to Iran. Non-Arabs felt a sense of liberation, and Persians occupied, for a time, the chief positions in the new government. The doctrine of Arab supremacy was made obsolete, and a large number of the Arabs themselves, who had emerged from the desert only a short century before, receded to the desert not to be heard of again until the twentieth century. To be sure, the Abbāsids were Arabs, but they ruled actually only until 842, and only nominally until 1258. Islam remained, but its destiny was not in the hands of the Arabs alone.

The Abbāsids had come to power with the help of many groups, and each group saw in the Abbāsids its own triumph. The Abbāsids, however, were not interested in any of these groups except as a means of gaining power. No sooner had the new caliphate been established than Saffāh, the first Abbāsid caliph, and his more unscrupulous successor, Mansur, began to rid themselves of those who had been their allies. It is said that Mansur had four obsessions: hatred for the Shi'is; hatred for Abu Moslem; love for his son; and an exaggerated dislike for spending money.[21]

In any case, his hatred of Abu Moslem was reciprocated. It is said that Abu Moslem wanted to get rid of the Abbāsids after using them to destroy the Omayyads. The Abbāsids had already used Abu Moslem and did not need him anymore. Mansur tricked Abu Moslem into accepting his invitation to a feast in 754 and then put him to

19. Ibid., p. 129.
20. Rafi', National Uprisings, p. 209.
21. Abbas Eqbal, Tārikh-e Iran az Sadr-e Eslām tā Estilā-ye Moghol (A History of Iran from the Advent of Islam to the Mongol Conquest) (Tehran: Chāp-e Khodkār, 1939), p. 88.

death. This treacherous deed caused such an uproar in Iran that it took the Abbāsids a century to suppress it; and in the process they weakened themselves to the point of extinction. Soon after the Abbāsids came to power they realized that it was not politically expedient to antagonize the majority Moslems in favor of the minority Shi'is and checked their own pro-Shi'i proclivities. This did not endear them in the eyes of the Shi'is, who thenceforth became the enemies of the caliphate.

With two of their main groups of supporters turned against them, about the only base of support left to them was the majority of orthodox Moslems; they had supported the Abbāsids because of their alleged piety as opposed to the alleged worldliness of the Omayyads. To be sure, the Abbāsids were not any less worldly than their Omayyad cousins, but they kept up the pretense of piety. Unlike the Omayyads, they imposed Islam upon the masses of Iran and became dogmatic to the point of organizing the first inquisition in Islam.

When the Abbāsids came to power, a large segment of the population of Iran, especially in the rural areas, was not Moslem. The Abbāsids, however, who had discarded Arab supremacy, concentrated on religion and aroused the animosity of the masses. The history of Iran during the first century of Abbāsid rule is the story of religious uprisings all over the country. After the first century, the Abbāsid caliphs were only figureheads and were used by leaders of principalities in Iran who had such an important part in the creation of the Persian renaissance.

Persian opposition to the Abbasids took three forms—religious, literary, and political. The most spectacular and the noisiest of the three was the religious uprising, mainly because it was the movement of the masses. It is of interest to note that the Zoroastrian mobads did not have any part in these uprisings. Shorn of their power by the Moslem rulers, and rejected by the masses even in the Sasānian times, the mobads had created an isolated existence for themselves. These uprisings are so numerous that they cannot be described here.[22] They had many common characteristics, however. They were anti-Arab and sometimes anti-Islamic; they had speculative and bizarre beliefs and an exaggerated system of eschatology; they were communal and took care of the social and economic needs of the members; and practically all of them attached themselves to Abu Moslem Khorāsāni by preaching the doctrine of transmigration of souls to show that the leader was the incarnation of the fallen hero. These uprisings began in 755, when Sinbad the Magian, a good friend of Abu Moslem, set out to destroy the Ka'ba, and slackened with the execution of Bābak in 839. In between were uprisings led by Eshāq (Isaac) the Turk, Ostādsis, Yusof Barm and others.

22. For a detailed description of each one see Rafi', *National Uprisings*, pp. 248–402.

The most famous was the "Veiled Prophet of Khorāsān," who rebelled in 766 and claimed that he was the reincarnation of Abu Moslem. His followers, who numbered in the thousands, wore a white uniform and are known as the "White Shirts." They robbed caravans, destroyed mosques, and killed those who prayed or gave the call to prayer. Equally as famous as the Veiled Prophet is the rebellion of Bābak Khorramdin, whose religion was a mixture of Zoroastrian and Mazdaki beliefs, called *Khorramdin*, or "Happy Religion." It can also be translated "red religion." His followers, who kept the forces of two caliphs occupied for over twenty years, were called the "Red Shirts." In the end Bābak was captured in 838 by Afshin, a Persian general in the service of caliph Mo'tasem and was executed in Baghdad.

The second form of Persian opposition to the Abbāsids was literary. During the Omayyad period when the Byzantine and Persian secretaries and other officials could not tolerate the claims of Arab superiority any longer, they started to combat these claims by writing about the good points of their own nationality and the weaknesses of the Arabs. They were called the *Shu'ubiyeh*, or nationalist writers. As the people of Syria became Arabized, the movement became more and more Persian and reached its peak during the Abbāsid caliphate. Through original writing and translation of Pahlavi books, they tried to revive the Persian culture and reestablish the Persian tradition and social structure. They were avant-garde literary critics and dominated the Mo'tazelite movement, which was a rationalist movement that questioned, among other things, many Islamic dogmas, especially the dogma of the infallibility of the Koran.[23] The caliph Ma'mun came so much under their influence that he raised the green flag of the Shi'is and appointed the eighth Imām, Ali al-Rezā, as his heir. The uproar created by this move forced Ma'mun to leave Baghdad. After two years of struggle he recanted and is accused of having ordered the execution of Imām Rezā. He also removed his support of the liberals, but the intellectual and religious controversy continued until after the middle of the tenth century. Two of their most important members, the literary genius ibn-Moqaffa and the blind poet Bashshār ibn-Bord, were executed for heresy by the caliphs Mansur and Mehdi, respectively. Ibn-Moqaffa, whose real name was Ruzbeh Pārsi, was a secretary in the court of the Omayyads and continued in the same position with the Abbasids. He translated *Khodāynāmeh* (*Book of Lords*) into Arabic and called it *Siyar al-Muluk al-Ajam* (*Attributes of the Kings of Iran*), for the use of the caliphs. His more popular translation was the ancient Sanskrit classic, *Panchatantra*, which had been rendered into Pahlavi by Borzu under the name of the "Fables of Bidpāy." Ruzbeh translated it into Arabic as *Kalileh va Demneh*. This is a delightful animal story in which the animals take

23. Orthodox Moslems believe that the Koran is the uncreated word of God and coexisted with Him, but the Mo'tazelites believe that it was created by man.

on the characteristics of humans and discuss all sorts of philosophical and moral questions. Both of these translations set the norm for Arabic writing until recent times. It is said that Ruzbeh claimed that his Arabic was much better than that of the Koran. He was accused of being a *zendiq*, a heretic, and was burned to death.

The third form of Persian opposition was political. Afshin, the Persian general who captured Bābak, was typical of this group. He was an aristocrat and an anti-Arab, but he did not care for the masses and felt that their uprisings confused the issue. The main issue was to control the government from the top. They indeed did penetrate the early Abbāsid caliphate and were quite successful in "Persianizing" the administration. The aristocratic Persian family which exerted the most influence was named Barmak, whose distinguished members, Khāled, Yahyā, Fazl and Ja'far, occupied ministerial posts for half a century. They had charge of civil and military affairs and appointed and deposed governors and generals at will. They organized the postal service, inherited from the Sasanids, to serve the public. They built roads and caravanserais and made Baghdad the hub of commerce and industry. They also established a bureau of translation in which manuscripts from many languages were translated into Arabic. Due to the fact that the Barmakids were Shi'is, coupled with a probable scandal that involved the sister of the caliph Hārun al-Rashid and Ja'far, the latter was executed while Yahyā and Fazl died in prison.

On the whole the early Abbāsids kept the pretense of piety and dealt harshly with non-Moslems. Even the zemmis could not build a house of worship, could not have homes taller than their Moslem neighbors, and their testimony against Moslems was not admitted in court. The Omayyad doctrine of Arab supremacy was resented by the Persian aristocrats, but the Abbāsid religious zeal persecuted the rest of the population. Freedom came with the rise of independent principalities and the renaissance of Iran.

5

The Persian Renaissance

The Persian renaissance, which began roughly about the end of the ninth century and reached its peak in the twelfth, only to be arrested temporarily by the Mongol invasion, had basically two aspects. One was political and the other cultural, namely religious, intellectual, and literary. The origins of the renaissance are to be found in the almost constant struggle of the Persians to exert their national and cultural identity and in the ability of the Persians either to dominate the culture of their conquerors or to "Persianize" it to suit their mood and needs. Two centuries after the conquest of the Arabs the Persian political and cultural renaissance became possible because of the weakness of the Abbāsid caliphs.

During the first century of their rule, the Abbāsid dynasty had relatively strong and distinguished caliphs like Mansur, Hārun al-Rashid, and Ma'mun, and without them they probably would not have been able to establish themselves. The Omayyads had deliberately relied upon an Arab base. Their satraps and military commanders were always Arabs and could be depended upon to enforce the use of the Arabic language and values. The Abbāsids, on the other hand, had abandoned their Arab base. They chose Persian satraps who, in the end, did not remain loyal, and they themselves were not strong enough to impose their will. On the whole, however, they did not use their enormous wealth to weld the different elements and keep the empire intact. The Golden Age of Islam did not begin until the tenth century when all the Abbāsids could do was to keep themselves alive, and some of them did not succeed in even that. The period of borrowing, however, in which most of the available manuscripts of the non-Islamic world were systematically collected and translated into Arabic, was begun during the early Abbāsid period. Hārun al-Rashid and especially Ma'mun, who had come under the influence of the Mo'tazelites, did support the intellectuals and strengthened the foundation which made the Golden Age possible.

After Ma'mun, whose espousal of the Shi'is had alienated the orthodox Arabs and whose later recantation had not left many friends for him among the Persians, the caliphs felt even more insecure. The last of their Khorāsāni bodyguards, who had been weakened because of the murder of Abu Moslem, had left in disgust. In the struggle between Ma'mun and his older brother Amin for the caliphate, the Persians had sided with Ma'mun and brought about the death of Amin. Fazl ibn-Sahl, a Shi'i convert from Zoroastrianism, became powerful in the court of Ma'mun and further alienated the orthodox Arabs.[1] Ma'mun's change of heart and his alleged order for the execution of Imām Rezā, fanned the fires of revolt in Khorāsān. The *coup de grace*, as it were, was delivered by Ma'mun himself when he sent his trusted general, Tāher, to quell the rebellion. Tāher, who was from Khorāsān and also was close enough to the center of power in Baghdad to know its weaknesses, joined the rebellion as its leader. He founded the Tāherid principality in 823 and was the first to omit the mention of the caliph's name in the Friday prayers.[2]

Notwithstanding all the difficulties the Abbasids were having with the Persians, the Arabs did not come to their aid. They continued their own intertribal feud between the north and south and practically abandoned the caliphs to their own devices.[3] To protect himself and his household, the caliph Mo'tasem (833–842) brought in the Turks to act as his bodyguards. These Turks, who were from the easternmost part of the empire, were devout Moslems and as brave and obedient as they were uncouth and unlettered. Furthermore, they were innocent of the feuds, intrigues, and the struggle for power going on in Baghdad and could be trusted. Unfortunately for the Abbasids, however, these stalwart Turks proved to be a Frankenstein monster. After several years, their debauchery and rowdyism caused so much uproar in Baghdad that the caliph was forced to move his capital to nearby Samarra and take his bodyguards with him. But the change of venue did not solve the problem. By 861 they had become strong enough to kill the caliph Motavakkel and replace him with his son. Soon they were making

---

1. See Zarrinkub, *Do Qarn Sokut*, p. 214 ff.

2. It was customary to mention the caliph's name in the Friday prayer as a sign that he was the real ruler. This was done even when the caliph was no more than a figurehead, in order not to antagonize the public. A few principalities, however, refused to follow this custom.

3. That is, to the feud between the Qaysites and the Kalbites. For detail see Phillip Hitti, *History of the Arabs* (7th ed.) (New York: St. Martin's Press, 1961).

and unmaking caliphs and became the virtual rulers of what was left
of the empire. Under such circumstances, it is not surprising that
independent principalities mushroomed all over the empire.[4]

PERSIAN PRINCIPALITIES

The principalities in Iran from the middle of the ninth century
to the coming of the Mongols in the second decade of the thirteenth
century were so numerous and overlapping that it takes more than the
limits of this small volume to describe them.[5] In order to get a general
idea of this confused patchwork of principalities, they may be divided
in two different ways. One way would be to divide them into Persian
and Turkish principalities. Almost invariably the Persians, such as the
Saffārids, Sāmānids, Buyids, and the like were more nationalistic and
revived the use of the Persian language and traditions. Even the Turkish
leaders were Persianized and became patrons of great Persian poets and
scientists. But they were doing it for the sake of prestige, however, and
would not go out of their way to establish Persian culture. A second
way would be to divide the principalities into Shi'i and Sunni. All the
Persian principalities, with the major exception of the Sāmānids were
either Shi'is or Khārejis, which meant that they did not hesitate to
attack the caliph or omit the mention of him in Friday prayers. The
Turks, on the other hand, with the exception of Khārazmshāhis were
all Sunnis and were eager to get a letter of investiture from the caliph;
and even though they did not take orders from the caliph, they did
mention his name in Friday prayer. The one thing that they all had
in common was that their base of operation was either north of the
Alborz mountains or in the eastern part of Iran, neither of which areas
was readily accessible to the forces of the caliph.

The first consciously Persian principality was the one established
by Ya'qub ibn-Leys-e Saffār in 867.[6] Inasmuch as Saffār means coppersmith, it shows that Ya'qub did not belong to the Persian nobility and
rose from among the common people. Since this would have been
almost impossible in the stratified Sasanid society, and since it had
become a common occurrence in Iran, it is safe to say that it had come
about by the egalitarian preaching of Islam. In any case, in his youth
he helped his father who was a coppersmith, and later he joined a band
of brigands and eventually entered the service of the local chieftain in

4. The general attempt to form principalities independent of Baghdad was
not confined to Iran. Indeed, the Idrisids of Morocco (788–974) were the first to
establish a kingdom of their own. The impotence of the caliphs encouraged such
activities all over the empire.

5. For a description of these principalities, see Percy Sykes, *History of Persia,*
Vol. I (London: Macmillan, 1951), and Eqbal, *Tārikh-e Iran,* p. 109 ff.

6. Although the Taherids were Persians, they were not particularly interested
in the revival of Persian culture.

Sistān. Eventually he overthrew the chieftain and, with the help of his three brothers became the ruler of Sistān.[7] From then on, it was a series of campaigns against the petty rulers of Sistān, Fārs, and Khorāsān, the Tāherids, and also against the caliph in Baghdad. So far as is known, he was the first to try to overthrow the caliph, and he almost succeeded. A number of sources indicate that one of the reasons for Ya'qub's defeat was the fact that he fought on Easter Sunday, even though he knew that the group of Christians in his army would not take part. But he thought he could win without them. This is indicative at least of the religious distribution in eastern Iran. Ya'qub tried a second time but died in Gondishāpur. His brother succeeded him, but the dynasty came to an end in 892. There is a controversy about his religion, some believing that he was a Shi'i and others that he was a Khāreji. In this writer's view he was neither, but was very much a free thinker. His fame in Persian history is his insistence that all correspondence be in Persian, a subject which will be discussed later.

Another Persian principality which had a very important role to play in the Persian renaissance is the Sāmānid (874–999). They claimed descent from Sāmān, a Persian nobleman. The famous writer, abu Reyhān Biruni, who wrote about A.D. 1000, reports that the Sāmānids were descendants of Bahrām Chubin, the Persian general who rebelled against the Sāsānid king Khosro Parviz.[8] Their area of suzerainty was Khorāsān, Transoxiana with Bokhārā as their capital. The founder of the dynasty was Esmā'il ibn-Ahmad (874–890). He defeated the Saffārids and a few other principalities to carve out a kingdom for himself. The other well-known prince in this line is his son Nasr, who became Amir at the age of eight and died at the age of 38. Nevertheless, thanks to able ministers, during his reign the Sāmānids conquered the most territory.

During the Sāmānid period, Persian literature came into its own; these rulers attracted such Persian scientists and poets as Rāzi, Avicenna, Rudaki and others to Bokhārā. The Sāmānids were devout Sunnis and always saw to it that their conquests were approved by the caliph, who readily issued letters of investiture. Even though as Persians they encouraged the revival of the Persian language, as Sunnis they upheld

7. The best primary source on the Saffarids is *Tārikh-e Sistan* (*History of Sistan*), author unknown, edited by M. T. Bahar (Tehran: Zavvar Press, 1936). Nearly half of the book was translated into English by this writer in connection with a thesis on the Saffarids, and a good portion of the rest was translated by R. Park Johnson in his thesis on Sistan, both at Princeton, 1939 and 1942 respectively.

8. The *History of Sistan* traces the ancestry of Ya'qub to the Sasanids, as is true of all the leaders of Persian principalities. Even though such reports should be interpreted with caution, they show the prestigious position of the pre-Islamic dynasties in the mind of the Persians. Even the Safavids in 1500, who were Turks, claimed descent from the Sasanids.

orthodoxy and obedience to the caliph. For a time they held their own, but in the end they were defeated by the Ghaznavids.

A third important Persian principality arose in Deylamān, the mountainous and wooded slopes north of the Alborz range overlooking the Caspian Sea. This region today is part of the province of Gilān. The Moslem soldiers were not able to cross the difficult Alborz mountains to subdue the inhabitants. During the years between 847 and 867, in the caliphates of Motavakkel, Montaser, and Mosta'in, the Shi'is were persecuted. A large number of them took refuge in the Alborz mountains and later they found the *Alavi* (Shi'i) kingdom of Tabarestān. During their sojourn among the Deylamites, they converted a number of their leaders to Shi'i Islam. Consequently the Deylamites, because of their strong Persian nationalism and Shi'i proclivities, were bitter enemies of the Abbasids.

The Deylamites are divided into two branches, Āl-e Ziyār, known as Ziyārids and Āl-e Buyeh, known as Buyids. They ruled contemporaneously and sometimes fought each other, the Ziyārids from 911 to 1041, and the Buyids from 934 to 1055. Perhaps because the Ziyārids remained mostly in the Caspian littoral and did not mingle with the flow of events in the south, they were less influenced by Islam. A look at their names as well as their deeds indicates this conclusion.

The Buyids, however, crossed the Alborz and expanded their domain all the way south to the Persian Gulf and west beyond the Euphrates River. So far as is known, Buyeh was a fisherman, but he is claimed to have descended from Yazdger, the Sāsānian king. He had three sons, Ali, Hasan, and Ahmad, who were at first in the service of the Ziyārid prince Mardāvij and later crossed the Alborz range and started a kingdom for themselves. It was through the cooperation and ability of these brothers, especially Ali and Ahmad, that the Buyids became masters of western Iran and most of Iraq.

The impotence of the caliph and the near anarchy in the court at Baghdad may be surmised by the fact that in the fourteen years between 931 and 945 the caliphate changed hands five times. It is said that the hapless caliph Mostakfi, in his desperate desire to be rid of his Turkish "protectors," asked a staunch Shi'i like Ali Buyeh to rush to his aid. Very likely the Buyids would have gone to Baghdad on their own initiative. Ali, who was in Fārs at the time, asked his brother Ahmad, who had already captured Ahvāz on the Kārun River, to advance to Baghdad. Ahmad did not have much difficulty in defeating Tuzun, the commander in chief of the Turkish guard, and entering Baghdad. The deliriously happy Mostakfi, forgetting the fact that Ahmad was a Shi'i, made him the new commander in chief, presented rich gifts to all the three Buyeh brothers, and bestowed upon each of them high-sounding titles.

Notwithstanding these honors, however, the Buyids went out of their way to insult the caliph. Indeed only a month after these events,

Mostakfi was literally dragged to Ahmad's presence, blinded, and thrown into jail. His successor Moti' (946–974), whose name ironically enough means "obedient," obeyed every whim of Ahmad. He was not allowed to appoint his own officials and was wholly dependent on Ahmad for his daily sustenance. It is said that Ahmad was seriously considering deposing the Abbasids altogether and appointing a member of the house of Ali as the new caliph. He was advised against the move, however, on the ground that as long as the Abbasids were caliphs, the Buyids could treat them in any way they pleased without arousing the criticism of their own Shi'i supporters. But if a scion of the house of Ali was made a caliph, then all the Shi'is would follow him as the only legitimate ruler and discard the Buyids altogether.[9] Many a Shi'i king in Iran has vouched for the soundness of the advice!

The Buyids during more than a century of their rule used Shiraz as their capital because there they had a better base of support and also because Baghdad had lost its luster. To emphasize their Persian origin, they were the first among the principalities to use the title of Shāhanshāh, "king of kings." In time they were divided into three groups with bases of operation in Fārs, in Khuzestān and Kermān, and in Hamadān and Esfahān. Gradually the Buyids lost their territory to the rising Turkish principalities.

It has already been stated how the Abbasid caliphs, in order to protect themselves from the machinations of the Persians on the one hand and of the Arabs on the other, formed a Turkish guard in Baghdad. This opened the way for the Turks of the eastern shore of the Caspian and of Central Asia to come west. At first they came in small groups, and their numbers increased in later years. They came as soldiers, servants, and sometimes as slaves. As they saw the political confusion in Iran and they heard of the weakness of the caliphs, some of the adventurous among them joined the continuous battle among rival principalities and carved out kingdoms for themselves. It must be remembered that the Turks did not come as conquerors and it cannot be said that they came with any great or established cultural background except their tribal mores and social values. The main motivation was love for adventure and personal ambition. Inasmuch as they were devout Sunnis, some of them, after they had been established, did feel the responsibility of propagating Islam through conquest and did feel it their duty to protect the Abbasid caliphs from their enemies. The collapse of Persian dynasties did not mean the end of the Persian renaissance. The Turks were swallowed up by the tremendous cultural activity of the Persians and became its enthusiastic patrons. Persian was the official language of their court and they conducted themselves in the manner of Sāsānian kings.

9. Eqbal, *Tārikh-e Iran*, p. 159.

THE GHAZNAVIDS

The founder of the Ghaznavid kingdom was a Turkish slave by the name of Sebük-tegin who was bought in the Sāmānid slave market. Dealing in slave trade or charging transit taxes for the slaves who were being taken to the western markets in Baghdad and Syria was a lucrative source of income for the Sāmānid rulers. Later he was given to another slave named Alp-tegin who had made himself very useful to the Sāmānid governor of Ghazneh, in modern Afghanistan. After the death of Sāmānid governor, Alp-tegin took over the governorship. At his death Sebük-tegin, who is reputed to have been his son-in-law, announced himself independent of the Sāmānids.

The actual founder of the Ghaznavid dynasty and the one who gained real independence and made a name for himself was his son Mahmud (988–1030). During the thirty-two years of his reign, Mahmud carved out a large kingdom, which included all the possessions of the Sāmānids, Saffārids, and a good portion of the Buyid kingdom. In addition to this, he conquered western India and opened that subcontinent to the influence of Islam.

Mahmud combined his love of war and riches with his piety. As a devout Sunni he felt it his duty to carry on the holy war against the infidels of India. During a span of twenty-four years he was involved in at least twelve small and large campaigns against India. The caliph gave him the title of the "Right Hand of the Realm," and Moslem historians have referred to his sorties into India as a *ghazwa*, the same name that is given to the battles in which the Prophet participated, and have called Mahmud a *ghāzi*, 'holy warrior.' One of his better known battles was the capture of the famous Hindu temple of Somnath, which has been immortalized by the poetic description of Farrokhi Sistāni. It is not certain whether Mahmud got enough loot out of his adventures in India, but there is no question that Islam gained a strong foothold in that subcontinent.

Sultan Mahmud is well-known in Persian history as the patron of men of science and letters. He was the contemporary of such luminaries as Avicenna, Biruni, Onsori, Farrokhi, and, the most famous of them all, Ferdosi Tusi. All of the above men, with the exception of Avicenna, served at his court, some willingly and others by force. Mahmud was unlettered and did not understand Persian well enough to appreciate its literature. Futhermore, as a devout orthodox Sunni, he was suspicious of philosophy and new learning. Nevertheless the love of learning and Persian literature was so prevalent in his day that the mark of distinction for any prince was to have a number of intellectuals around him. Mahmud craved this respectability even if he had to kidnap some of the men of letters, which he did. Ferdosi, who completed his famous *Shāhnāmeh* in Mahmud's court, had a great deal of trouble with him and in the end had to escape to save his life. Five centuries later, the poet Jāmi, assessing the life of Mahmud, wrote:

> Gone is the greatness of Mahmud, departed his glory,
> And shrunk to "he knew not the worth of Ferdosi," his story.[10]

As it has been stated, the power of the Ghaznavids began to decline after the death of Mahmud. Even though the dynasty lasted in ever-shrinking territory until 1186, they did not amount to much and had to make way for the larger Turkish dynasty of Saljuq.

THE SALJUQS

By far the most important Turkish rulers to establish a kingdom in Iran were the Saljuqs, who overran not only Iran but also the west of Baghdad. They were the first Moslem soldiers who were able to defeat the Byzantines in the famous battle of Manzikert (now Malazkirt) north of Lake Van, in 1071,[11] and establish the Saljuq kingdom of Rum in Asia Minor.

The Saljuqs belonged to the Ghuzz Turkman tribes, who roamed in central Asia east of the Aral Sea. They were part of a nine-tribe confederation. The Sāmānian princes had, for their own expediency, brought them from their home and settled them west of the Amu Daryā (Oxus). They became Moslems, and one of their number, by the name of Saljuq, with the aid of three of his sons, Esrā'il, Mikā'il, and Musā Arslān, were destined to found a dynasty and a strong empire. At this stage the Saljuqs cannot be viewed as much more than a band of organized marauders, who because of the weakening of the traditional *Marzbāns* (border guards) under the Sāsānids and later the Taherids and the Sāmānids, could penetrate the defenses and enter the plateau of Iran. Furthermore, the mountainous terrain of Iran was similar to the highlands of Palmir and suitable for the grazing of sheep and the customary migration between *yeylāq*, 'highlands,' and *qeshlāq*, 'lowlands.' It must also be emphasized that the ease with which the Saljuqs took over Khorāsān was to a considerable degree due to the misrule of the Ghaznavids. Sultan Mahmud, who was more interested in the plunder of the riches of India than in building a tranquil kingdom, did not find as rich a loot as he expected. The result was heavy taxation on the merchants, small shopkeepers, and peasants in order to make Mahmud's wars possible. During the reign of his son Mas'ud, the situation became worse and the misrule intensified. The turnover in dynasties was so frequent that people did not have time enough to form loyalties. This was especially true of artisans and merchants, who

---

10. E. G. Browne, A *Literary History of Persia*, II (Cambridge: Cambridge University Press, 1964), p. 95.
11. The Turks celebrated the 900th anniversary in 1971.

supported any leader who could give them and their caravans protection. When Toghrol, the grandson of Saljuq, came into the Ghaznavid strongholds, he did not have much difficulty. In 1037 he was crowned king, and, as a good Sunni, as "the Client of the Commander of the Faithful," that is, of the caliph in Baghdad.[12]

Toghrol (1037–1063) not only advanced the Saljuq arms to cover the whole of Iran, entering Baghdad in triumph in 1055; he also developed a reason for being, or a motivation for the Saljuq empire. This purpose was to protect the caliphate from its Shi'ite enemies, the Buyids in the east and the Fātemids in Egypt; and to uphold Sunni orthodoxy against the encroachments of foreign and liberal ideas, be they Twelver Shi'is, Esmā'ilis, Mo'tazelis, or free thinkers of all description. What the Ghaznavids had started to do through zeal and fanaticism, the Saljuqs carried out through zeal and organized political and intellectual planning. The fact that the celebrated and able Persian vazir Nezāmal-Molk, who undoubtedly had a great deal to do with the formation of the above policies, held the same office under two Saljuq kings for thirty years, was responsible for the strengthening and success of that policy.

About the time that Toghrol was busy establishing himself in Khorāsān the Fātemids of Egypt had become a threat to the Abbasids. The Fātemid caliphate was founded by Esmā'ili Shi'is, who were bitter enemies of the Abbasids. Even though it had become expedient for the Buyids to keep the caliph in power, the Fātemids had no such intention. During the Fātemid caliphate of Mostanser (1045–1095), who had advanced to Aleppo, the Abbasids were in special danger. After his entry into Baghdad in 1055, Toghrol had to leave the capital to settle difficulties in the east. In 1057 Arslān Basāsir took Baghdad, drove away the caliph Qā'em (1031–1075), and read the name of the Fātemid caliph in Friday prayers. He had control of the city for a year before Toghrol was free to drive him out and reinstate Qā'em.

Toghrol died in 1063 at the age of seventy. During the reigns of his nephew Alp Arslān (1063–1072) and the latter's son Malekshāh (1073–1093), the rank and file of the Persians witnessed thirty years of comparative peace and prosperity while the intellectual advance, which had already started, kept pace with the prosperity. The intellectual ferment of the period is shown in the fact that Nāser Khosro, Mohammad Ghazāli, and Omar Khayyām flourished at this time. The first was an Esmā'ili poet missionary, the second was the famous orthodox theologian opposed to the Esmā'ilis, and the third was a mathematician and poet of no particular religious view.

These were also the thirty years in which Nezām-al-Molk was in firm control of the office of vazir of both Alp Arslān and Malekshāh. Ac-

12. J. A. Boyle, ed., *The Saljuq and Mongol Periods*, Vol. 5 of *The Cambridge History of Iran* (Cambridge University Press, 1968), is full of useful information on the subject and very important.

cording to H. Bowen, Nezām al-Molk was perhaps responsible for preparing a five-point policy to be carried out by the Saljuqs after the death of Toghrol.[13] First, the Turkman tribesmen should be sent to raid the Christian territories of Asia Minor in order to free the populace from the unbridled activities of the Turkmans. Second, the sultan must always demonstrate the irresistibility of his power but at the same time show clemency toward those who submit. Third, local rulers should always be supervised by a member of the Saljuq family. Fourth, to avoid rivalry and bloodshed for succession, a capable heir should be announced early. And fifth, good relations should always be maintained with the Abbasid caliphs.

After the death of Malekshāh there was the usual struggle for succession, despite Nezām al-Molk's provision to prevent it. With the exception of the reign of Sanjar (1119–1157), when there was some stability, the Saljuqs could not rule the empire they had created. Eventually they were divided into three main groups. One is known as the Saljuqs of Iran (also Great Saljuqs) 1037–1194, who after Sanjar were fragmented into smaller principalities. Another is known as the Saljuqs of Syria (or Shām) who had their capital at Aleppo (1094–1117). The third is the Saljuqs of Asia Minor (or Rum) with their capital at Konya (1071–1299). During most of these years the Crusaders were engaged in warfare against the Arabs, but the Saljuqs of Iran not only did not heed the plea for help from their fellow Moslems but did not go to the aid of the Saljuqs of Syria. Perhaps the most important effect of the Saljuq rule in Iran was the saving of the Abbasid caliphate. They repulsed the Fātemids of Egypt and they broke the Buyids' heavy hand on the caliphate. Even though the Esmā'ili activity continued in Iran, for a time at least, they strengthened the foundations of Sunni orthodoxy. The early Saljuqs did not deal much better with the caliphs than the Buyids but as the Saljuqs weakened, relatively capable caliphs, such as Nāser (1176–1222) exerted some power for a short time.[14]

THE KHĀRAZMSHĀHIS

The region of Khārazm (ancient Charasmia) is located in the lower reaches of Āmu Darya as it flows into the southern coast of the Aral Sea. It was originally populated by Iranians, and the people spoke a dialect of Iranian related to Sogdian. The encroachment of the Turkish tribes from the steppe gradually diluted the Iranian nature of the culture, and by the time they established a dynasty they were Turks with perhaps some Persian proclivities.

Anush-Tegin, the first of the Khārazm rulers, and his descendants, were hereditary governors appointed by the Saljuq sultans. It was not until

13. C. E. Bosworth, "The Political and Dynastic History of the Iranian World," in *The Saljuq and Mongol Periods*, p. 57.
14. Ibid., p. 201.

the last years of Sanjar that Atsez (1127–1143), the very able Khārazmi
ruler, took advantage of Sanjar's defeat at the hand of the Qara Khatay,
and took Khorāsān. Later, as the Saljuqs' power waned, the Khārazmshāhis increased their territory and power. Among the increasing number of petty principalities that arose after the fall of the Saljuqs, the
Khārazmshāhis have been chosen for consideration for two reasons. One
is to show that despite the new lease on life that the caliphs received
from the Saljuqs, they were still in danger. The Khārazmshāhis, though
Turks, were Shi'is, or had strong Shi'i proclivities and constituted a
threat to the caliphate. Indeed, Sultan Mohammad Khārazmshāh
(1217–1238) omitted the name of the caliph Nāser from Friday prayers.
The second reason is that Mohammad Shah might have been able to
transfer the caliphate from the Abbasids to the house of Ali had it
not been for the attack of Chengiz Khan and his Mongol hordes, which
swept aside everything in their way, putting an end to the Kharazm-
shāhis and eventually the caliphate itself.

SOCIAL AND ECONOMIC CONDITIONS

Unfortunately our sources speak very little about the social and
economic life of the people, especially the common people, in the five
centuries under discussion. A good part of it has to be surmised. A very
resourceful author by the name of Abol Faraj Esfahāni (897–967)
wrote a book called *Ketāb al-Aghāni* (*Book of Songs*) in which he collected anecdotes, songs, poems, games, pastimes, and jokes about the
Omayyad and Abbasid men and women of wealth and power. Judging
by his observations, one can readily see that even proximity to the
life and times of the Prophet did not prevent the cities of Mecca and
Medina under the early Omayyad period from becoming centers of
leisure, pleasure, and vice. There were clubs and cabarets, houses of ill
repute and elegant salons, belly dancers, serious musicians, and songsters
from all parts of the empire. If such things did go on within a stone's
throw of the Ka'ba and the tomb of the Prophet, then one can readily
surmise that other cities throughout the period had such facilities for
the enjoyment of those who could afford them.

Hunting and polo were the sports of kings and princes, and they
shared chess with men of lesser ranks, while practically everyone played
nard (backgammon) as they do today. The common people of Iran, as
well as the nobility, enjoyed themselves at festive occasions such as
Noruz (New Year's) and *Sedeh* (autumnal equinox) except at times
when such celebrations were forbidden by the orthodox Saljuq kings.
Parents could buy their children toys of stuffed animals, wooden swords,
and clay pipes.[15] In *Tārikh-e Sistān*, we read that Ya'qub, the founder

15. Ibid., p. 278.

of the Saffārids, as a boy, used to play "Shah-Vazir" using the knuckle of a sheep, a game that was still played in this writer's boyhood in northern Iran. The Buyids, who were Shi'is, are reputed to have started passion plays, ta'ziyeh, which depicted incidents in the life of the Imāms, especially the martyrdom of Hosayn. Traveling troupes of actors would go from town to town and put on performances for the edification and entertainment of the public. The common people had ample opportunity to use the bath houses in the cities, and even small towns and larger villages claimed such accommodations. Strangers were cared for in hostels, and if they were poor they could always sleep in the mosque.

Women were segregated, and their duty was in the home, except for slave girls, who would amuse the men by their song and dance. Polygamy was permitted to the extent of four legal wives. It being a slave society, we may assume that men of the upper classes availed themselves of the opportunities to have concubines. The upper classes sat on raised divans covered with mattresses and cushions, and the lower classes used mats. Then as now, the people used to warm themselves in the winter by the use of korsi, a brazier which held a charcoal fire under a low stool and was covered with a quilt. The security and welfare of the people depended very largely on the nature and power of the caliph, the prince, or the local governor. During the period of principalities, which lasted some three centuries, wars, pestilence, famine, invasions, banditry, and heavy taxation must have made the lot of the people hard to bear. Thanks to the vastness of the empire, the existence of fairly good roads, the numerous military campaigns, polygamy and concubinage, Arabs, Persians, Turks and Indians became mixed.

In spite of the disruptive effects of war and frequent changes in dynasties, commerce continued and merchants transported their wares to different parts of Iran as well as outside the country. The system of roads built in pre-Islamic times and improved upon during the early Abbasids was still functioning. Insofar as Iran was concerned, Esfahān seems to have been the hub to which roads converged from Tabriz, Zanjān and Ray; Baghdad, Kermānshāh, and Hamadān; Baghdad, Ahvāz, and Shiraz; and extended northeastward to Nishāpur, Marv, and Sir Daryā; and eastward to Kermān, Sistān, and through the Ghur desert to India. To be sure, highway robbery was prevalent, especially during troubled times (which were many), and local brigands exacted security fees from caravans. But travel was possible and caravans took to the road. In 1052 Nāser Khosro, the famous Esma'ili missionary, visited Esfahān and reports that there were some fifty good caravanserais in the city as well as 200 brokers who handled the transaction of money for the merchants.[16] Nearly two centuries later, even in a more troubled

16. Ibid.

period, another famous Persian writer, Sa'di, was able to travel to India, Khārazm, and west to Syria.

The old idea that all land belonged to the king continued into the Islamic times with the difference that the *umma* (the Islamic community) replaced the king. The caliph, as the chief executive of the *umma*, administered the land. Later when different princes and sultans became powerful, they took the job over. Land grants, called *iqtā*, were temporary depending upon the desire of the king. The grant did not include the land itself or the peasants who were working the land; only the income from it. At first these land grants were given to military leaders in return for the support of the army; and later they were also used to secure the support of the bureaucracy; and the expenses of the court came from revenues from the king's lands. For example, in the court of Malekshāh the expenses of the royal pantry came from the revenues of Khārazm, and the man in charge there was responsible for collecting them. Inasmuch as Atsez, who was actually in charge, became an independent ruler, it is quite evident what could be accomplished with judicious land grants. The four chief bureaus of administration, namely secretariat, revenue, military records, and audit, each had an *iqtā*.[17] There was always tension between the bureaucracy, *divān*, headed by the chief minister, and the court, *dargāh*, headed by the king. Since the military was under the king, usually the *dargāh* was victorious.[18]

RELIGION, SCIENCE, AND LITERATURE

In this circumstance of general dynastic struggle and warfare interrupted by only short intervals of stability, Iran experienced one of the most brilliant eras of cultural renaissance in the history of any people. Inasmuch as most of the cultural activity during the early Abbasids was made up of the translation of available material from different parts of the known world, the period of creativity coincided with the turbulent period of principalities. During this time Persian theologians, scientists, philosophers, historians, and poets produced original works and in the process revived the Persian language into a beautiful vehicle of expression.

Two of the most important problems facing Islam were the theological problems created by its contact with other religions and ideas, and the problems conneccted with the caliphate. We have already discussed the Mo'tazelites and the question whether the Koran was coexistent with God and therefore infallible, or created by the mind of

17. Ibid., chapter entitled "Internal Structure of the Saljuq Empire," by A. K. S. Lambton, pp. 231–39.

18. The same kind of tension exists in all governments, as for example between the White House staff under the President of the United States and the State Department.

man and subject to mistakes. There were a number of other questions such as free will and predestination, the attributes of God and His unity, the anthropomorphic connotations of the names of God in Islam, and others. These did not remain purely theological questions, but perhaps because the *Shu'ubiyeh* were involved in the controversy, national rivalry got somehow mixed in it. According to the observation made by H. A. R. Gibb, the problem facing the Islamic society was whether it should "become a reembodiment of the old Perso-Aramaean culture into which the Arabic and Islamic elements would be absorbed, or a culture in which the Perso-Aramaean contributions would be subordinated to the Arab tradition and the Islamic values." [19] Professor Gibb is of the opinion that in the end the Arabic-Islamic tradition won the contest. On the other hand, Professor Frye believes that "In the case of Persia there was no question, but that the former [Perso-Aramaean] view should prevail, while in the Arabic-*speaking* parts of the caliphate it would seem the latter triumphed." [20] While I am inclined to agree with Professor Frye, it must be pointed out that inasmuch as the main intellectual and political battles were fought in Iran, the result was not certain, depending on whether the Sunnis with Arab proclivities were in power or the Shi'is with Persian leanings. The Persian tradition won only after the Mongol invasion, when Iran became free from the inhibitions that the Arabic-Islamic tradition had imposed. Although Shi'ism and Sufism have their roots in Islam and have branches among the Arabic speaking peoples, they became Persian vessels in which Arabic-Islamic traditions and values were diluted.

It is not within the scope of this volume to discuss this important question except in a brief outline. It was not until the middle of the century that orthodoxy found a capable defender in the person of Abol-Hasan Ali al-Ash'ari. He declared the uncreated nature of the Koran and the arbitrary nature of God by rejecting free will. He said that man was responsible for his actions only because God willed it. He further stated that the meaning of the attributes of God are different from the meaning of the same attributes as applied to man, thus separating God and man altogether and removing God from the knowledge of man. The scholastic school somehow had to reconcile Islam with the new learning. This task, ironically enough, was accomplished to the satisfaction of the orthodox by a Persian, Abu-Hamid Mohammad al-Ghazāli, and was politically enforced by another Persian, Nezām al-Molk.

This dean of Moslem theologians, Ghazāli, was born in Tus, Khorāsān in 1058, and after a tumultuous life died in his birth place in A.D. 1111. He studied every philosophy and religious thought and was converted to some in turn. He ended up in orthodoxy and taught at the Nezāmiyyeh College in Baghdad founded by Nezām al-Molk. In his

19. Quoted by Frye, *Persian Heritage*, p. 274.
20. Ibid.

book, *The Revival of the Sciences of Religion,* he had tried to reconcile Islam, Greek rationalism, and Persian mysticism into one harmonious whole. Thomas Aquinas, who had a similar task in reconciling Christian revelation with Greek rationalism, read Ghazāli's work, which had been translated into Latin, and was influenced by it. Although Thomism was challenged by the Protestant Reformation and the philosophical systems which came after it, Moslem orthodoxy is only beginning to be challenged in the twentieth century.

The other main problem facing Islam involved the theory and the practice of the caliphate. Aside from the thorny question of succession, the main reason for the existence of the caliphate was to enforce the law of God as revealed in the Koran and practiced in the daily life of Mohammad. This is known as the *Shari'a,* which could not be enforced without a state, which in turn could not be held together without a caliph. With the gradual weakening of the caliphs and the rise of rival caliphates, the situation was quite confusing. The institution was forced to go through changes and suitable substitutes and justifications had to be found. Consequently the Koran and the Tradition did not remain the only sources of Islamic political philosophy. At least two other sources were added during the period of Persian renaissance. One was the contribution of Moslem political philosophers; the other was the "practical precepts" written for the guidance of princes, which were taken from the Irano-Turkish tradition and mores.

All of the political philosophers were by no means Persians. Indeed one of the foremost among them was Abu Nasr al-Fārābi (870–950), a Turk from Transoxiana. To the Greek, law was the product of man's mind, while to the Moslem it was the will of God. Plato wanted a philosopher-king while Islam already had a prophet-king. To resolve the dilemma, Fārābi combined the two. He said that imagination was the function of prophecy and intellect the function of philosophy. By having a prophet-philosopher for a king, we have a person with intellect and imagination.

He was followed by one of the great geniuses of all times, Abu Ali Hosayn ibn-Sinā (980–1037), a Persian from Bokhārā. He is known as Avicenna. A distinguished philosopher as well as a prominent physician, he wrote learned essays on half a dozen other subjects. For a while he was at the court of the last Sāmānid prince in Bokhārā, then in Khārazm and then from city to city until his death in Hamadān. Part of this time he was escaping the kidnappers of Sultan Mahmud Ghaznavi, who wanted him at his court. Nevertheless, he found time to write two works of encyclopedic proportions, one on philosophy called *Shafā,* and the other on medicine called *Qānun (The Canon).* In political philosophy, he acknowledges his debt to Fārābi, but goes a step further by declaring prophecy to be the result of the highest human intellect. In other words a prophet was a philosopher with highest intellect. There is no dichotomy involved. One could conclude that since prophecy was the result of intellect, revelation was not necessary. He agreed with Fārābi that in the absence of a prophet, it was possible to have a good society. Furthermore, Avicenna integrated his political philosophy with the old Persian system of social classification and added a sociological dimension to the process of secularization. He divided society according to professions, such as rulers, administrators, artisans, and so forth, as against the division of society by lineage preferred by the Arabs. This gave an aura of legitimacy to powerful men who considered it their profession to rule even though they were not remotely related to the Prophet.

More palatable to the tastes of the orthodox and more understandable to the rulers, were the "Practical Precepts," or the "Mirrors to the Princes," which became popular during this period when so many strong men wanted to behave like the kings of old but did not have the proper education. Among these, one is *Qābusnāmeh*, written by Qābus Vashmgir, of the Ziyārid principality, and the other is the better known *Siyāsatnāmeh*, by Nezām al-Molk written for the edification of Saljuq princes. They deal with every royal duty from playing chess to the administration of justice. The art of government is taught through anecdotes, maxims, and examples taken from Sāsānid kings and other sources.

Even though the ideas of Fārābi, Avicenna, and others were considered heretical to the orthodox, the Shi'is, Esmā'ilis, and free thinkers discussed them and were influenced by them. All along the caravan routes there was a string of large cities in which the merchants, artisans, and poets were affluent, cosmopolitan, and fascinated by new ideas. The Esmā'ilis, with their network of missionaries, had a cell in every city. They not only fanned the grievances of the miserable masses against the caliphs and the Sunni rulers; they also organized discussion groups and encouraged the integration of Islam with Persian culture. They formed semisecret fraternities called "Brethren of Purity" and encouraged political activities against the government. It is important to note that philosophers like Fārābi and Avicenna, scientists like Rāzi and Omar Khayyām, and men of letters like Ferdosi were all accused of heresy, and a large number of them were either Shi'is, Esmā'ilis, or served under Shi'i rulers. It must also be noted that there was no talk of anti-Islamism at this time. They were all Moslems and eager to propagate the faith, but they wanted a broader Islam than the one brought from the desert.

The orthodox, however, were not satisfied; sustained by the power of the Saljuqs, they tried to stamp out these heretical ideas. Nezām al-Molk, the most effective champion of orthodox theologians, placed orthodox civil administrators in all departments of the government. He established colleges in different cities, the most important being the Nezāmiyyeh College in Baghdad, in which bureaucrats were trained to apply Moslem Shari'a to every aspect of government and society. He forbade the celebration of Persian festivals and took punitive measures against the Shi'is and Esma'ilis. Indeed some parts of *Siyāsatnāmeh* reads like witch hunting. He not only attacks these "heretics" but includes the members of the tolerated religions as well, and he supports the statement that "It is better that enemies should not be in our midst." This led to an Esma'ili revolt under the leadership of Hasan Sabbāh, who was leader of the group in Deylamān from 1090 until his death in 1124. He fortified the fortress of Alamut, in the Alborz mountains north of Qazvin into an impregnable fortress. It remained their stronghold until 1257 when it was destroyed by the Mongols. Sabbāh used terror and assassination as a political weapon. He organized the Esma'ili cells in the cities into armed bands. The devotees who were sent on missions of assassination were fearless, believing that their mission was holy and that if they were killed they would go to paradise as martyrs. One of their first victims was Nezām al-Molk himself.[21]

The Persian renaissance produced great physicians, mathematicians, astronomers, and historians as well. We have mentioned that Gondishāpur was a medical center in Sāsānian times and remained so in Islamic times. Hārun al-Rashid built a hospital in Baghdad after the Persian model and called it by its Persian name *bimārestān*. The most original work in medicine was done by two Persians, Rāzi and Avicenna. Mohammad ibn-Zakariyya al-Rāzi (865–985) was born in Ray near modern Tehran, and lived most of his life under the Sāmānid patronage. For a time he was the chief physician in Baghdad. His book on medicine, *Al-Hāwi*, is a comprehensive work in medicine in which he reports his clinical studies on the kidney stone, small pox, and measles and describes his invention of seton (a method of suturing) in surgery. Avicenna, who has been discussed as a philosopher, was a physician at the Sāmānid court at the age of 16. His encyclopedia of medicine, *Qānun (The Canon)*, was used as a text in Europe well into the seventeenth century.

In mathematics and astronomy we must single out Mohammad al-Khārazmi, whose works introduced "Arabic" numerals, algorism, and algebra to the West; Abu Reyhān Biruni, who figured the latitude and longitude of many cities on the basis of the rotation of the earth on its axis; and Omar Khayyām, who in addition to his works on Euclid, helped inaugurate a new solar calendar which is in use in Iran. Of the contributions of these men, as well as scores of historians, geographers, and others to what is sometimes called "Islamic civilization," suffice it to quote the late E. G. Browne: "Take from what is generally called Arabian science—exegeses, tradition, theology, philosophy, medicine, lexicography, history, biography, even Arabic grammar—the work con-

---

21. For a detailed treatment of Esmā'ilis see Boyle, ed., *The Saljuq and Mongol Periods*, chapter 5.

tributed by Persians and the best part is gone." [22] Very likely their work would not have been possible had it not been for the weakness of the caliphs and the freedom which this gave to the intellectuals to become creative. After the Saljuqs restored orthodoxy, scholarship and creativity began to languish in the world of Islam wherever orthodoxy was in power.

During this period almost all the intellectuals wrote their scientific and philosophical treatises in Arabic, which was still the language of the learned. Persian, however, was not forgotten, for this period saw also the renaissance of the Persian language, which eventually became the medium through which the meditations of the soul and the thoughts of the intellect were expressed. "New Persian," as it is called, is new in that it has borrowed a large number of Arabic words, but it is old in that it is the same as Pahlavi (also called "Middle Persian") which was connected with "Old Persian," and so on to the original Aryan language.

The language which is spoken in Iran, Afghanistan, Tajikestan, and the neighboring regions is one of the few languages of the world with an unbroken literary history going back to ancient times. It was kept alive by the masses with practically no literature during the two centuries of Arab rule; it was encouraged and made official by leaders of principalities, who had emerged from the masses and did not know Arabic; and it was formed by men of talent, who enriched their spoken tongue by blending into its unencumbered grammar and syntax words from the Arabic vocabulary.[23]

Since all of the philosophical and scientific writings were done in Arabic, Persian was used in poetry. Generally Ya'qub Saffar is given credit for ordering the use of Persian in poetry and correspondence, partly because he did not know Arabic and also because he was a Persian "nationalist." It was during the Sāmānid period, however, that Persian poetry took form and beauty by persons like Rudaki and Daqiqi. The latter had come upon a source that contained the history of the kings of Iran from the earliest times. He set out to render the whole thing in poetry but had not done much before he died. Some thirty years later, Ferdosi found both the original manuscript and the couple of thousand lines written by Daqiqi. Ferdosi rendered the whole story until the conquest of Iran by the Arabs in epic poetry. The volume, *Shāhnāmeh*, was dedicated to Sultan Mahmud Ghaznavi, who did not comprehend the value of the book nor appreciate the worth of the poet. The *Shāhnāmeh*, however, has enjoyed prolonged and enthusiastic popularity wherever Persian is spoken, and Ferdosi is considered one of the great-

22. Browne, A *Literary History*, Vol. 1, p. 192.
23. At certain times in Persian history when Persian has been poured into an Arabic mould, either because of religious zeal or as a show of learning, it has rendered both languages artificial.

est poets. All who read the *Shāhnāmeh*, heartily agree with its author, who said: "Much agony did I suffer in these thirty years, but I resurrected Ajam [Iran] with my Persian."

It is of course impossible to write even a few lines about each of the score of famous poets of Iran during this period, and the simple listing of the names will be tiresome reading indeed. The main branches of Persian poetry are first *ghazal*, 'ode,' used mostly for the expression of love, beauty, and other mystical sentiments. Second is *qasideh*, 'purpose poem,' which is longer than the ode and is usually descriptive of an event, condition, or experience. Most of the Persian poets have used these two forms and among the great in this period are Rudaki, Anvari, Farrokhi, and Khāqāni. The third form is *masnavi*, which by its form of multiple rhyme is suited to storytelling. There are different rhythms of *masnavi* from martial (like the verses of Ferdosi) to relaxed (like the mystic stories of Rumi). In between are the *Quintet* of Nezāmi. Four poems of the *Quintet* are stories. Two of them *Bahrām nāmeh*, and *Eskandar (Alexander) nāmeh*, describe the life and deeds of the two heroes. The other two are love stories, *Khosro and Shirin*, taken from Persian lore, and *Leyli and Majnun*, taken from Arabic. There are other delightful love stories such as *Yusof and Zoleykhā*, *Vis and Rāmin*, *Vāmeq and Azra*, and others which are written by different poets. The fourth popular form of Persian poetry is *robā'i* 'quatrain,' which is always relaxed and describes a passing mood or thought. The most famous poet of this form is, of course, Omar Khayyām; less known to the West is Bābā Tāher Oryān.

It must be emphasized here that almost all of these poets knew Arabic, and some wrote excellent poetry in that language. One of the greatest of Persian poets is Sa'di of Shirāz, who in his writings uses Persian and Arabic at will. He is best known for his *Golestān (Rose Garden)*, which is required reading in all Persian schools. In short anecdotes written in prose and poetry, Sa'di moralizes on all sorts of conditions and relations. His ethics is situational, sometimes cynical, and always existential.

The poets were supported by patronage of the princes who were more interested in flattery than in literature. The poets had to satisfy this craving in order to make a living and some of them became very rich indeed. Every occasion, whether it be birth, death, marriage, war, victory, or what have you, was a suitable subject for poetry. These poems would bring gifts of money or clothing. The patron was always in danger of being ridiculed—in exquisite poetic form—if he aroused the poet's displeasure.[24] These same poets, however, on their own time wrote some of the lasting poems which take the readers' soul to heights of aesthetic experience.

---

24. Ferdosi's ridicule of Sultan Mahmud, after he was rebuffed by the latter, is among his best.

The Mongols

The Mongol avalanche which started in 1219 in Sinkiang had by 1224 destroyed a chain of cities on the Iranian plateau such as Balkh, Bokhārā, Samarkand, Marv, Harāt, Nishāpur, and Ray; it had killed men and women by the thousands; and it had left maimed the few who had escaped with their lives. Why the Mongols came so far from their base of operation in China is still vague. All that can be ascertained is that the governor of the border town of Utrar, under the principality of Khārazmshāh, killed a number of Chinese merchants who were sent by Chengiz Khan and confiscated the rich merchandise. Chengiz Khan sent his envoys to the ruler of the dynasty, Mohammad, and would have been satisfied if the governor had been punished, but Mohammad was too proud to punish him and killed the envoys instead. This started the avalanche. On the other hand, Chengiz, who had become emperor of a settled and civilized Chinese empire, had difficulty controlling the restless Mongol tribesmen. The only alternative was to keep them fighting. In any case, in the words of a contemporary, "they came, they looted, they killed, they burned, and they left." Actually they did not leave. Many remained and were absorbed by the Persian people and culture. That the advance of the Persian renaissance was arrested there is no question, but it did not last long. Indeed, the speed with which the Persians were able to rise again is nothing short of a miracle.

After the death of Chengiz, his vast empire was divided into three parts. First was China proper, with Peking as capital; its ruler had titular authority over the whole empire. The second, in Russia, was known as the "Golden Horde," with its capital at Sarāy. The third was in Iran, called the "Ilkhan," with its capital at Marāgheh in Azarbāyjān. Destructive as Chengiz had been in Iran, Holāgu, the founder of the Ilkhan dynasty, was a builder and a patron of arts and sciences. Marco Polo, who traveled through Iran to Peking around 1271, describes the thriving industries of Tabriz, Kāshān and Kermān. Holāgu is also responsible for ending the Abbasid caliphate with the capture of Baghdad.

The Mongols, as pagans, were very tolerant of people of all religions. Some of the Ilkhan rulers were Christians and the Vazir of Argun in 1289 was a Jewish physician. But in the end Islām won, when Ghāzān Khān (1295–1304) became a Moslem and with the zeal of a convert destroyed the "heathen" temples as well as the Christian and Jewish houses of worship.

The arrest of the Persian renaissance was short-lived. The Persians not only restored their own culture but they also civilized the Mongols. Unlike the Arabs, the Mongols had not come with an ideology and therefore did not impose any restrictions on the Persian artists and scientists. The famous Persian miniature paintings show the freedom under which the artists worked. The very power that was so destructive at first also freed the Persian culture from the limiting tendencies of orthodox Islam and brought Iran and Islam into contact with the cultures of Asia.

By the time the Crusaders were driven away and the Mongols had been absorbed, the geopolitical pattern of the Middle East reverted to what it was before Islam. Iran was separated from its neighbors to the west along the same line as the Sāsānids had been separated from the Byzantines. Furthermore, Persian language replaced Arabic in practically everything except the recital of the Koran and prayer. The Persians, however, had changed considerably since the Sāsānian days. Their blood was mixed with Berbers, Arabs, Greeks, Turks, Mongols, Indians and a few other nationalities. Their loyalty was not to a land but to a language and culture. It was a form of "culturalism" or cultural nationalism in which the Persians found their identity. Two centuries later political unity followed in the establishment of the Safavid dynasty.

6

The Isolation of Iran

Professor C. E. Bosworth begins his erudite essay on "The Political and Dynastic History of the Iranian World (A.D. 1000–1217)" [1] with the statement: "For nearly a thousand years—indeed, until our own century—Iran has generally been ruled by non-Persian dynasties . . ." This is, of course, a truism; but it must be stated because a casual reader of Persian history does not realize it. What is more important is the fact that the Persians themselves are not conscious of it. Very few Persians really think of Mahmud Ghaznavi, Malekshāh, Sanjar, or even Timur-e Lang (Tamerlane) as "alien" rulers. Indeed they will smile with incredulity if one suggests that Shah Abbās the Great was not a Persian. This is important because it underlines the idea of culturalism or cultural nationalism discussed at the conclusion of the previous chapter. The Persian race—if it ever existed—was so mixed by intermarriage (voluntary and enforced) with Greeks, Romans, Arabs, Turks, Mongols, and others that it lost its meaning. The experience of the Persians in absorbing the culture of all comers and blending it with theirs and producing something new was so enriching and rewarding that land and boundaries became insignificant. It did not make any difference whether this activity was carried out in Baghdad or Balkh. What was important was the culture, the outlook, and not land. What was considered essential was the language as the medium of that culture, and not race. Such a concept is more of a fulfillment of the tolerant and cosmopolitan ideals of the Achaemenids than the limited nationalism imported from nineteenth-century Europe, which is based on a national state and race.

1. C. E. Bosworth, in *Land of Iran*, p. 1.

This concept of cultural nationalism was strengthened during the Mongol period. As has been stated, the absence of a strong caliphate to impose orthodoxy had provided the intellectuals and artists in all fields the freedom to be creative and to inaugurate the Persian renaissance. The Mongols, who did not have an ideology to impose, obliterated even the partial sanctions imposed by some of the Saljuq rulers. The result was a period in which the Persian artists and writers were not bound by many restrictions imposed by the dogmas of religion or government.

It is agreed by all historians of Iran that the four centuries from the founding of the Ilkhan dynasty in 1250 to 1650, or a century and a half after the founding of the Safavid dynasty, was one of the brightest periods of cultural advance in the long history of Iran. In art, architecture, philosophy, history, mathematics, and astronomy, the record is from excellent to brilliant as compared with any other period in Persian history. It is also agreed that from 1650 to the beginning of the twentieth century is a period of cultural decline in Iran. How is this to be explained?

Some modern Persian historians are in the habit of lamenting the Arab conquest of Iran while praising the religion of Islam which the Arabs brought.[2] They denounce practically every Arab ruler of the Omayyad and Abbasid dynasties while extolling the virtues of the Persian and Turkish principalities that encouraged the renaissance of Persian culture. When it comes to the Mongol period, however, they seem to execute an intellectual somersault and state that the four centuries of cultural excellence was a "continuation of the brilliant scientific and literary movement of the Abbasids" and believe that the three centuries preceding the twentieth, was nothing but the manifestation of the "destructive rule of the Mongols and Timurids." [3]

It is hard to believe that, if the Mongol conquest was as destructive as it is claimed, it would take four centuries for its crippling effect to show itself. Furthermore, we know that the Abbasid caliphs, including the enlightened ones like Ma'mun, were more interested in stamping out religious and political heresy than in the advancement of learning. Most of the scientists and philosophers were accused of heresy; and had the situation not been so fluid that no principality had absolute power over the whole country for a long time, it is difficult to believe that they would have been allowed to be creative. It is quite evident that cultural advance becomes possible in a free society. In this case a free atmosphere was created by the weakness of the caliphs during the period of principalities. It was encouraged by the princes of these principalities either because of their own desire or out of rivalry with other

2. As for example, Eqbal, Falsafi, Zarrinkub, Rafi', and others.
3. Abbas Eqbal, *Tārikh-e Mofassal-e Iran az Estilā-ye Moghol tā Enqerāz-e Qājāriyyeh*, (*A History of Iran from the Conquest of the Mongols to the Fall of the Qajars*) (Tehran: Chāp-e Khodkār, 1940), p. 199.

leaders. It was given special impetus by the ferment of the Twelver Shi'i and Esmā'ili opposition to Sunni orthodoxy. This state of affairs continued during the Mongol period when there was no dogma to worry about and the scientists, philosophers, and artists had freedom of inquiry and expression. Under the circumstances it is not surprising to witness the galaxy of writers and artists during the Mongol period. Cultural activity slackened, however, when the Safavids made Shi'ism the state religion and carried out a period of forced conversion. By the time of Shah Abbās (1587–1629) the last bright light of the cultural advance was still in evidence. After that, when Shi'i heterodoxy became orthodoxy, state and religion became one, and the kings with very few exceptions had to enforce the dogmas of the established religion, then the light of learning began to dim.

The purpose is not to minimize the destruction wrought by the Mongols; but it is important to note that it did not break the Persian spirit, nor did it destroy the Persian cultural advance except for the temporary arrest during the invasion and a few years after that. The Persians did manage to become advisors and ministers for the Mongols from Holāgu on. They did survive the invasion through artistic creativity which reached its heights as evidenced by the magnificence of miniature paintings. Furthermore, they did withstand the onslaught through Sufism which minimized the significance of the real world which had crumbled around them. Sufism was a reaction to the transitory nature of life—a phenomenon which was heightened by Mongol destruction—so that the mystic experience, which is the union of the self with God, became a means by which to free the soul.

SUFISM

It is generally thought that Sufism derives its name from the woolen (suf) garment which the adherent wore. It has its roots in the Koran and one of the earliest Moslem mystics was Rabi'a (d. 801), the celebrated Arab lady from Kufa. Sufism must not be identified with Shi'ism. It was thanks to the influence of Ghazāli that Sufism was given a niche in the orthodox temple and was tolerated by the Sunnis. Perhaps because it was tolerated by the Sunnis, the Shi'is did not have much use for it until after the Mongol invasion. There was not much love for the Sufis among the orthodox because Sufism was a reaction to the orthodox theology of the separation of God and man. According to the Sufis, there is true similarity between the attributes of God and man through which man can become "one" with God. The law of Islam, Shari'a according to the majority of the Sufis, is like a "shell" which protects the kernel. Sufis are not all agreed, however, on what to do with the shell once it is broken and the kernel is reached. Some believe that it is still useful as a protection; others think that it should be honored for having contained the kernel; and still others like the prince of all mystics, Jalāl al-Din Rumi, believe that it is only good for animal fodder.

The Sufis, like the early Christians, called themselves "People of the Way," *ahl-e tariqat*. The idea is that the soul of man, which is the breath of God, has been separated from its source and longs to return to be lost in Him. Since there are different "ways" by which man may reach God, the Sufis are not only tolerant of all religions and philosophies, they themselves have been affected by them. Religious influences from Christianity, Mithraism, Buddhism, and Hinduism, and philosophical concepts such as gnosticism, monism, and pantheism can readily be seen in Sufi literature. The venerable Persian mystic, Attār of Nishāpur, who in his old age was massacred by the Mongols in 1222, has a beautiful allegorical poem called "The Conversation of the Birds." In this the birds (humanity) want to go and be with their king (God) whose name is Simorgh. They pass through seven valleys (conditions) of search: love, understanding, detachment, communion, wonder, union, and/or extinction. Of the thousands that started out many perished and many even killed each other to save themselves. In the end only thirty birds (Persian *si* = 30 and *morgh* = bird) arrived. When they were ushered through the portals of the king's palace, the veil which covered their eyes was rent asunder. They gazed at each other and realized that they were thirty birds (*si morgh*) and that Simorgh (God) was none other than they the *si morgh!*

Another great mystic was Hāfez of Shirāz (d. 1389) who must be ranked among the top five poets of Iran. He had gnostic (*erfān*) tendencies and like other mystic poets, used wine, roses, and love both as allegory and as aids to spiritual life. He was accused of agnosticism and heresy by the local clerics but these did not bother him. To him life continued to be supremely joyous and, like the wine which he enjoyed, also bitter. He could see the "Light of God [even] in the Magian house of worship" and the "Countenance of the Beloved in a cup of wine." He pitied the "witless fellow who could not see that God was with him all the time and was calling for Him from far off."

Perhaps in imitation of the Christian or Buddhist order of monks or both, the Sufis also organized orders, *tariqeh*. They met in their head-quarters, *Khāneqāh*, under the leadership of an abbot, *pir*, who had attained spiritual insight, discipline, and wisdom. The Christian or the Buddhist monk who wanted to attain salvation or nirvana found the world transitory and decided that he could not enjoy any part of it and became an ascetic. The majority of the Sufis, however, disavowed the world as a whole but at the same time enjoyed the parts which were within their reach. Jalāl al-Din Rumi (1207–1273) was the founder of the *Molavi* order which flourished in Turkey and Iran. His book of parables and anecdotes, *Masnavi*, is one of the most popular books in Persia. Because his followers played music and danced for the joy of knowing God, they are called the "whirling dervishes."

The Safavids

As we have seen, the Turkish tribes accepted Islam with great zeal and fanaticism and were loyal to its institutions. Perhaps because the discipline, devotion, and obedience to the leader practiced in the Sufi orders were similar to the life in the tribes, the Turks were attracted to these orders. Gradually the coming of the tribesmen added an economic and military dimension to the life of the orders. In addition to the spiritual leader, there were "lay" brothers who took care of the economic needs of the order. There were also warriors who protected the community and fought for the advancement of Islam. There were quite a number of these orders in Asia Minor and Azarbāyjān.[4] As the Ilkhan kings became Shi'i, a number of the Turkish tribes did the same and there came into being Sufi orders which were Shi'i. In the Shi'i orders, however, the leader of the order and the commander of the warriors was usually the same person; consistent with Shi'i tradition, the position of the leader was hereditary.

One of these orders which had a large following among the Turkish tribes was called Safi or Safavi, in honor of the first leader Sheykh Safi who died in 1334. Since these warriors had a red headgear, they were called *qezelbāsh*, or "red heads." Sheykh Heydar, a direct descendant of Safi, was killed in 1490, and left the leadership to his thirteen-year-old son Esmā'il.[5] With the help of the devoted *qezelbāsh*, who comprised seven clans, this remarkable youth revenged his father by defeating the prince of Shirvān, and took Armenia and Azarbāyjān. He proclaimed himself king with Tabriz as his capital. In the next fifteen years of almost constant warfare, Esmā'il was the master of Iran, from the borders of Syria to the Oxus and from the Caucasus to the Persian Gulf.

It was apparent that the Safavi dynasty founded by Esma'il was not just another principality established by the adventurous ambition of a warrior. From the very beginning the dynasty was established on two foundations. One of these was Shi'i and the other Persian, and Esma'il concentrated more on the first than the second. His hatred of the Sunnis knew no bounds and his persecution of the Sunnis was ruthless. The alternative for the majority of the Persians who were Sunnis at the time, was either conversion to Shi'ism or death. Conversion must have been rapid, because half a century later Iran was a Shi'i country and gradually became an isolated island surrounded by a sea of Sunni Islam. While regretting the cruelty of forced conversion, modern Persian historians are generally agreed that the establishment of Shi'i religious hegemony saved Iran from being incorporated into the Ottoman empire.

4. The founder of the Ottoman empire, Osman, was a *ghazi* warrior in one of these orders.
5. His mother was a Greek princess from Trebizond named Martha.

The Ottomans, who had had extraordinary success in Europe and had sealed the fate of the Byzantine empire by the capture of Constantinople, were eager to go eastward and occupy the traditional lands of Islam. Indeed, Bāyezid II (1481–1512) was in touch with the Uzbek chief Sheybak Khan in an attempt to nip Esmā'il's ambitions in the bud. Eventually the Ottomans did conquer Arabia, the Fertile Crescent, and North Africa, and they would have extended their empire to Central Asia had it not been for the Safavids. In his letters to Esmā'il, Bāyezid gave him "fatherly" advice and asked him to refrain from shedding Sunni blood and desecrating Sunni graves and cautioned him to be wary of the Persians because they "are a people who will not obey a king who is not one of them." [6] This reference to the fact that Esmā'il was not a Persian when he was claiming that he was a descendant of the Sāsānian kings, must have cut him to the quick. When Esmā'il defeated and captured the Uzbek leader, he had his skin filled with straw and sent it to Bāyezid. Then he had the man's skull made into a gold-rimmed bowl from which he drank wine the rest of his life. The devotion of the qezelbāsh to Esmā'il as the supreme religious and political leader was so great that at his order they actually ate the victims' raw flesh.[7]

The inevitable contest between Esmā'il and the Ottomans, whose new ruler Selim I (1512–1520) was as hotheaded and cruel as Esmā'il, took place at the battle of Chāldirān in 1514. On his march eastward Selim destroyed some 40,000 Shi'is in Asia Minor. At the battle of Chāldirān, the Ottomans won a resounding victory, but it did not prove conclusive, partly because the Janissaries refused to pursue Esmā'il farther east, and partly because richer prizes were awaiting Selim, namely Syria and Egypt. The Battle of Chāldirān was a contest between the Ottoman artillery and muskets and the Safavid spears, bows, and swords. Furthermore, the Safavids found out that religious fanaticism and courage were no match for muskets and cannons. Chāldirān was also the beginning of a senseless and inconclusive struggle between Iran and Turkey which lasted for nearly three hundred years.

From the death of Shah Esmā'il in 1524 to the accession of Shah Abbās the Great in 1587, three Safavid shahs turned their attention eastward and carved out an empire which was fast approaching the size of the Sāsānian empire. Because Tabriz was too close to the borders and vulnerable to attack and occupation by the Ottomans, the capital was moved to Qazvin. The qezelbāsh warriors formed the backbone of the state, and their leaders were each given a district as a fief. In return they provided the shah with soldiers and with revenue. These leaders had power of life and death over the population and were given the

6. Nasrollah Falsafi, *Chand Maqāle-ye Tārikhi*, (*A Few Historical Essays*) (Tehran: University of Tehran Press, 1962), p. 6.
7. Ibid., p. 12.

task of converting them to Shi'ism. The proof of conversion was cursing the first three caliphs as "usurpers." Those who refused were summarily executed.

Even though the Shah as leader of the order was considered supreme, the *qezelbāsh* leaders who had become rich and powerful tried to interfere in the question of succession. Each supported his own favorite among the sons of the deceased shah, and all of them preferred to have a weak person on the throne so that they would be able to do what they pleased. During the early Safavid period we witness a standard struggle between the oligarchy and autocracy and the infighting between the oligarchs themselves for position of leadership. During the reign of the mild-mannered and ascetic Shah Mohammad Khodābandeh, the *qezelbāsh* became especially unruly; and in order to insure that they would have another weak person on the throne, they killed the crown prince, his mother, and most of the Safavid princes. A younger brother of the crown prince, however, was rescued and a few years later, in 1587, he assumed the throne as Shah Abbās. Under Shah Abbās Iran reached the zenith of its power and at the same time, the beginning of its cultural and political decline. While his predecessors concentrated on forcing all the people to conform to Shi'ism, Shah Abbās emphasized the Persian aspect of his rule. The cultural advance, which had continued through the Mongol period and had experienced a setback by the ruthless imposition of Shi'i dogma upon the people, had still some life in it and Shah Abbās kept it alive a little longer. It was his good fortune to be king at a time when the neighboring countries had their own difficulties. The Ottomans were fast declining; the Russians had their "Time of Troubles"; and the Mongols of India had lost their hold on the country. Shah Abbās gained territory at the expense of all three of them, especially Russia and the Ottoman empire.

One of the first things which he did was to destroy the power of the *qezelbāsh*. He took land away from them and killed most of their leaders. He still maintained a *qezelbāsh* corps but it was mostly ceremonial and the men were armed with antiquated weapons. He built a base of support for himself among the people. In place of the *qezelbāsh*, he organized two armies, one made up of Christians from Georgia and Armenia, and the other made up of Persians. He equipped both armies with modern muskets and artillery. This act of Shah Abbās broke the back of the militant Sufism in Iran, which considered its mission to be the conversion or destruction of the Sunnis rather than the advancement of Islam. Around 1597 when Shah Abbās was fighting the Uzbeks, there came to Iran two young Englishmen, Anthony Sherly and his eighteen-year-old brother Robert. They had military experience, and some of their English companions knew the art of casting cannons. Shah Abbās was attracted to these brothers both as persons and as means of improving his army. He trained and equipped his new forces with the help of the Sherly brothers. They took part in the wars between Iran and Turkey and later were sent by Shah Abbās on diplomatic missions.[8]

GOVERNMENT

In the last chapter while discussing the governmental structure of the Saljuqs, we mentioned the tension which existed between the palace, *dargāh*, and the chancery, *divān*. In the Safavid period this same tension between the two groups continued. The system of land grants was also continued. The expenses of the office of the grand vazir as well as those of the provincial governor, district supervisor, aided by a county commissioner (*khān*) and his assistant, the local supervisor (*soltān*),[9] were all paid from the income of the land assigned to each. It was their job to collect taxes, pay the soldiers in their locality, and send a specific amount to the Shah. They also sent gifts to the king. Some of the provincial officers had friends who were close to the Shah, who in return for appropriate gifts would speak well of them in the presence of the Shah.

The Shi'i nature of the Safavid dynasty created another tension within the government which has continued in Iran to the present. Inasmuch as the hidden Imām was the true ruler of the empire, he had spokesmen who could interpret the law of Islam according to the needs of the time. These spokesmen were called *mojtahed*; their opinions were binding on all the Shi'is. This would take all power from the hands of the Shah had there not always been more than one *mojtahed* at a given time. Sometimes there were four or five who, naturally, did not agree on all questions. This division among them gave a free hand to the Shah or the government to carry out its program. There was more than one spokesman for the hidden Imam because of a lack of any hierarchical provision to appoint a *mojtahed*. In addition to proper academic training, anyone aspiring to be a *mojtahed* had to have a reputation for piety, wisdom, and common sense. Since always more than one person had the above credentials, a person would be considered a *mojtahed* by unofficial and popular consensus. Seldom did all the *mojtaheds* agree on a given question, and the shah or government could get by with a great deal of innovation and deviation, both of which are anathema in Shi'i and Sunni Islam alike.

The Safavid kings had a special position and the early shahs of the dynasty tried to maintain it. It has already been stated that the Safavid

---

8. Eqbal, *Tārikh-e Mofassal*, p. 279.

9. In order to belittle the Ottomans, the Safavids gave the title of high Ottoman personages to the low functionaries in their own government. "Sultan," which was the title of the Ottoman emperor, was a very low officer in the Safavid hierarchy. The same was true of "Sheikh al-Islam," "Belerbey," and others. Perhaps the Turks reciprocated with the title of "Padeshah" or "Pasha."

rulers combined in their persons, as leader of the Safi order, both temporal and religious powers. The Shah was called "the most perfect leader." They also claimed that they were descendants of the Prophet and tried to extend their power over all the Shi'is as the spokesmen for the Imām. They could not, however, do away with the office of the *mojtahed* but they did not endow the office with any actual political or administrative powers. The Safavids created another office called *sadr*, headed by a religious leader who, with the help of a large bureaucracy, administered all the courts, religious endowments, marriage and divorce, and also the police.[10] The *mojtahed* was a "chaplain" to the shah, and his influence was in direct proportion to the power and personality of the king. After Shah Abbās, when the power of the king declined, the *mojtaheds* became powerful.

Shah Abbās himself had friendly relationships with the religious leaders and called himself "the dog of the threshold of Ali." He built a beautiful mausoleum over the tomb of the eighth Imām, Ali al-Rezā, in Mashhad and, when it was completed, walked all the way from Esfahān on a pilgrimage. The honorary title of *Mashhadi*, given to those who made the pilgrimage became as important as *Hāji*, for going to Mecca, and *Karbalā'i* for going to Karbalā. There were other kings, however, like Nāder Shah (1736–1747) and Rezā Shah (1924–1941) who did not have any use for religious leaders or *mojtaheds*. Most of the rest of the kings were subservient to them in differing degrees. The tension between the two has continued to the present day.

SOCIAL AND CULTURAL LIFE

Shah Abbās moved the capital from Qazvin to Esfahān and built it into such a beautiful city that to this day it delights visitors. Some of the most beautiful mosques and buildings still stand. He encouraged architecture and painting. He did much to revive some of the old festivals of Iran such as the festival of water, of roses, and of lights. He was especially fond of the festival of lights, when he would order fireworks.[11] Other pastimes engaged in by the populace were cock, wolf, bull, and ram fights; card games; acrobatics; tightrope walking; and puppet shows. The aristocracy, as usual, played polo. The brotherhood of men who spent their leisure in physical exercise was perhaps in existence before the Safavids. This brotherhood, which is still in existence, called their place of exercise "a house of strength" and had a hierarchy with a special code of honor. The drummer would usher in the leader with special beats on the drum and then would sing the

10. Until the twentieth century the police in both Shi'i and Sunni countries had the duty to see that people performed their religious duties as well as to prevent religiously illegal acts from being committed.

11. Nasrollah Falsafi, *Zendegāni-ye Shah Abbas* (*Life of Shah Abbas*), III (Tehran: Ibn Sina), p. 168.

adventures of Persian heroes from the *Shāhnāmeh*, as they went through their exercises.

The Safavids, as Shi'is, encouraged the passion plays and the religious processions commemorating the tragic events at Karbalā. In cities all over the country, the processions were the most important social events and districts vied with each other in the excellence of their productions and sometimes actually fought with each other. A major procession involved the cooperation of over a thousand people. Hundreds participated in them in fulfillment of their vows. Some beat their breasts and some beat their bare backs with a cluster of chains, all in unison and to the rhythm of the dirges they chanted. The climax came on the tenth day of Moharram, when a new group joined the procession. They were clad in white shrouds and each held a sword in his right hand while with his left he clung on to his companion's belt. They marched sideways in two lines facing each other, and inflicting wounds on their shaved heads. Each of these "sword beaters" had a friend marching behind him with a stick in his hand. He would bring his stick between the sword and his friend's head if he noticed that the sight of blood and the frenzy of the occasion might cause the participant to inflict fatal wounds on himself.

The shahs, of course, had their harems, which were guarded by black eunuchs. The Safavids took their women with them to wars, and some of them were good marksmen and actually participated in battle. In cases of defeat, the eunuchs had orders to kill the women. Prostitutes were brought under strict supervision and were housed in a special quarter of the city called "veil-less." In campaigns, they were allowed to follow the camps and each would be charged a special tax.[12] Sometimes there were "women's days" at the bazaars when no men except the shopkeepers would be allowed. There were also "women's evenings" in the boulevard that had been built in Esfahān where the women of the city would promenade up and down the treelined streets. It is not difficult to imagine that such occasions were eagerly awaited by the women who otherwise led secluded lives.

Shah Abbās was especially popular with the peasants and the masses. Cruel though he was, the victims of his ruthless rages were the *qezel-bāsh* leaders and members of the officialdom whose liquidation brought respite to the people. He frequented bazaars and in his trips to different sites he walked in the streets and talked with the passersby. He had the habit of inviting himself to peoples' houses without previous notice and sharing their meals with them. The true and embellished accounts of such activities have become part of the lore of Iran which grandmothers tell their grandchildren to this day. As a popular and powerful shah, he set the style also. He popularized shaving and actually ordered men to shave their beards.[13] He frequented tea houses where

12. Ibid., Vol. 3, p. 55.
13. Ibid., Vol. 2, p. 280.

he would listen to poets and story tellers and exchange pleasantries with the people.

ECONOMIC SITUATION

The theory that everything belonged to the Shah continued. There was no distinction made between the personal expenses of the Shah and the government. The main sources of revenue for the Shah and the government were these:

1. Taxes levied on each province. These were paid in cash and in kind.
2. Income from the private domains of the Shah. When he destroyed the *qezelbāsh*, Shah Abbās confiscated their lands and realized tremendous income from them.
3. Income tax. This included an annual tax of one-half of all livestock, one-third of all silk and cotton, bridge and road tolls, head tax for non-Moslems, import duties, etc.
4. Taxes on the sale and cultivation of tobacco were very important.

Shah Abbās himself did not like to smoke and no one dared to smoke in his presence, but it was popular and became more so after his death. By the end of the nineteenth century, as we shall see, the cultivation and use of tobacco, introduced into Iran probably by the Portuguese, became a factor in international relations and national uprising.

To the above we must add such miscellaneous revenues as confiscation of property, gifts from foreign embassies, and the fact that craftsmen worked for less wages when engaged in the Shah's construction program. It is estimated that the annual income of the empire was between 700,000 and 900,000 *tomans*. The annual expenditure is not known, but it was less than the annual income, and the coffers of the early Safavids were full. In the finance department there was one official responsible for the mint. All silver and gold coins were minted in the capital while copper coins were produced locally. What seems to be an innovation of Shah Abbās was an officer in charge of fair prices. The guilds, which had their beginnings during the period of principalities, had become well organized institutions and remained so until the first decades of the twentieth century. Every three months or so, the officer of price stabilization met with the leader, *white beard*, of each guild and determined a fair price. Until the early years of the twentieth century offenders were paraded in the bazaars and sometimes met with severe punishments.

CONTACT WITH THE WEST

One of the most interesting episodes in the history of Iran after the Mongol invasion is its contact with the West. The main reasons

were political and economic and had religious and cultural implications
as well. All sorts of people from Europe, diplomats, merchants, soldiers,
priests, and adventurers, made their way to Iran. As early as the twelfth
century, the Crusaders had become aware of the differences which
existed between Iran and the Arabic speaking parts of the Moslem world.
They tried unsuccessfully to involve the rulers of Iran against Syria.
When the pagan Mongols invaded Iran, Europeans were eager to seek
their friendship in order to counteract the aggressive conduct of Moslems in the Fertile Crescent and also to convert the Mongols to Christianity. Pope Innocent IV sent embassies to the Mongols. The adventures of Marco Polo did much to encourage traders and adventurers to
journey to Iran. By the middle of the fourteenth century, because of
the constant wars of expansion waged by the Ottoman sultans, it was
Tabriz rather than the blockaded Constantinople that was an important
center of commerce.

In the sixteenth century two factors helped to increase the contact
of Iran with the West. One was the avowed anti-Ottoman policy of
the Safavids, which coincided with a similar policy on the part of the
rulers of Europe. The second was the fact that the sixteenth century
ushered in the age of exploration. Trade routes had shifted from the
Mediterranean, and Europeans were seeking other routes. It was not long
before the Portuguese were bringing spices from India and had established themselves in the Persian Gulf. In 1508 Shah Esmā'il signed
a treaty with the Portuguese over the trade of the Persian Gulf and
mutual military assistance against the Ottomans. Even though the
military clauses were never implemented, the Persian Gulf ports of
Muscat, Bahrain, and Hormoz became important trade centers.[14]

Since the cape route had been monopolized by the Portuguese and
the Spaniards, the British, for a time, tried the northern route that
had been opened to them. They made contact with the court of Ivan
the Terrible and formed the Muscovy Company. In 1561, a representative of this company, Anthony Jenkinson, went by way of the Caspian
to Qazvin, the capital of the Safavid Shah Tahmāsp I. The dangerous
and costly route, the lack of market for English woolens, and the
reluctance of the fanatic Tahmāsp to have anything to do with infidels,
all worked together to persuade the British to give up the project; Shah
Abbās's attitude, however, was very different from his predecessors. He
used his contact with the Europeans to equip his army with artillery
and muskets, to open excellent markets for Persian products, especially
silk, and to try to subdue the Ottomans. In the first two he was successful.

When Shah Abbās was improving Esfahān, he brought a large
number of Armenian families as hostages from their homes in Jolfa

14. The importance of Hormoz as a world trade mart has been recorded by
Milton in his *Paradise Lost*.

and settled them across the Zāyandeh Rud (river) from the city. As the "New Jolfa" flourished, more Armenians migrated voluntarily and settled in many parts of Iran. He never failed to impress the European ambassadors and Christian monks with his tolerance toward the Armenians. They were permitted to build their own homes, ride horses, and wear any kind of clothes they pleased, a privilege which non-Moslems did not have before or very long after Shah Abbās until modern times. The Shah had a monopoly of the silk trade, which was one of the most important items of export, and he let the Armenian merchants administer it for him.[15] He gave special privileges to Catholic monks and allowed them to open a mission in Esfahān proper. Indeed, by his remarks he had led some of the Christian monks from Rome to think that he himself was about ready to be converted. He was lavish in his entertainment of foreign visitors and gave the European merchants special privileges. All provincial governors were given strict orders to facilitate travel arrangements for European merchants and do everything in their power to satisfy their needs. The Europeans were also given the privilege of being subject to their own laws while in Iran. This was an extension of the privilege given to the "People of the Book"; later this was used as a means of imperialism by the countries of Europe and continued until the second decade of the twentieth century.

The Shah sent a number of embassies to the capitals of Europe. In 1599 he sent a large embassy accompanied by Anthony Sherly and in 1608 another one accompanied by Robert Sherly. The main purpose of these embassies, which was to launch a simultaneous attack on the Ottomans, was not accomplished. No doubt these contacts provided Shah Abbās with enough information to know that the power of Spain was on the decline. He entered into a trade agreement with the British East India Company in 1616 and by 1622 a joint Anglo-Persian force expelled the Portuguese and Spanish traders from the Persian Gulf. Shah Abbās built a new port on the Persian Gulf, Bandar-e Abbās, and the British did most of their business there with branches in Shirāz and Esfahān.

The Dutch also appeared on the scene in 1581 and were received with enthusiasm. They made a barter arrangement exchanging Dutch merchandise, mainly textiles, for Persian silk, rugs, wool, and brocade. This arrangement was more popular with the Persian merchants, and by the time of Shah Safi (1629–1642), the Dutch had virtual control of the Persian trade. They were exempt from paying import duties, but instead they had to buy 600 bales of silk annually.[16] Toward the last decades of the seventeenth century, trade in the Persian Gulf began

15. Falsafi, *Life of Shah Abbas*, Vol. 3, p. 206 ff.
16. Nasrollah Falsafi, *Tārikh-e Ravābet-e Iran va Orupā dar Doreh-ye Safaviyyeh* (*A History of Irano-European Relations During the Safavid Period*) (Tehran: Ibn Sina, 1939), p. 95.

to slacken. This was partly because Europeans had found greener pastures in east Asia and partly because the weak Safavid Shahs could not maintain peace and security.

Even though there were brisk and varied economic activities throughout these years, cultural interaction was practically nil. The reason is perhaps not hard to find. On the one hand, Shi'i orthodoxy had strengthened its hold ever since the coming of the Safavids and had created such a dogmatic and fanatical shell that it had stultified almost all intellectual investigation or artistic expression. Iran was insulated not only against an intellectual ferment from Europe, but was isolated from contact with the world of Islam.

On the other hand, the Catholic monks, who represented the European intellectuals in Iran, were similarly closed minded and were unaffected by and opposed to the Reformation which was going on in Europe. Both sides were convinced that there was not anything they could learn from the other, and they came together without being aware of each other's existence. The intellectual interaction between Iran and the West had to wait until the middle of the nineteenth century.

NĀDER SHAH

Notwithstanding his many good qualities, Shah Abbās was a cruel person, and it is reported that he kept his five hundred executioners busy. He who had done so much to build an empire destroyed it by his thirst for blood, even that of members of his own family. Like his contemporary, Ivan the Terrible of Russia, he killed his own son, the Crown Prince. Not satisfied with that he blinded his other two sons so that by the time he died there was no one except his grandson Safi, a youth of seventeen, to become king. The death of Shah Abbās was a signal for the old enemies of Iran to rise for revenge. The excesses of the Shi'i cruelty against the Sunnis could not be tolerated by the Ottoman sultans, who were caliphs and protectors of all Moslems, especially Sunnis. While the Ottomans were weak they did not have much choice, but when Shah Abbās died and each of his successors proved weaker than the previous one, the Ottomans moved against Iran from the west and encouraged their fellow Sunnis, the Uzbeks and the Afghans, to attack from the east. It took a number of years of warfare, for neither the Ottomans nor the Afghans were strong enough to win a decisive victory. Among the many weak successors of Shah Abbās, Shah Soltan Hosayn (1694–1742) was the worst. He was an indecisive and extremely superstitious man and was so much under the influence of the Shi'i clergy that he would not take a drink of water without a *fatva* (religious sanction) from the *mojtahed*. In 1722, the Afghan leader Mahmud invaded Iran and defeated the Persian forces on May 8, 1722, in the village of Golnābād, some twelve miles from Esfahān.

Shah Soltan Hosayn surrendered, but his son Tahmāsp II, who had fled to Qazvin, continued the struggle.

Tahmāsp himself could not accomplish very much, were it not for the rise of Nāder Qoli, a soldier of fortune, who was destined to be called the "Napoleon of Iran." Nāder was a Turk and belonged to the Afshār tribe loyal to the Safavids. He was an officer in the Persian army and did much to help Tahmāsp II push the Afghans back. In the meantime the victory of the Afghans had whetted the appetite of the Ottomans and the Russians against Iran. The Russians had to withdraw because of the death of Peter the Great in 1725, but the Ottomans continued the attack. The Turks defeated the Persians while Nāder was in the east, and Tahmāsp signed a treaty in 1732 by giving up five cities in the Caucasus. Nāder, who was against such a treaty, led a revolt against Tahmāsp and chose his infant son Abbās III as king with himself as regent. During the next three years he defeated the Turks, pushed the Russians back, and secured eastern Iran against the Afghans. In 1736 the infant Shah died and Nāder assumed the throne as Nāder Shah Afshār. He was crowned in the plain of Moghān in Āzarbāyjān. During the next eleven years, his main work was to retake the territories lost by the later Safavids and further to expand the empire. His spectacular campaign was against India. He captured Kābol, Peshawar, and Lāhore in 1738, and the next year he defeated the Moghul emperor Mohammad Shah and entered Delhi. Because of a misunderstanding, he ordered the plunder of the city and the massacre of the population from 9 A.M. until 2 P.M. It is estimated that some 20,000 perished and a large part of the city was burned. The price of the plunder brought with him from India has been estimated at from thirty to eighty-seven million pounds. Among these were the Peacock Throne and the famous diamond Kuh-e-Nur.[17]

Nāder Shah might have become an enlightened founder of a dynasty had he not succumbed to the senseless cruelty which had become the habit of kings. When he became Shah, he did so on condition that the people of Iran would stop cursing the first three caliphs and would cease molesting the Sunnis. He realized the danger to Iran of needlessly arousing the hostility of the Sunnis. Furthermore, he wanted to break the power of the clergy. There is a difference of opinion about whether Nāder Shah was a Sunni or Shi'i. It seems that he was a freethinker. He gathered the representatives of all religions and told them that since there was only one God there should be only one religion. He ordered the Old and the New Testaments and also the Koran to be translated into Persian. He is reported to have commented that if he had time he would devise a new religion.[18] He cer-

17. Eqbal, *Tārikh-e Mofassal*, p. 319.
18. Reza Zādeh Shafagh, *Nader Shah* (Tehran: University of Tehran Press, 1961), p. 65. This is a translation of western writers such as Minorsky, Lockhart, and others.

tainly wanted to end the strife between the Sunnis and the Shi'is by uniting them and made this five-point proposition for unity:

1. That the Shi'i doctrine be recognized officially as the fifth school of thought in Islam.
2. That the Shi'is should have special accommodations in Mecca.
3. That every year there should be a special leader of pilgrimage, *Amir al-Hāj*, from Iran.
4. That the Ottomans and Persians should exchange prisoners of war.
5. That the Ottomans and Persians should exchange ambassadors.[19]

The Shi'i leaders were greatly perturbed over this news and supported the revolt that was brewing against him. He had become cruel and suspicious. He killed his own son and in the end was assassinated in 1747. Nāder's accomplishments were transitory, but they came at an opportune time and gave Iran a continued existence.

The period between the death of Nāder Shah and the coronation of Āghā Mohammad Khan, the founder of the Qājār dynasty in 1795, lasted fifty years. The first twelve years were spent in warfare among the many claimants to the vacant throne. The victor was Karim Khan, the head of the Zand tribe. For twenty-one years this kindly man ruled most of Iran without the aid of an executioner, and it seemed that he might save Iran; but his untimely death ended that hope. He never called himself Shah, but his title "The Advocate of the Peasants," seems to anticipate the thoughts of the French Revolution. He was eager that everyone in his capital, Shirāz, and in the rest of the country live in peace. He was so very different from what was considered the characteristic king that, rather than destroying the son of his bitterest enemy, he kept him as an honored guest in his house. At Karim Khan's death this same man, Āghā Mohammad Qājār, fled Shirāz and after seventeen years of warfare crowned himself Shah of Iran in 1795 at Tehran. During the Qājār period, Iran was ushered into the nineteenth century and the era of European imperialism, which contact with the West destroyed the isolation of Iran.

19. Ibid., p. 71.

7

Imperialism, Awakening,
and Revolution

When the nineteenth century dawned, Iran was so isolated that it was oblivious of what was happening in the world and so insulated that what little information came through was ignored altogether. If the Safavids had encouraged freedom of thought rather than suffocation of the Persian spirit with religious dogma, and if the brightness of the reign of Shah Abbās had been the beginning of an era of excellence rather than the end of an intellectual ferment which had ushered in the Persian renaissance, then the nearly two centuries of relationship with the countries of Europe would have produced leaders who were at least aware of the tremendous movements that had rejuvenated the western world. But unfortunately the main seed sown by the Safavids was religious fanaticism, and the main crop harvested was superstition and ignorance. Compared to the whole Safavid period, the age of Shah Abbās had the permanency of a beautiful bubble and the Iranian people had only been treated to a spectacle of pomp which had degenerated into effeteness leading to ruinous defeat.[1] Religious fanaticism was so strong that even the attempts of Nāder Shah were not able to dislodge it, and the reign of cruelty and lawlessness was so pervasive that the humane rule of Karim Khan Zand was not able to soften it. Even men of letters felt the spirit of restriction. In writing about the poets of his period, Azhar (1711–1781), said that the situation was such that "No one has the heart to read poetry, let alone compose it." [2]

The Qājār dynasty, which ruled Iran from 1795 to 1924, produced

1. Peter Avery, *Modern Iran* (New York: Praeger, 1965), p. 18.
2. Quoted by Browne, *A Literary History*, IV, p. 282.

kings who, on the whole, were inept, unimaginative, superstitious, and selfish. The founder of the dynasty, Āghā Mohammad Khan, was a eunuch who had been castrated by an enemy of the Qājārs at the age of five. He grew up to become a conniving, vindictive, cruel, and stingy misanthrope. He was assassinated by his own servants in 1796. His nephew, Fath Ali Shah, whose reign of thirty-six years coincided with some of the momentous events in the history of modern Iran, was no better. In addition to presiding over the diminution of the country, he is also known for his unusually long beard and a progeny of some 2000 princes and princesses. He had all of his uncle's bad traits and none of his good ones.[3]

The Russian Advance

Notwithstanding the decline of its fortunes, Iran was still a power to be reckoned with in west Asia and important enough to be wooed by European rivals. During the first decades of the nineteenth century European politics were dominated by Napoleon. British animosity toward Napoleon was constant while the Russian attitude fluctuated between friendship and animosity depending upon the situation. On the other hand, Russian and British interests in Iran were constant, while Napoleon's interest in Iran, and in India, for that matter, was only in how far it could be used as a tool to defeat Great Britain or force Russia to come to terms. The rulers of Iran, however, neither cared nor knew how to benefit from this rivalry and shifting of alliances. Indeed, practically every time Iran was caught for having made the wrong alliance. The cornerstone of British policy in west Asia was to safeguard the route to India, while Russian policy was to have access to the Persian Gulf through Iran. It is not certain whether Russia was interested in India, but its supremacy in the Gulf area would certainly threaten Great Britain. Consequently, Great Britain did not want Russia to annex all of Iran, which in the early years of the nineteenth century included most of Afghanistan.

At the turn of the nineteenth century Great Britain sent a mission to Iran and persuaded the Shah to sign a diplomatic and commercial agreement in which Iran promised to follow an anti-French policy. Commercially, Iran exempted British and Indian merchants from paying taxes and allowed the importation of British broadcloth, iron, steel, and lead without duty. In return Great Britain promised to provide Iran with necessary weapons in case the Afghans or the French attacked Iran. The enemy of Iran was not France but Russia, about whom there was no provision in the treaty simply because at the time Great Britain was friendly toward Russia. To the pleas of Iran for help against Russia, Great Britain lent a deaf ear. In the meantime

3. Nafisi, *Tārikh-e Ejtemā'i*, p. 75.

France and Russia had one of their periodic quarrels. Accordingly Napoleon sent a mission to Iran in 1805 proposing an alliance against Russia provided Iran would repudiate its treaty with England.[4] The Shah, who had become disappointed in the British attitude, agreed to this and the result was the Treaty of Finkenstein in May 1807. A large French mission under General Gardanne came to Iran for the purpose of training the Persian army and making cannons and other weapons. The French general concluded a commercial agreement to facilitate the importation of French goods and services into Iran. It is indicative of the vision of the Shah to note that in Article Six of this agreement, Iran wants France to send a painter, printer, crystal cutter, china maker, cabinet maker, stone cutter, watch maker, diamond cutter, carriage maker, and so on.[5]

All this came to naught, however, because Alexander of Russia and Napoleon became friends, albeit temporarily, and signed the treaty of Tilsit in 1807. This freed Russia to carry on its campaign of expansion against Iran. Now it was Napoleon's turn to lend a deaf ear to Iran's request for assistance against Russian aggression. This gave the British an opportunity to send a mission to Iran in 1808 and sign a treaty against France and Russia. The French military officers in the Persian army were replaced by British officers, and evidently the change of military advisers confused the Persian soldiers. The Crown Prince, Abbās Mirzā, who has the reputation of being the most able of the Qājārs, was in command of the Persian army. He did not have the support of the Shah, who was reluctant to spend any money for the defense of the country. The major battle was fought in Aslānduz in 1812. Very likely the Persians would have been defeated anyway, but there is no question that they were demoralized when all the British officers withdrew. Once more Russia and Great Britain had become friends and Iran was expendable. Qā'em Maqām, one of the two enlightened Prime Ministers of the Qājār period, accused Great Britain of causing the defeat of the Persian forces.[6]

Iran signed the Treaty of Golestān on October 13, 1813. Iran lost five cities in the Caucasus, gave up the right to maintain a navy on the Caspian, and gave up its claim to Georgia and Dāghestān. Perhaps the most damaging provision was Russia's promise to support the claim of Abbās Mirzā to the throne. In accepting this support, the crown prince was inviting Russia's interference in the internal affairs

---

4. The attitude of Russia toward Napoleon was ambivalent. Fear of losing Poland tempted Russia to join Napoleon against Great Britain. Napoleon, however, expected his allies to join the blockade against England, which would have been hard on Russia because most of its foreign trade was with England, through the ports of Murmansk and Archangel.

5. Nafisi, *Tārikh-e Ejtemā'i*, p. 118.

6. Ali Akbar Binā, *Tārikh-e Siyāsi va Diplomāsi-ye Iran* (*Political and Diplomatic History of Iran*) (Tehran: University of Tehran Press, 1959), p. 171.

of Iran. Not to be outdone, Great Britain also promised its support. From then on every Qājār crown prince was escorted to the capital by the Russian and British ministers when he came to ascend the throne.

The war, which had lasted some ten years, created staggering financial problems for Iran which in turn weakened the central government. Some of the tribes rose in rebellion. The war was especially hard on the people of Āzarbāyjān, who had to carry the burden of the war for ten years without any help from any other part of the country. As far as the Shah was concerned, the war was in the territory under the care of the crown prince and he had to raise the money for it. After the war, the Shah did not help in any program of reconstruction and the people of Āzarbāyjān were groaning under heavy taxes. The result showed when the war was resumed some twelve years later.

The need for money on the part of Iran and the need of Great Britain to reciprocate the actions of Russia resulted in a new treaty between Great Britain and Iran in 1814. It is referred to as the "Definitive Treaty," [7] in which Iran promised to break its alliance with any European power at war with Great Britain; to prevent armies hostile to Great Britain from entering Iran; and to help Great Britain in case the latter is attacked through Afghanistan. On its part Great Britain promised to come to Iran's aid if it was attacked by a European country; not to interfere in the affairs of Iran with Afghanistan; to pay Iran an annual subsidy of £150,000; and to help Iran settle its boundaries with Russia.

The last item seems to support the contention of Persian historians that the Golestān Treaty had not settled very much and should be regarded as a truce agreement rather than a peace treaty. Furthermore it could not be expected that the Russian program of expansion was over. Inasmuch as the majority of the population of the recently annexed cities was Moslem, there were credible reports of the Russian persecution of these Moslems. There is no doubt that the Persians felt humiliated and wanted revenge.[8] The Russians did persuade Abbās Mirzā to attack the Ottomans while the latter had their hands filled with the Greek rebellion. Perhaps the crown prince succumbed to this temptation because he wanted to regain his prestige, which had suffered at the hands of the Russians. The war against Turkey was, as usual, inconclusive and ended with the Treaty of Erzerum. This was the last war between the two nations. The struggle had continued ever since the battle of Chāldirān in 1514.

The desire for revenge on the part of Iran, the maltreatment of the Moslems, which eventually resulted in the declaration of a "holy war," and the Russian encroachment on Persian territory all brought

7. It is also called the Tehran Treaty.
8. Bina, *Political History*, p. 187 ff.

about the renewal of hostilities in 1825. The Persians were unable to maintain the success they had gained in the early months of the war. The Shah's avarice prevented him from appropriating any funds so that a good number of the army disbanded because of lack of pay. There was erratic leadership and lack of discipline. Great Britain, who had signed a treaty of friendship with Russia, refused to honor its agreement of 1814 or to come to the aid of Iran on the ground that Iran was the aggressor.[9] The Russians occupied Tabriz in 1827 and the Persians sued for peace.

The Treaty of Turkmanchāy in 1828 gave all of the Caucasus to Russia and set the boundary following the Aras River, and then south to include Lankarān and east to Āstārā on the Caspian. Iran officially accepted the principle of extraterritoriality and the payment of an indemnity amounting to three million pounds. Furthermore, a commercial agreement set a maximum duty on Russian imported goods at 5 percent *ad valorem*. The Treaty of Turkmanchāy ushered in a new era because for nearly a century Iran became a buffer state between Russia and Great Britain. It was not entirely a colony of either power and yet not free to chart an independent course internationally or internally. For a long time the leaders in Iran were either "Russophile" or "Anglophile." Later on the "Iranophiles," who brought about the Persian revolution, felt that Iran needed a third western power to save them from the Russians and the British.

THE BRITISH ADVANCE

The crown prince Abbās Mirzā, who was reputedly the most able leader among the Qājārs, died in 1833, just a year before his father Fath Ali Shah. This was unfortunate, for not only was Iran deprived of his leadership, but the throne went to his own son Mohammad Shah, who proved to be as narrow-minded, superstitious, and incapable as his grandfather. The young Shah entered Tehran with an army commanded by the British General Sir Henry Lindsay Bethune and was accompanied by the Russian and British ministers. Even so, there were some claimants to the throne who foolishly persisted for a time.

Russian desire to control Istanbul and the Straits was so important a part of the "Eastern Question" that the powers of Europe had left Russia alone in its ambitions in Central Asia and regions east of the Caspian Sea. There were no stable relationships between Iran and the different khanates of this region, which was populated by Uzbeks, Tājiks, Turkmans, Afghāns, and others. Some were independent at times; some paid tribute to Iran; and some were under the suzerainty of Iran. The Persians considered Herāt to be the capital of Khorāsān

9. For a justification of British actions see Sykes, *A History of Persia*, II, chapter 76.

and felt that most of Afghanistan was part of Iran. Indeed, judging by the treaties signed between Iran and Great Britain, it would seem that Great Britain recognized this fact. After Turkmanchāy, however, the situation had changed drastically. The British policy to defend the approaches to India was still valid, but there was a definite change in the British appraisal of Iran. Great Britain was no more willing to let Iran have a free hand in Afghanistan and east of the Caspian. When Mohammad Shah tried to strengthen his hand in Afghanistan, Great Britain intervened contrary to the promise made in the "Definitive Treaty" of 1814.

There was disagreement among the members of the British government in India as to where the line should be established for the defense of India. Some believed that the Indus was the best, which would have left Iran free in Afghanistan. Others, recognizing the Russian interest in that region, felt that they could cooperate much better with the Russians than with the "Mohammedan races of Central Asia and Kābul," which would presumably give Russia a free hand in Afghanistan. There were still others who felt that the defense of India would be made easier by the British supremacy in Afghanistan, which included the Hindu Kush mountains.[10] Apparently the last option won acceptance.

Mohammad Shah spent most of his thirteen years in office strengthening his position in Afghanistan, but Great Britain intervened and the Shah was forced to retreat. The British believed that Iran was not strong enough to stop the Russians, and they also felt that Qājār kings had Russian proclivities and might enter into an alliance with them against the British in India. They were probably correct in both. Consequently the history of Iran from Turkmanchāy until the turn of the twentieth century is the story of the slow but sure advance by Russia from the northeast and by Great Britain from the southeast.

The internal affairs of Iran in these years were reflections of what was going on in foreign affairs. Iran had lost initiative in its relations with Great Britain and Russia and lagged behind in internal reform and reorganization. The very able Abol Qāsem Qā'em Maqām, who showed much awareness of the need for reform, was put to death by Mohammad Shah. The new prime minister was Hāji Mirzā Āghāsi, whose lewdness, ignorance, fanaticism, and avarice have made him a detestable character in the Qājār administration.

The question of Afghanistan and more especially Herāt remained on Iran's agenda during the early years of Mohammad Shah's successor, Nāser al-Din Shah, who ascended the throne in 1848. Herāt was the center of a Persian speaking area with great ties with Iran.

10. Avery, *Modern Iran*, p. 37 ff.

The Persian forces occupied the city in 1856, but Great Britain considered the move serious enough to declare war on Iran. While a British column was marching toward Herāt, another army went by way of the Persian Gulf. After occupying Bushehr, the British took the port of Mohammareh, now called Khorramshahr, at the confluence of Kārun and Shatt-al-Arab rivers. Later a flotilla sailed up the Kārun and captured Ahvāz. Most of this was accomplished without much resistance on the part of the Persian forces. As the treaty of peace was concluded in Paris in 1857, according to which Iran agreed to evacuate Afghanistan and recognize its independence, it also agreed to use the "good offices" of Great Britain in any border disputes with Afghanistan.[11]

Most of this was during the Crimean War, which had kept Russia busy. It was not until 1868 that Alexander II had enough stability at home to venture into Central Asia by occupying Bokhārā. Two years later the Russians took Kokand. In 1884 Russia annexed Marv and thus became master of the region east of the Caspian Sea and all of Central Asia. Iran was forced to accept the Atrak River as the new boundary, thus ceding to Russia the most fertile part on the north bank of the river. In all these advances, Iran sought the aid of Great Britain to stop Russia. Great Britain, however, either could not or would not help. Since India was secure through British control of the affairs of Afghanistan, it did not really matter to them if the Russians controlled the territories east of the Caspian and Central Asia.

In the same way that the British virtually gave Russia a free hand in northeastern Iran, the Russians reciprocated by looking the other way when Great Britain annexed territories south of Afghanistan to the Persian Gulf. The story is too long and devious to be recounted here. The British did not use military campaigns to gain their ends although the threat was always present. From 1870 to 1903 there were boundary disputes in Afghanistan and minor revolts in Baluchestān. In all these disputes and uprisings Great Britain offered its good offices to settle them. There were the Mokrān Boundary Commission of 1871, the Sistān Arbitration Commission of 1872, the Perso-Baluchestān Commission of 1892, and the Second Sistān Commission of 1903. When all of this was over, the western boundaries of British India had somehow expanded considerably at the expense of Iran. In annexing the territory west of the Caspian Sea, Russia had cut Azarbāyjān in two, calling its half "Russian Azarbāyjān." In the same way Great Britain cut Baluchestān in two, calling its half "British Baluchestān."

11. In 1879 a Conservative British government was seriously considering returning Herat to Iran, but in the elections the Liberals won and the plan was abandoned. Ibid., p. 68 ff.

ECONOMIC IMPERIALISM

By the beginning of the twentieth century the annexation phase of Anglo-Russian imperialism had come to an end. Neither country allowed the other to annex any more Persian territory. While it is true that if it were not for the presence of Great Britain, Russia would have annexed all of Iran, it is equally true that if it were not for the presence of Russia, Great Britain would have controlled Iran. It was the fate of the country to be a buffer state in which Russia and Great Britain wielded economic and political power without having any responsibility for the welfare of the people.

Long before the end of the nineteenth century, however, what is known as economic imperialism had started. It lasted for about fifty years from 1870 to 1921. When Great Britain assumed full responsibility for India after the well-known "Mutiny" in 1857, speedy communication between London and Delhi became of utmost importance. In 1863 the overland Telegraph Convention was signed in Istanbul, connecting London to Baghdad. A year later the Shah agreed to have the line extended to Kermānshāh, Hamadān, Tehran, and Bushehr. The Indo-European Telegraph Company, formed in 1870, operated the communication between London and Delhi through Iran with several branch lines in the country itself. There is no question that the telegraph lines connected the different cities and made the governing of the provinces from the capital easier. Furthermore it ended the isolation of Iran and put her in close touch with the capitals of Europe. Nevertheless, it opened the way to many more concessions granted to Great Britain and Russia which eventually put the resources of the country under foreign control. It can readily be seen that some of these concessions were nothing but evil exploitation of the people, while there were others which were profitable to both sides. Unfortunately the good was more than offset by the superior attitude of the foreign managers which, at best, was suffocatingly paternalistic and, at worst, destructively humiliating. It must also be said that all concessions were granted by the members of the ruling class, from the Shah down, with the sole purpose of advancing their own selfish interests. One may excuse the British and the Russians for wanting to make a profit, and one may even praise some of them who were sincerely laboring under the ideology of the "white man's burden," but one cannot forgive the Persian leaders who received bribes and made themselves rich at the expense of their own people.

In 1872, Baron Julius de Reuter, a naturalized British citizen, received a seventy-year concession for a gigantic monopoly for the building of railroads, exploitation of mines, establishment of a bank, building of water works, regulation of rivers, and so forth. The Shah was insistent that negotiations be kept secret. Before signing, Nāser al-Din Shah went through the motions of asking the opinion of his ministers. They all assured him that if he placed his "most blessed name to the concessions, this one stroke of his pen will vouchsafe to the people of this land more benefit than they have received from all the kings of Iran over thousands of years." [12] It is important to note that this concession was granted without knowledge or pressure from the British government. The greed of the Shah and his ministers made them give away the resources of the country, and their appalling ignorance of the European business scene made them do it for a miserably low sum. "The pretty phrases about benefiting the country by bringing the fruits of European progress to Iran and the pretence at concern for the well-being of the people made the actions of the corrupt ruler and his equally corrupt ministers still more offensive by adding hypocrisy to treasonable greed." [13] Fortunately for Iran, the Russians were against the concession, as the Shah found out when he made his first trip to Europe soon after signing it. The British government was not in favor of it either and so it was cancelled.

When Nāser al-Din Shah made his second trip to Europe, he was impressed with the smart uniforms and riding ability of the Russian Cossack detachments. He expressed the wish that he would like to organize a similar force in Iran. The Russian government was delighted at the idea and offered to send an officer to help the Shah in the project. The Persian army, it will be recalled, was trained by the French and the British, followed by Italians and Austrians. When it came to the Russians' turn, the British tried to stop it. But the Shah was adamant and refused to approve the British project to develop the lower Kārun for navigation. The British acquiesced and, as a result, they had their Kārun River concession, while the Russians trained a Persian Cossack Brigade, which was commanded by Russian officers and was the only organized force in Iran until 1921.

Baron de Reuter, who had not stopped his efforts to salvage something out of his ill-fated concession, was given a new concession for the establishment of a bank, to be called the Imperial Bank of Persia, with the right to issue bank notes. In order to keep the appearance of impartiality, a concession was given to the Russians to open the Banque D'Escompte de Perse. The Imperial Bank printed money and each bill carried the name of the city in which it could be used. Individuals traveling from city to city had to pay a commission to exchange their money for the bill which would be accepted in that city. Not only were the profits from this scheme astronomical, but Persians were given the feeling that they were traveling in a foreign country.

By far the most notorious of all concessions and the most far-

12. Ebrahim Teymuri, *Asr-e Bikhabari yā Tārikh-e Emtiyāzāt dar Iran* (*The Uninformed Period or a History of Concessions in Iran*) (Tehran: Eqbal va Shoraka, 1954), p. 107.

13. Firuz Kazemzadeh, *Russia and Britain in Persia, 1864–1914* (New Haven: Yale University Press, 1968), p. 108.

reaching was the Tobacco Régie of 1890. This concession was also negotiated secretly by the Shah and a certain Major Gerald F. Talbot with the good offices of the British minister in Tehran, Sir Henry Drummond Wolff. The concession gave the British company a monopoly for the production, sale, and export of all tobacco in Iran. The Shah was to receive an annual payment of £15,000 while the promoters of the company in England claimed in their advertisement for the sale of shares that they expected a profit of £500,000 per annum. While the abortive Reuter concession of 1872 dealt with the undeveloped wealth of the country, the Tobacco Concession of 1890 affected the lives of thousands of growers, merchants, and users of tobacco. The vehement, well-coordinated, and general opposition to this concession surprised everyone, especially the Shah. The opposition was somewhat slow in forming, but when it was organized it acted with such a fury that it forced the Shah and the British government to retreat.

Among the leaders of the opposition were the merchants who stood to lose their income; the Shi'i clergy who were afraid that hundreds of foreign employees scattered all over the country would undermine Islamic beliefs and practices; and a small band of "Europeanized" liberals. They were followed by peasants who were led to believe that they would suffer; and by hundreds and thousands of smokers who could not see the necessity of buying from a foreign company the tobacco which they themselves had grown. All of these groups were encouraged, one way or another, by the Russians.[14] The Shah, who was not used to such large-scale opposition, responded by imprisoning the opponents of the concession. The struggle continued until December 1891, when the leading Shi'i *mojtahed*, Hāji Mirzā Hasan Shirāzi, issued the following *fatva* from his residence in Samarra, Iraq: "In the name of God the Compassionate and the Merciful. Today the use of *tanbāku* and *tutun* in any form is tantamount to war against the Imam of the Age; may God hasten his advent." [15]

Obedience to the ban was universal. Dr. Feuvrier, the French physician of the Shah reported, "Suddenly, with perfect accord, all the tobacco merchants have closed their shops, all the *qulyāns* [water-pipes] have been put aside, and no one smokes any longer, either in the city; or in the Shah's entourage, or even in the women's apartments." [16] The Shah was forced to cancel the concession, but the cancellation cost

14. Nikki R. Keddie, *Religion and Rebellion in Iran, The Iranian Tobacco Protest of 1891–1892* (London: Frank Cass, 1966), p. 65 ff.

15. In Persian there are two words in common use for tobacco: *tanbāku* was used for the plant itself and also for the chunky cut used in smoking *qalyān*, the water pipe; *tutun* is a powder form used in the long-stem pipes prevalent at the time.

16. Quoted by E. G. Browne, *The Persian Revolution, 1905–1909* (Cambridge University Press, 1910), p. 52.

Iran £500,000 in damages. This sum was borrowed from the Imperial Bank at 6 percent interest. The loan was to be paid in forty years, and the customs duties of the Persian Gulf were pledged as collateral. This was the first loan and there were many more to follow. Eventually most of the resources of the country were mortgaged to the British and Russian creditors. An eyewitness Persian author reported "notwithstanding this loss, Iran has come to herself and is on its way to awakening. From the settlement of the Régie concession, the nation of Iran has learned that it is possible to stand in front of the king and demand one's rights." [17]

According to the lunar Moslem calendar, which was prevalent at the time, 1896 was the fiftieth year of Nāser al-Din Shah's reign. On Friday, May 1, just a few days before the jubilee celebrations were to begin, the Shah went to Shah-Abdol-Azim, a shrine about ten miles south of Tehran. There he was shot dead by Mirza Reza of Kerman, a disciple of the notorious Pan-Islamist agitator Sayyed Jamāl al-Din Afghani, who had been ousted from Iran by the late Shah in 1891.

The crown prince, Mozaffar al-Din, arrived from Tabriz accompanied by the British and Russian ministers. He was an amiable man of forty-three, ineffective and uninterested in the affairs of government. He was also sick and felt that he should go to Europe for cure. With no money in the treasury, search for ready money became the main preoccupation of the Shah. The Russian bank offered a loan of £2,400,000 at 5 percent against the customs receipts of the whole country except the Persian Gulf. It will be recalled that Iran already owed £500,000 to the British. Since the Russians wanted to be the sole creditors, one condition was that the British loan be paid out of it. After payment of the British debt, discounts, commissions, and other obligations, just enough was left to pay for His Majesty's trip to Europe in 1900.

Almost as soon as he returned from the European tour, he made plans to go again. His father had been to Europe three times, but he had been there only once and was still sickly. Russia again came forth with a loan of over a million pounds at 4 percent. In return Iran gave a concession for the Russians to build a road from Jolfa, on the Russo-Persian border in Āzārbāyjān, to Tabriz, Qazvin, and Tehran. Another condition of the loan was a revision of the tariff regulation. The Belgian customs advisor to the Shah, Joseph Naus, has usually been derided for working against the interests of Iran, but evidence does not support this accusation. The Shah wanted money and Naus revised the tariff and produced more revenue.[18] It was the Shah and his court

17. Nezam al-Islam Kermani, *Tārikh-e Bidāri-ye Iranian* (*History of Persian Awakening*) (Tehran: Bonyad-e Farhang, 1966), p. 13.
18. See Marvin L. Entner, *Russo-Persian Commercial Relations, 1828–1914* (Gainesville, Florida: University of Florida Press, 1965).

who were working against the interests of Iran. All that can be said is that Naus's "solution" favored the Russians, who had given the loan, rather than the British, who had refused.

Great Britain, however, did not have to wait too long to be of service to the Shah, for he returned home penniless and needed more money. This time the British offered a loan of £300,000 at 5 percent payable in twenty years from the receipts of the Caspian fisheries. There were more loans and the competition between the British and Russian banks was fierce to the point of being ridiculous.[19] The back-breaking loans, the rivalry between the corrupt Russophile Persians and their equally corrupt Anglophile compatriots, the concern of the merchants for their own future, the fear of the clergy for the future of Islam, and the general awakening caused by contact with the West, culminated in the demand for a "House of Justice." This meant different things to different groups. To the common man the important word was *justice*. To the clergy it meant the establishment of Shi'i theocracy, while to the Europeanized Persian it meant constitution. Whatever it was, the disinterested Shah granted it, with a little pressure, in a royal rescript of August 5, 1906, that limited the power of the monarchy and ordered the establishment of an assembly, called the Majles, and the creation of a constitution.

Background of the Revolution

In order to understand better the awakening of Iran and the revolutionary movement that was the symbol of it, we should recall three points which have been discussed in the pages of this book. The first is the Persians' consciousness of their identity. This identity was started during the Achaemenid period and has continued with different degrees of intensity until the present. During the Islamic period it manifested itself religiously in such movements as the "Black Shirts," "White Shirts," "Red Shirts," the "Brethren of Purity," and the Twelver Shi'i and Esmā'ili Shi'i heterodoxies. Sometimes it has manifested itself politically as in the Barmakids, Saffārids, Sāmānids, and others. It has also appeared culturally as in the Shu'ubiyeh movement, in poets like Ferdosi, in scientists and philosophers like Avicenna and Rāzi, and on to the Mongol period when the Persian culture became fully independent. Perhaps it was the strength of this consciousness and the sense of belonging which enabled the Persians to absorb their conquerors and Persianize them.

The second point mentioned in these pages is the fact that creativity and intellectual and spiritual advance is possible in a society where there is intellectual and religious freedom. This is true about any people, but we have seen in these pages the creativity of the

Achaemenids when there was tolerance as compared with the period of cultural stagnation during the last part of the Sāsānids when religion and state joined in imposing dogma upon the people. In the Islamic period during the Omayyads, who were more interested in Arab superiority than in imposing Islam, there was freedom for the intellectually curious to translate the known knowledge of the world into Arabic and the religiously sensitive to discuss Islam in the context of the Greek and Persian religious thought. The Abbasids, however, who had come to power on a religious platform, so to speak, introduced religious inquisition in Islam, executed writers, and accused philosophers and scientists of heresy. Fortunately their power did not last very long. As they became weak and unable to impose any dogma, we witness the "Golden Age" of culture which, in the case of Iran especially, continued throughout the Mongol period, when there were no dogmas or inhibitions to amount to much. It was again during the Safavid period when Shi'i heterodoxy became the state religion and was imposed upon the people that we witness a cultural retrogression.

The third point to recall is the isolation of Iran, which was the inevitable result of the religious and political dictatorship during the Safavid period. Notwithstanding the extensive political and commercial relationship between Iran and various European countries, there was no intellectual or spiritual interaction. Iran was even separated from the rest of the Moslem world. It was considered to be *in* the world of Islam but was certainly not *of* it. As the power of the clergy increased, the isolation of Iran became more complete. The various movements in nineteenth-century Iran can be understood in the light of this isolation; Babism certainly dealt a severe blow to the spiritual authority of the clergy. The Pan-Islamism of Afghāni was an attempt to destroy the wall which separated the Shi'is from the rest of the Moslems. The purpose of the Europeanized constitutionalists was definitely to raze the wall that isolated Iran from the rest of the world. In all this the identity with the past was used to arouse the populace and only when the walls crumbled and religious dogmas weakened did the resurgence of a new Iran become a possibility.

BĀBISM

Bābism or Bābi-Bahāism was an indigenous reform movement in Shi'i Islam with no influence from abroad. It grew out of the Shi'i tradition and remained so until Bahāism carried it abroad and made it a "world faith." According to the Sheykhi sect, the absent twelfth Imam, who shall someday appear, is in touch with the believers through one person, who is called the *Bāb* or gate. The leader of this group, Mirzā Ali Mohammad of Shiraz, claimed to be the Bāb in 1844. Later, in his book *Bayān*, in which mystic and esoteric terms abound, he refers to himself as the Imam himself, or the "Point of

Revelation," or the "Point of Explanation," and speaks of "Him whom God shall Manifest." Insofar as the date 1844 was one thousand years after the disappearance of the twelfth Imam, the new movement was considered the beginning of a new dispensation with a new calendar, laws, and so forth.

The fact that Mirzā Ali Mohammad gained a ready following from all walks of life in many parts of the country is indicative of the disappointment of the people in the life and message of the clergy and in conditions in general. Typical of most Islamic movements, the Bābis, as they were called, took up arms and set out to establish the new kingdom. Perhaps the fact that it started in Shirāz and had an important center in Yazd, has led Professor Avery to think that Bābism happened to be a movement of the southerners against the north.[20] As a matter of fact it spread so fast that the north became the real battle ground and the leaders of Bābism after the death of the Bāb were northerners. The Shah was against it and the clergy preached against it, but the movement grew. Soon after the execution of the Bāb in 1850, the abortive attempt of two of his followers to assassinate Nāser al-Din Shah reopened the wrath of the government against them. The severe persecution which ensued and the courage with which the Bābis endured it helped their cause tremendously.

The designated successor of the Bāb was a man named Yahyā, with the title of *Sobh-e Azal*, the "Morning of Eternity." His half-brother, Hoseyn Ali, must have also been close to the Bāb, for he had the title *Bahāullāh*, the "Splendor of God." Both brothers were exiled to the Ottoman empire. In 1866 *Bahāullāh* claimed that he was "Him whom God shall Manifest," whose coming was foretold by the Bāb. Yahyā, however, did not accept his brother's claim, and the ensuing struggle between the two and their followers caused the Ottoman government to separate them. Sobh-e Azal was sent to Cyprus and Bahāullāh to Acre in Palestine.

It appears that Sobh-e Azal wanted to keep the movement limited within the bounds established by the founder, while Bahāullāh wanted to broaden it in scope. Bahāullāh won and the movement was changed from Bābism to Bahāism. The Bābis were active in the social and political movement in Iran while the Bahāis kept aloof. It cannot be said that Bahāism, as a faith, spearheaded the modernization of Iran or had anything to do with the constitutional movement. Nevertheless, the movement created a ferment, and the Bahāis were more receptive to new ideas even though they were not interested in propagating them. The Shi'i clergy certainly accused them of every innovation with which they disagreed and all modern concepts were attributed to them. The Bābi-Bahāi movement shook the foundations of Shi'i orthodoxy. A

20. Avery, *Modern Iran*, p. 53.

large number of Jews and Zoroastrians became Bahāis and as such broke the religious barriers which existed.[21]

PAN-ISLAMISM

As a religiopolitical movement, Pan-Islamism was not popular in Shi'i Iran. It is ironic, therefore, that the most famous Pan-Islamist of the nineteenth century should be a Persian by the name of Jamāl al-Din Afghāni (1839–1897). The activities of most of his life do not belong to the history of Iran, but his writings and his correspondence with a number of Persians contributed a great deal to breaking the wall of isolation around Iran. He was a controversial figure, and possessed a remarkable personal magnetism. His life was so tumultuous, his writings so incendiary, and his ideas so inconsistent that the last word has not been written about him.[22]

He claimed to be from Afghanistan even though he was a Persian known as Asadābādi. He paraded as a Sunni, though he was a Shi'i. He is considered a forerunner of the Persian Revolution,[23] though he might not have supported it had he lived. He does not seem to have had any scruples and was willing to appear in any guise that would gain him his end of appearing "to the Shi'i ulama as a pious Shi'i, interested in preserving the existing faith against the infidel Shah; to his followers as an excoriator of the backward clergy; to a mass Islamic audience as a defender of Islam against Western inspired materialism; and to a Western audience as a defender of science and philosophy against religion." [24] In the light of this some are tempted, and this writer is among them, to dismiss him as a paranoiac political agitator, and his claims for freedom and progress as only means to his main purpose which was Pan-Islamism. And yet it is wrong to reach such a conclusion because some of the influential Persians of the nineteenth century were impressed by him; some of the Shi'i clergy were goaded by him into action; and Persians, to this day, quote his writings.

Afghāni visited Iran twice. The first time was in 1886, when his vituperous utterances so infuriated the Shah that he asked him to leave the country. The second visit of Afghāni happened to coincide with the tobacco protest. Again he aroused the Shah's displeasure and in order to save himself from expulsion took sanctuary, *bast*, in the nearby shrine of Shah Abdol-Azim. Later he was forcibly expelled from Iran.

21. The number of Christian converts to Bahaism in Iran has been negligible.
22. Nikki R. Keddie, *An Islamic Response to Imperialism: Political and Religious Writings of Sayyid Jamal al-Din "al-Afghani"* (Berkeley: University of California Press, 1968); this is the best account so far, but the author is preparing a more complete biography.
23. Cf. Browne, *Persian Revolution*, p. 14 ff.
24. Keddie, *Islamic Response*, p. 45.

Since Afghāni has been given credit for having played an important role in the tobacco strike, it must be said that only after he was rebuffed by the Shah did he start writing letters to the Shi'i leaders against the injustices of the Shah.

The Pan-Islamic group in Iran was very small. One of its leaders was Sheykh Ahmad Ruhi, a poet from Kermān. His poetry denouncing Nāser al-Din Shah and praising Abdul Hamid as the "Sultan of Islam" leaves no doubt as to Afghāni's plan for the union of Islam and Iran's position in such a union. As has been stated, one of his disciples killed Nāser al-Din Shah. Pan-Islamism, like Bābism, was not a major factor in the awakening of Iran, but it served to penetrate the wall of isolation behind which Iran had been imprisoned.

CONTACTS WITH THE WEST

In the nineteenth century Iran was invaded by European nations, who had high intellectual attainment and material prosperity as well as, what seemed to Persians, military invincibility. The recognition of this fact was the first step in the long slow process which culminated in ending the isolation of Iran. Perhaps it was the crown prince Abbās Mirzā's bitter defeat at the hands of the Russians that induced him to send seven students to England between 1811 and 1815 to "study something of use to me, themselves, and their country." [25] So far as is known, these were the first Persian students to study abroad. Of these seven one died; the rest returned a physician, gunsmith, engineer, chemist, artillery man, and teacher-printer. The last one went to Oxford and his memoirs described life in England, which he called the "country of freedom," compared it with Iran, and blamed the Moslem clergy for the backwardness of Iran.[26] In 1845 five more students were dispatched to study in Paris. Throughout the century more students were sent and they came back not only with technical knowledge but with observations on the life and culture of Europe.

The person, however, who laid the foundation of modernization was Mirzā Taqi Khan Amir-e Kabir, the astute grand vazir of Nāser al-Din Shah. He was the son of a cook and a protégé of Qā'em Maqām, the able and ill-fated vazir under Mohammad Shah. He was the chief officer to Nāser al-Din, when the latter was crown prince residing in Tabriz. In that position he had occasion to go to Turkey and observe the "Tanzimat" reforms in that country. He also went to Russia and knew the language well enough to absorb what he saw and heard. When Nāser al-Din was crowned in 1848, Amir-e Kabir, who was the new

25. Hafez F. Farmayan, "The Forces of Modernization in Nineteenth Century Iran," in William Polk and Richard Chambers, eds., *Beginnings of Modernization in the Middle East, The Nineteenth Century* (University of Chicago Press, 1968), p. 120.
26. Ibid., p. 123.

Shah's brother-in-law, became the grand vazir. This was a very auspicious beginning if only it had been allowed to continue. However, during his three short years in office, he did more than any other individual to push Iran toward modernization.

This remarkable man, whose capacity for work seemed unlimited, did not leave a single stone unturned, and made his presence felt in every facet of government. He established a newspaper which published articles on a wide range of subjects from parliamentary government in Europe to the headhunters of Borneo, and from building of railroads and opening of mines to planting American cotton in Iran.[27] He reorganized the court system, the army, and postal service. He built jute, sugar, and textile factories. Perhaps his greatest accomplishment was the establishment of the Dār al-Fonun, "Polytechnic Institute," with departments in medicine, mining, and military science. It had a press of its own for publishing scientific and technical works, and employed European instructors.

Both the reforms and the energetic way the Amir-e Kabir was carrying them out aroused the opposition of many groups and individuals. Among his enemies were the Shi'i clergy, about whom he had remarked to the British Consul, "The Ottoman government was able to regain its authority only after breaking the power of the clergy." [28] In 1849 it was noised about that the shrine of Sāheb al-Amr in Tabriz had performed a miracle and that the city should be exempt from paying taxes. The British Consul, to encourage the idea, sent a gift of a chandelier to the shrine. Amir-e Kabir arrested the leaders of the clergy, including the Sheykh al-Islam, and had the British Consul recalled home. "Never again did the Sāheb al-Amr shrine perform a miracle." [29]

The clergy found a powerful ally in the person of the Queen Mother, who had great influence over her son and was a mortal enemy of her own son-in-law. Amir-e Kabir was dismissed in 1851 and, a year later, he was executed by the Shah's order, in Kāshan. About the only person who stood by him until the end was his devoted wife, the Shah's only sister. It is said that the Shah "never forgave himself for the role he had played." [30] Perhaps so, but it is difficult to believe this in a Shah who wanted a citizenry so ignorant that they would not have known whether "Brussels was the name of a city or a kind of cabbage."

Another person who must be mentioned as a forerunner of the westernization of Iran is Mirzā Malkam Khan (1833–1908). He was

---

27. Fereydun Adamiyat, *Fekr-e Āzādi* (*The Thought of Freedom*) (Tehran: Sokhan, 1961), p. 46. According to the author, an American missionary imported the seed for the Amir. Since the American missionaries did not arrive in Tehran until 1872, he must have learned about it through the missionaries in Āzarbāyjān.

28. Ibid., p. 50.

29. Ibid., p. 51.

30. Farmayan, "Forces of Modernization," p. 127.

the son of an Armenian from Esfahān, whose stormy life can easily fill a volume, and who was in and out of favor with Nāser al-Din Shah. A good portion of his life was spent as the Shah's representative abroad. During the years when the granting of concessions was popular, as Persian Ambassador in London, he persuaded the Shah to sign a concession for a national lottery system. Later the Shah changed his mind and cancelled the concession and recalled him. Keeping this secret, Malkam sold the worthless concession to a British company for £40,000. There was a scandal and Malkam Khan, who was dismissed from service, stayed in Europe and edited a Persian paper which he called *Qānun*, 'law.' This paper was smuggled into Iran and became very influential and a thorn in the flesh of Nāser al-Din Shah.

Malkam Khan, who had studied extensively in the West, was influenced by Auguste Comte and John Stuart Mill. He translated part of the latter's book, *On Liberty*, into Persian.[31] He was a pamphleteer and wrote on all subjects such as the need of a new alphabet, distribution of land, revision of law, westernization, and so on.[32] His main message was the rule of law, and his style of writing did very much to end the bombastic style prevalent during the Qājār period. He also introduced freemasonry, *Farāmush-Khāneh*, 'House of Forgetfulness' into Iran.

There has been speculation about his religion and whether he was a Christian or a Moslem. It appears that his father was a convert to Islam. He himself never mentioned his own faith but let it be taken for granted that he was a Moslem. He was a humanist at heart and one of the most interesting results of his work is the organization of humanist societies in Iran. At one time they had over three hundred very influential members, most of whom became active in the Persian constitutional movement. The Persian humanist (*Ādamiyat*) societies were on the whole theistic. The members were called "brothers," and new members were received with special ceremony and had to sign the following pledge: "O Creator of the world, I confess that thou hast bestowed upon me the nobility of humanity. In return for such a glorious gift of God, notwithstanding my former shortcomings, I now [stand] before thee and swear by Thy Truth and Almighty Power, that I shall try with all my strength to uphold the honor of this position, as long as I live. If I ever fail in my undertaking, may I be cut off from Thy grace and compassion both in this world and in the next." [33]

OTHER INFLUENCES

Newspapers also played a great role in the westernization of Iran. Most of the papers were published in "diaspora," to borrow the apt

31. Adamiyat, *Thought of Freedom*, p. 98.
32. Adamiyat lists twenty-six pamphlets, pp. 101–2.
33. Ibid., p. 222.

phrase from Professor Avery. Besides *Qānun* which was published in London, there was *Akhtar*, published in Istanbul, *Habl al-Matin* in Calcutta, and *Sorayyā* in Cairo. The publication of books helped in destroying the walls of isolation in Iran. Mirzā Yusef Khan Mostashār al-Doleh, who was in and out of the government foreign service and died in prison, probably by torture, wrote two books on the two subjects which he considered to be essential to progress. One was *Ketābche-ye Banafsh* (*The Purple Handbook*) in 1877, on railroads, and the other volume was called *Yek Kalameh* (*One Word*) in 1878, concerning law and constitution.[34] Two other writers who wrote popular books on the necessity of social change, were both merchants from Āzārbāyjān. One was Abdol Rahmān Tālebof, whose popular book *Ahmad* is a dialogue between father and son on the causes of Iran's backwardness. The other author was Zeyn al-Abedin Marāgheyi, whose *Travels of Ebrāhim Bey* is the story of a young Persian residing in Cairo who went to see what Iran was like. The effect of these two books on the general population cannot be exaggerated.

We have already mentioned the opening of the Polytechnic Institute in 1851. That was about the only school opened by the government in the nineteenth century, but liberal merchants of Āzārbāyjān, Gilān, and other provinces opened private schools along western lines. These were modeled after the schools which had been established by the American, British, and French missionaries. The Americans opened a school in Rezā'iyeh in 1836, the French Lazarites in Tabriz in 1839, and the British in Esfahān in 1870. Before the end of the century the Americans and the British missionaries had schools or hospitals or both in Tabriz, Hamadān, Tehran, Kermānshāh, Mashhad, Esfahān, Yazd, Kermān, and Shirāz. It was the deepest desire of the missionaries to change Iran by converting the people to Christianity, but realizing the impossibility of that, a large number of them were happy to change the attitude of the young through education and the introduction of the best values of the West. The missionaries, whether they were teachers, doctors, nurses, or evangelists, were all harbingers of change. To many Persians they were the embodiment of the very change they desired for their country.

The values that the missionaries taught were dignity of labor, the virtue of service, importance of the individual, equality of women, democracy, and patriotism. All of this was included in what was called the "building of character." Without doubt the most influential and popular missionary in Iran was the American, Dr. Samuel Jordan, who arrived in Iran in 1898. He was an educator and did as much as any man, if not more, in the modernization of Iran. He wanted to establish a college in Iran because "The young oriental educated in Western lands as a rule gets out of touch with his own country. He loses sym-

34. Farmayan, "Forces of Modernization," p. 139.

pathy with his own people. He loses all faith in his old religion and gets nothing in its stead. In mission schools and colleges we adapt the best Western methods to the needs of the country. While we retain all that is good in their civilization, we also inspire their students with enthusiasm for the high ideals and the pure standards of the Christian lands." [35]

He taught the dignity of labor by leading his students in leveling ground for a soccer field. As early as 1902 he bemoaned that "the better class of young Moslems are utterly lacking in patriotism." [36] Jordan was in the habit of calling his program a "constructive revolution," and the Persians liked what he had to offer. The presence in modern Tehran of a Jordan Hall, Jordan School, Jordan Library, Jordan Boulevard, and a statue of Dr. Jordan attest to this approval.

The missionaries were the first to establish schools for women in Iran. In 1889 when the first missionary female physician, Dr. Mary Smith, arrived in Tehran, scores went to stare at her and to find out how it was "possible for a woman to have enough knowledge to be a doctor." They were also the first to publish a magazine for women. The *World of Women*, edited by Mrs. Arthur Boyce with the assistance of the graduates of the American girls' school in Tehran, continued the publication for twelve years and was a forerunner of many similar magazines for women.

PERSIAN REVOLUTION

The Persian Revolution is perhaps unique among the revolutions of the twentieth-century Middle East in a few points. In the first place, it was not a military revolution. The Cossack brigade, which was the only effective military unit in the country, was not aware of it. In the second place, no one person had charge of it. The revolution was directed, somewhat haphazardly, by the merchants, the Europeanized liberals, and the moderate clergy. In the third place, the Persian revolutionists did not have to fight to get a constitution and a parliament. Rather, they were forced to fight in order to defend what they already had achieved. Finally, it is indicative of the nature of the Persian culture to note that the Persian constitution granted in 1906 is the oldest constitution in all of Asia. Unlike so many other countries, Iran has never thought of scuttling it and writing a new one. It has been amended many times but never discarded. Even Rezā Shah Pahlavi, who disregarded the constitution so many times, always participated in the anniversary celebration on August 5.

35. East Persia Mission Microfilm, Presbyterian Historical Society, Vol. 186, no. 15.

36. Shokrollah Naser, *Ravesh-e Doktor Jordan* (*The Method of Doctor Jordan*) (Tehran: Pākatchi, 1945), p. 16.

It has been mentioned that Mozaffar al-Din Shah had mortgaged the future of the country for his two trips abroad. He had negotiated a loan of £300,000 with the British; but that did not seem to be enough, for he was negotiating a joint Anglo-Russian loan of £400,000. As a result of Naus's effort to increase the revenue, the price of sugar had been raised. On December 11, 1905, a group of merchants called a strike and closed the bazaar. When the government retaliated by flogging the merchants, some two thousand merchants and clergymen, headed by two moderate *mojtaheds*, Sayyed Mohammad Tabātabā'i and Sayyed Abdollāh Behbahāni, took sanctuary at the shrine of Shāh-Abdol-Azim and asked for a "house of justice."

The Shah was perhaps willing to acquiesce but his advisors persuaded him to make a halfhearted promise and dragged on the affair until the summer of 1906. In July, a large number of the clergy and their followers took sanctuary in Qom, 60 miles south of Tehran. Not to be outdone, some 13,000 Westernizers, merchants, and others took sanctuary in the grounds of the British Legation in Tehran. The taking of sanctuary, *bast*, has been an honored tradition in Iran, but never before had anyone done it in a foreign legation. This was of course done with the British consent. It was then that the Shah granted the contitution.

It was impossible that, in such an important transition, the two rival powers, Great Britain and Russia, would not intervene. The Russian Tsar, who had been forced to grant a constitution to his own people and was disbanding the Duma as soon as it was elected, did not want such a thing to occur in Iran. Since Russia was against the constitution, Great Britain was for it. Their support of the constitutionalists was dictated purely by self-interest and did not have anything to do with the ideology of freedom or democracy.

The young revolutionary movement experienced two severe blows in 1907. The first was the death of the Shah on January 8, 1907 and the accession of his son Mohammad Ali, who was known to be a Russian puppet and against the revolution. From the beginning he started to undermine the work of the Majles, and in this he was encouraged by the Russians. The reactionary activities of the Shah were challenged in two ways. One was by the "people of the pen." Ever since the granting of the constitution and its corollary freedoms, the number of newspapers had increased by the month. They attacked and lampooned the Shah and the reactionaries in poetry, prose, satire, humor, and cartoons. Songs were written on revolutionary topics and troubadours used to sing these, instead of love songs, at weddings and other gatherings.

The other means was the appearance of the *anjomans*, 'Councils'. More than anything else it proved that the revolution was not the sole monopoly of the clergy or of the European educated elite. It had a wider base among the people. There were literally hundreds of these all over the country and each had from half a dozen to one hundred members. Some opened schools, some had discussion sessions, others conducted literacy classes, and still others wrote pamphlets. There were some *anjomans* who volunteered to help the deputies in their work. There were also terrorist *anjomans*. Even the women, secluded as they were, had their *anjomans*. There was no central group to direct these activities.

One of the first acts of the new Shah was to recall the reactionary Amin al-Soltan from Europe and make him prime minister. On August 31, 1907, as the prime minister was leaving the Majles, he was shot dead by a terrorist, who immediately committed suicide. On the assassin's body was found a paper with the inscription "Abbās Āqā, money changer of Āzarbāyjān, member of the anjoman, national Fedā'i, ['devotee'] no. 41." On this same day the Majles heard its second bad news of the year, namely the signing of the Anglo-Russian Convention. This dealt with Iran, Afghanistan, and Tibet, and was directed against Germany. It divided Iran into three sections. The territory north of the line from Kermānshāh to Yazd to the Afghan border south of Mashhad, was designated as a Russian sphere. The territory east of the line from Birjand to the Persian Gulf west of Bandar-e Abbās was the British sphere. The rest was not designated, which probably meant that it was for both. This very uneven division shows that Great Britain was still obsessed with the defense of India.

Persian reaction was one of dismay turned into anger against Great Britain. It was upon Great Britain "the Mother of Parliaments," that the revolutionaries had depended; and now that they had their backs to the wall, Great Britain not only had violated the independence of Iran but had also betrayed the revolution by joining with the opposition.

The revolutionaries, however, did not have time to brood over this, for the Shah was closing in on them. No doubt encouraged by the Anglo-Russian Convention, the Shah ordered Colonel Liakhov, commander of the Cossacks, to bombard the Majles. A large number of the revolutionists were arrested, their leaders were executed, and the rest went into hiding or fled the country. It seemed that the revolution was over, and it would have been if it had not had support among the rank and file of the population. Overnight three centers rallied to the defense of the constitution: Tabriz, under the leadership of Sattār Khan and Bāqer Khan; Rasht under the leadership of Sardār Mohi and the Armenian Dāshnāk nationalist, Yefrem Khan; and the Bakhtyāri tribe in Esfahān.

Tabriz was besieged for nine months by the Shah's and Russian troops. Everyone seems to have joined in the defense of the city including Howard Baskerville (Princeton, 1907) a young teacher in the American Mission School who resigned his post to join the revolutionaries. He was killed on April 12, 1909, when he led a sortie to bring food for the starving population. The determined resistance of the Tabrizis gave time to the Bakhtyāris in Esfahān and a volunteer army from

Rasht to move toward Tehran. They took the capital on July 13, 1909, and deposed the Shah. The siege of Tabriz was lifted and the constitutionalists were in power again. During all this time when so much atrocity was committed by the Shah and the Russians, Great Britain did not raise her voice in protest. Oil was discovered in the "neutral zone" of Iran in 1908, and in order to prevent the Russians from coming to the southwest where the oil was, they left the Russians free to do as they pleased in the northwest.[37] Upon the good offices of Russia and Great Britain the revolutionaries agreed to exile the ex-Shah with a pension, and chose his young son Ahmad as the new Shah.

When the second Majles convened on November 15, 1909, it was confronted with two major problems, both of which had arisen during the first session. One was the ideological differences among the deputies and the other a desperate need for money. Two distinct political factions had emerged, one revolutionary and the other evolutionary. The former or the "Social Democrats" wanted separation of temporal and religious powers, compulsory military service, land distribution, compulsory education, and so on. Most of the European-educated middle-class merchants and young writers belonged to this group. The second faction, called the "Social Moderates" included the moderate clergy, and some of the landlords and nobility who were simply against the excesses of the ex-Shah.[38] The Europeanized nationalists wanted a constitutional government, mashruteh, based on laws legislated by the elected representatives of the people. The clergy desired mashru'eh, or the rule of Moslem Shari'a as interpreted by the mojtaheds. Neither side was strong enough to subdue the other, and the compromise is apparent in the Supplement to the Constitution. Article II of this document requires that a committee of mojtaheds be present in the Majles with veto power over any legislation which they consider to be against Moslem law.[39] The fact that this article was never implemented shows that to the secular nationalists it was only a window dressing.

The bankruptcy of the country, however, knew no ideological boundary. The Majles felt the need of a financial advisor from abroad; in the light of all that had happened, the United States was the natural choice. Morgan Shuster, together with a number of assistants, arrived in May 1911 as Treasurer-General and was invested with extensive powers. At the same time a French lawyer, Adolphe Perni, was employed to draw up a new penal code, which he completed by 1912. The fact that the mojtaheds accepted such arrangements showed not only their lack of power but also the inadequacy of the religious law.[40]

Shuster's job was by far more difficult. He was in complete sym-

37. See Avery, Modern Iran, p. 134.
38. Malek al-Sho'ara Bahār, Tārikh-e Mokhtasar-e Ahzāb-e Siyāsi (A Brief History of Political Parties) (Tehran: Bahār Press, 1945), p. 8 ff.
39. For the full text see Browne, Persian Revolution, Appendix AO IV, p. 372.
40. Banani, Modernization of Iran, p. 68.

pathy with the goals of the Democrats and considered himself the employee of the Majles rather than of the Cabinet. Shuster felt that a good part of Iran's financial troubles would be solved if taxes were collected properly. He organized a treasury force which confiscated the property of the landlords, who were in the habit of declaring themselves "under the protection" of Russia or Britain in order not to pay taxes. The insistence of Shuster to place the treasury gendarmes under the command of a former British officer caused him a good deal of unnecessary difficulty. This indiscretion on Shuster's part, however, was not important because in the eyes of Russia and Great Britain the very existence of Shuster signified more independence for Iran than they liked to give.

Inasmuch as the Majles gave full support to every plan proposed by Shuster, the Russians sent an ultimatum on November 29 for his dismissal. A second ultimatum followed, which asked Iran to promise not to employ any foreign advisors without the consent of Russia and Great Britain. This was followed by a third in which Iran was asked to pay indemnity for the troops that Russia had dispatched to enforce the first ultimatum. The British not only supported all these Russian moves but brought up Indian troops ready to occupy south Iran.

The Majles sent cables appealing for aid from the parliaments of the world. This was the revolution's darkest hour and yet it proved to be its finest. The cabinet, headed by the Bakhtyāri chieftain Samsām al-Saltaneh, was in favor of dismissing Shuster and presented a resolution to this effect on December 1, 1911. It was a few hours before the forty-eight hours fixed by Russia ran out. One deputy arose and said: "It may be the will of Allah that our liberty and our sovereignty shall be taken from us by force, but let us not sign them away with our own hands." [41] Others spoke in the same vein, a roll-call vote was taken and the Majles rejected the Russo-British ultimatum with only a few abstentions. The people outside were ecstatic, Russian and British goods were boycotted, and hundreds volunteered for resistance. Pressure was brought to bear for the Majles to reconsider. When it was rumored that they might yield, a group of women representing their own *anjomans*, went to the Majles, some with revolvers under their veils, and told the President that they would "kill their own husbands and sons, and leave behind their own dead bodies if the deputies wavered in their duty to uphold the liberty and dignity of the Persian people and nation." [42]

The deputies held, and on December 24 the cabinet closed the Majles by force and dismissed Shuster. Thus came to an end the first

41. Morgan Shuster, *The Strangling of Persia* (New York: The Century Company, 1912), p. 182.
42. Ibid., p. 198.

phase of the Persian Revolution. It had failed because of the Anglo-Russian interference, because of the rift among the constitutionalists, and also because of their lack of unity and experience. It had also succeeded. The Constitution remained as a living symbol of their efforts, to which even the strongest dictator was obliged to pay lip service. It had succeeded because it inaugurated a period of freedom in which new poetry and prose flourished, new ideas were formulated, and songs of freedom were heard in the midst of the deprivation of war.

CULTURAL LIFE

The new poetry and prose showed a marked departure from the bombastic and flamboyant style prevalent in the early Qājār period. Some of the same persons responsible for the modernization of Iran were also pioneers in the reform of Persian literature. Ministers like Qā'em Maqām Farāhāni (1779–1835) and Taqi Khan Amir-e Kabir (d. 1852) began using more lucid Persian in their official reports and communications. Until recently their writings were used as models of good Persian in the high schools of the country. The simplification of Persian literature thus begun was advanced by the prolific pamphleteer Malkam Khan (1833–1908), who introduced the European style of writing, which became a model for the twentieth-century Persian writers. Malkam Khan and his contemporary reformer, the playwright Mirza Fath Ali Ākhundzādeh, were pioneers in the ranks of those unsuccessful individuals who have attempted to reform or change the Persian script.

Other writers began to express their social and political reformist ideas in the form of European-style novels such as *Ahmad*, by Tālebof, and *Travels of Ebrahim Bey*, by Marāgheyi. A work that received belated literary distinction is the Persian translation of that delightful book *The Adventures of Hajji Baba of Ispahan*, by James Morier, which appeared in England in 1824.[43] The translator, Mirzā Habib Esfahāni, combines colloquial Persian with the classical so skillfully that the result has been compared favorably with the *Golestan* of Sa'di.[44]

The Revolution of 1905, however, ushered in a period of literary creativity the significance of which has not been fully studied. This "literature of revolt," as it has been called, appeared in poetry and prose in over eighty newspapers, which sprouted like mushrooms all over the country. Even the naming of the distinguished poets and writers of the time would make too long a list for the brief discussion attempted here.

43. There is a controversy as to whether Morier wrote the book or a Persian author using Morier's name.
44. M. T. Bahār, *Sabk Shenāsi* (*Understanding Style*), Vol. III (University of Tehran Press, 1958), p. 366 ff.

What is important, however, is the fresh content and the new form of prose and poetry of this period. Among the poets may be mentioned Abolqāsem Āref Qazvini (1883–1934), who became the songster of the Revolution. He wrote more ballads than any other poet of the time. These did not deal with love and roses, as is usually the case, but with the burning political and social questions of the period. They were sung at parties and at wedding feasts all over the country.

Another writer of note was Ali Akbar Dehkhoda (1879–1956), whose column *Charand Parand* (*Balderdash*) in the revolutionary newspaper *Sur-e Esrāfil* was very popular. He wrote in colloquial Persian and by the use of popular expressions and idioms injected a new vitality into the Persian language. His subjects were the social and political ills of his day.[45] Later in life he eschewed politics and devoted his time to the writing of a four-volume *Amsāl va Hekam* (*Proverbs and Aphorisms*) and to the compilation of a more ambitious encyclopedic dictionary of the Persian language. This work, which is called *Loghat-nāmeh ye Dehkhoda*, is being arranged and published at an unusually slow pace by a commission appointed by the Ministry of Education.

Perhaps the most active and talented writer was the poet laureate, Mohammad Taqi Bahār (1886–1951), whose life spanned the revolutionary period through the hectic era after the Second World War. He was prominently active throughout, intermittently as editor, member of Parliament, minister, and university professor.

Music, frowned upon in Islam, did not enjoy periods of development in Iran. During the revolutionary period, however, it was brought into the service of social and political change. Musicians like Darvish, Shahnāzi, Shokri, and others cooperated with poets in the composition of ballads. Musical plays with political motivation were introduced. The most talented in this field was Mirzādeh Eshqi (1893–1924), who wrote a popular nationalistic opera but whose tragic assassination put an end to such activity. What is important to note, however, is that the melodies used were all Persian, with practically no influence from abroad.

Even though painting had Islamic restrictions, it had been "liberated" during the Mongol period. European portrait painting was introduced in Iran during the eighteenth century and continued throughout the Qājār period. Unimaginative imitation of European art was quite popular in the nineteenth century. The worst example of this copying can be seen on the minarets of the Sepahsālār Mosque in Tehran, built toward the end of the nineteenth century. All around the tile work of the minarets are medallions depicting French scenes such as the Louvre, Versailles, and others, copied from postcards. The best European in-

45. For an English translation of some of these see E. G. Browne, A *Literary History of Persia*, Vol. IV, pp. 469–82.

fluence can be seen in the works of the great master Kamāl al-Molk Ghaffāri, who flourished in the court of Nāser al-Din Shah, himself an amateur artist. His paintings, exhibited in the Golestan Palace in Tehran, reveal the gift for color and decorative pattern that has been a strong point of Persian artists.

8

The Resurgence of Iran

The young Ahmad Shah Qājār, having reached the age of eighteen, was crowned in July 1914. No one expected that the world would be engulfed by a war, and certainly no Persian present thought that he was witnessing the coronation of the last Qājār king. Everyone seemed to be happy, especially the constitutionalists, because the coronation brought the Constitution to mind and the Constitution demanded elections for the third session of the Majles, which had been closed since the ousting of Shuster in 1911.

The Third Majles still had the two factions of Liberal-Radicals and Conservative-Moderates.[1] The World War, however, had changed the situation drastically. Iran had declared neutrality but did not have the power to enforce it, with the result that it became the battlefield of hot war between the Ottomans and the Russians, and the scene of a "cloak and dagger" war between the British and the Germans. Great Britain formed a Persian militia in the south called the South Persia Rifles (SPR), and it was kept fairly busy quelling tribal uprisings caused by the German agents Niedermayer and Wasmuss.[2] There was brigandage and highway robbery, tribal raids on settled areas, and insecurity throughout the country. Persians suffered, but the greatest calamity befell the Nestorian Christians (also known as Assyrians and Chaldeans) in Āzarbāyjān. A large number of this group who lived in the mountainous regions of eastern Turkey were driven out as British

1. There was no political party in Iran in the accepted sense of the word until after World War II.
2. For an interesting account of German espionage, see Christopher Sykes, *Wasmuss, the German Lawrence* (London: Longmans, 1936); also Avery, *Modern Iran*, pp. 191–93.

sympathizers. They took refuge with their coreligionists, the Persian Nestorians, in the plain of Rezāiyeh. In Iran all of them were at the mercy of the Kurds, who burned their villages and massacred them at will. The fact that this region of Iran changed hands several times between the Ottoman and Russian forces added to their misery. Forsaken by Great Britain and Russia, who had promised them and the Armenians independence, and left unprotected by a Persian government that was absolutely helpless, they were doomed. Were it not for the American missionaries in Rezāiyeh who protected thousands of them, and for individual Persian Moslems, who helped as many as they could, the Nestorians might have been wiped out altogether.[3]

THE SOVIET REPUBLIC OF GILAN

The Third Majles was conspicuous in not having many sessions. Inasmuch as Great Britain and Russia were on the same side, most of the Persians and more especially the liberals felt that Iran would be divided between them. Consequently their sympathies were on the side of the Central Powers, and a number of them made the long trek to Istanbul. Some went to Germany, among them the fiery deputy Hasan Taqizādeh, who published the popular magazine *Kāveh* until 1921. Those who remained tried to bring about the defeat of the Allies by helping the Germans.[4] There were also a number of liberals who took matters into their own hands and set up revolutionary governments in Azarbāyjān, Gilān, and Khorāsān. The most important of these was the movement which was started in Gilān by a former theological student, Mirza Kuchek Khan. He was a nationalist who, together with his followers, had vowed not to shave or cut his hair until the foreign troops had withdrawn from Iran. Living as they did in the jungles of Gilān, they were called *Jangali*. Later when the German and Ottoman officers came to train the Jangalis, some undertones of Pan-Islamism crept into the ideology.

The October Revolution of the Bolsheviks in Russia changed the situation in Iran. It gave a new life to the Persian nationalists. In the Russian Revolution they did not see the triumph of an ideology but the breaking of an alliance with Great Britain that, in their minds, would have certainly divided and destroyed Iran. In a speech that one of these nationalists, the poet laureate Bahār, made in Tehran a few weeks after the Revolution, he said: "Two enemies had a rope around the neck of

3. The latest study on this group is by John Joseph, *Nestorians and Their Moslem Neighbors* (Princeton University Press, 1961). For the events in the Razaiyeh area during World War I, I am indebted to the unpublished memoires of the Reverend Hugo and Dr. Laura Muller.

4. See Movarraekh al-Doleh Sepehr, *Iran dar Jang-e Bozorg* (*Iran in the Great War, 1914–1918*) (Tehran: Bank-e Melli Press, 1957). The author was the Persian secretary in the German legation and was actively involved.

a man and were pulling from both sides. The poor fellow was struggling for his life. Suddenly one of the enemies let the rope loose and said, 'You helpless fellow, I am your brother,' and the man was saved. The man who let loose the noose around our neck is Lenin!" [5]

Immediately after the war Iran was occupied by British troops on their way toward Baku and the Caucasus to help the "Whites" in the civil war against the Bolsheviks. Mirza Kuchek Khan, like most of the Persian nationalists, was quite ambivalent toward communism, but his deputy Ehsanollah Khan was quite enthusiastic and wanted to set the Jangali revolt on the basis of class struggle. On the other hand there was disagreement in the Central Committee in Moscow as to whether Iran was "ready" for revolution. Nevertheless, the fortunes of the civil war gave the Bolsheviks the upper hand in the Caucasus; they got in touch with Mirza Kuchek Khan and eventually landed troops in Gilān. A Soviet Republic of Gilān was established in 1920 with Rasht as the capital and the combined Soviet-Jangali forces drove the Persian government troops near to Qazvin. There was a rift, however, among the leaders of the Jangalis. At the same time the Soviet government decided to give up the Gilān project and enter into negotiations with the Persian government. The Russian troops were withdrawn to the port of Anzali (now Pahlavi), and the government troops under the command of Colonel Reza Khan defeated the Jangalis. Kuchek Khan fled into the mountains and died of exposure.

Students of communism have wondered why the Soviet Union gave up Gilān and with it perhaps Āzarbāyjān and the whole northern littoral. Professor Zabih in his authoritative study finds it still difficult to interpret the events. "The Soviet habit of fitting historical data into changing ideological interpretations has clouded not only the facts themselves but also the background of the event." [6] As has already been mentioned, there was disagreement among the members of the Central Committee and especially the Baku Congress of 1920, whether Iran was ready for Marxism. There was also disagreement as to how to approach the intense nationalism prevalent in Iran.[7] Furthermore, there was still idealism among some of the old Bolsheviks to be against annexation as an act of imperialism. It is also significant to note that the Russians had just emerged from seven years of international and civil war, and were not strong enough to maintain an occupying force in Iran. It is also possible that they made a mistake. In any case the Russo-Persian relations took a turn from hostility to friendship.[8]

5. Bahār, *Political Parties*, p. 27.
6. Sepehr Zabih, *The Communist Movement in Iran* (Berkeley: University of California Press, 1966), p. 13.
7. For details on the Baku Congress, see ibid., p. 31 ff.
8. See George Lenczowski, *Russia and the West in Iran, 1918–1948* (Ithaca: Cornell University Press, 1949), pp. 59–60.

THE ANGLO-PERSIAN AGREEMENT

On the whole, the liberal nationalists of Iran looked with favor on the Bolshevik Revolution, not so much as an ideology to follow but as a tool to be used to save Iran from the "clutches" of Great Britain. The moderates, however, among whom were a large number of landlords and clergy, looked at the Revolution from a different point of view. Some of them saw in the Revolution an opportunity for Iran to regain territories lost to Russia during the previous century. They reasoned that Russia had become extremely weak through war, revolution, civil war, and famine. Furthermore, they were trying to maintain a regime which was hated by the rest of the world. Consequently, the Persian government sent a delegation to the Paris Peace Conference with instructions to ask, among other things, for the return of territories both east and west of the Caspian Sea, contiguous with Iran. They were not admitted to the Conference because of British opposition and nothing came of their demands.

The vast majority of the moderates, who were in control of the Persian government, looked upon the Bolshevik Revolution as a disaster. They were afraid of it for themselves and for their country. Any contamination with it might wrest from them their lands, their privileges, and their birthrights. Great Britain, to be sure, was not popular among the people but it was much better than Russia, especially a communist Russia. Even though British troops were in the country, the government was having trouble with Gilān in the hands of Kuchek Khan, Azarbāyjān under Khiyābāni, and central Iran pillaged by brigands, Nāycb Hoscyn-c Kāshi and his son Māshāllā Khan. The situation would have been worse without the British troops. Furthermore, Great Britain was paying the penniless Persian government a monthly stipend of £225,000.[9] Everything considered, it was rather natural for a landowning Prime Minister like Vosuq al-Doleh, a Foreign Minister like Prince Firuz, and their associates to come to the conclusion that it would be to the best interests of Iran to come under the protection of Great Britain, at least for a while.

The Russian Revolution had changed the situation for Great Britain also. It had rendered the Anglo-Russian Convention of 1907 obsolete, and had also created a vacuum which, if filled with Great Britain, would control the land and sea approaches to India as well as the oil wells of Iran. It had been a dream of Foreign Secretary Lord Curzon to create a "chain of vassal states stretching from the Mediterranean to the Pamirs" in which Iran was the "most vital link." In 1919,

9. Joseph Upton, *History of Modern Iran, an Interpretation* (Cambridge University Press, 1961), p. 41.

the veteran British diplomat, Sir Percy Cox, who was minister in Tehran, was given the task of implementing the above policy.

The agreement was concluded in secret between Great Britain and Premier Vosuq. According to the agreement Great Britain would provide advisors with "adequate power," at the expense of Iran for as many Persian departments as considered necessary. Great Britain would also train and equip an army at Persian expense. A loan of £2,000,000 at 7 percent was arranged to pay for the above and the pledge was to be "all the revenues and customs receipts" of Iran. Furthermore, "the purpose behind it" was, to put it in Professor Avery's words, "if not the only voice, Britain's was to be, so far as external powers were concerned, the supreme voice in Iranian affairs. Also, it was designed to ensure that Iran should prosper, but prosper in tutelage to Great Britain." [10]

The above agreement can be best understood in the light of the interpretation given in the above paragraphs. Whether there was any bribe involved cannot, of course, be ascertained. It is doubtful, however, whether there is a Persian historian who thinks that there was not. Ahmad Shah was against the agreement and refused to sign it or even endorse it when he visited England in November of 1919, saying "Let those who received money endorse it, I shall never endorse it." [11]

According to the Constitution, the agreement had to be ratified by the Majles to be binding. The British, who should have known better, showed their contempt for the document by not waiting for this. Prime Minister Vosuq did everything in his power to rig the election of the Fourth Majles, and the British were so sure of themselves that three chief advisors were dispatched to Iran. Mr. Armitage-Smith was sent for finance, General Dickson for the army, and Sir Herbert Smith for customs. When the agreement was announced in Paris, world reaction was immediate and negative. The United States was especially opposed, partly because of the Wilsonian antipathy to secret agreements and partly because the American oil companies who hoped to enter Iran were rightly apprehensive that the agreement would give Britain a virtual monopoly in Iran. The agreement was abandoned, Vosuq resigned, and the way was made clear for one of the most important events in the creation of contemporary Iran.

THE IRAN-SOVIET TREATY OF 1921

After the resignation of Vosuq, the new Prime Minister Moshir

10. Avery, *Modern Iran*, pp. 204–5. Pages 202–9 are an apology for the Anglo-Persian Treaty. Considering Mr. Avery's own statements, his analogy with the U.S. Point Four Program is misleading.

11. Bahar, *Political Parties*, pp. 36–38. Professor Avery states that the Shah did at last mention his "cordial acceptance."

al-Doleh showed an entirely different attitude toward the Soviet Union. He took advantage of the friendly gestures of the Soviet government and tried to put the relations between the two countries on the basis of confidence. His opposition to the Anglo-Persian agreement and his liberal attitude toward the Soviet Union did as much as anything else to persuade the Russians to withdraw their support of the Āzarbāyjān and Gilān separatists. The Treaty of 1921 was a direct result of the policy of reconciliation followed by Moshir al-Doleh.[12] It was also the implementation of the declaration of the Soviet Union cancelling all debts and credits existing between the Tsarist government and the other countries. As debtors in Europe, the Bolsheviks appeared as "thieves," and as creditors in Asia they were considered most generous. The Bolsheviks took care to put this treaty, as well as others which they concluded with Turkey and other countries in Asia, in the context of anti-imperialism and in contrast to the Anglo-Persian agreement of 1919.

By this treaty, which had twenty-six articles, the Soviet Union relinquished all Russian claims to assets, concessions, and properties to Iran. On its part Iran promised not to cede any of these to a third power but to "retain them for the benefit of the Persian people." [13] The treaty, however, retained some vestiges of Tsarist imperialism and made provisions for future Russian proletarian imperialism. The Caspian Fishery Concession of 1867, for example, and the tariff regulation of 1902 remained unchanged. In 1927 a new Irano-Soviet Fisheries Company was organized with a concession to operate for twenty-five years. The tariff, which was extremely favorable to Russia, remained intact and Persian trade suffered.

It was Article Six of the Treaty which caused Iran trouble in later years. It stipulated that if a third power attempted "to use Persian territory as a base of operation against Russia, Russia shall have the right to advance her troops into the Persian interior." Almost immediately the Soviet Union used this article not to withdraw its troops as long as remnants of the British army were still in Iran. It was also used as an excuse for invading Iran in September 1941, and at other times to object to Iran's security agreements with noncommunist countries. Even though the treaty as a whole was beneficial to Iran, the realization was not lost on a number of deputies of the Fifth Majles, which ratified it, that the old Anglo-Russian rivalry in Iran would continue with the only difference that Russia had a different tool to work with, namely communist ideology.

---

12. Rouhollah Ramazani, *The Foreign Policy of Iran, 1500–1941* (Charlottesville: University of Virginia Press, 1966), p. 167.
13. For the full text of the treaty see J. C. Hurewitz, *Diplomacy in the Near and Middle East* (Princeton University Press, 1956) 2, pp. 90–94; also Lenczowski, *Russia and the West in Iran*, Appendix I.

THE COUP D'ÉTAT

It could not be expected of Great Britain, which had been dealt such a great blow in the cancellation of the notorious 1919 agreement and which had sustained such a great loss of prestige, to sit on its hands and not do anything to recoup the losses. By the same token no modern historian should be expected to do so when interpreting the events before the coup. Reading through the mass of material on the background of the coup is as confusing (and also fascinating) as reading half a dozen detective stories at the same time. Perhaps the view that Great Britain planned every move and controlled every event is an exaggeration,[14] but it is equally unrealistic to think that Great Britain had given Iran up, especially when she knew about the Russo-Persian negotiation, and had let events take their course, come what may.[15] It is very reasonable to think, however, that having failed to have its own nationals in every department of Iran to safeguard British interests and to keep the Soviet Union at bay, the next best thing would be to create a strong central government which would be friendly toward Great Britain and fearful of Russia.

There is ample evidence that there was a good deal of talk about a coup d'état in those days. The very influential deputy and cleric, Modarres, reported that Reza Khan had invited him to help put an end to this chaos because, said Reza Khan, "I am afraid Iran will become Bolshevik." [16] Mr. Smart of the British Legation talked with Malek al-Sho'arā Bahār, a prominent member of the liberal faction of the Majles, about the necessity of "creating a strong government." They agreed on this but, "in the choice of the individuals to carry this out our tastes did not coincide," says Bahār; "all my difficulty was in this matter. We agreed to talk again but afterwards it became clear that had there been further talk the opportunity [for the coup] would have been missed." [17]

There is also ample evidence that Seyyed Ziya al-Din Tabātabā'i, one of the two actors in the coup d'état, was a gifted young editor of Ra'd, "Thunder." It is agreed that this paper was consistently pro-British and supported the 1919 agreement. He was suspect among liberals and was a member of the Pulād Anjoman, which was originally founded by the British in Esfahān. There was a good deal of coming and going between Seyyed Ziya and the members of the British Legation, during the days before the coup d'état. To say, as Professor Avery does, that the purpose was to recite and explain modern Persian

14. Cf. Hoseyn Makki, *Tārikh-e Bist Sāle-ye Iran* (*Two Decades of Persian History*), 3 vols. (Tehran, 1945).
15. Cf. Avery, *Modern Iran*, pp. 226–31.
16. Bahār, *Political Parties*, p. 61.
17. Ibid., p. 63.

poetry is to be as much of an ultra British nationalist as Mr. Makki is a Persian nationalist. Furthermore, on the very night of the coup d'état, the Shah and the Prime Minister heard that a Cossack contingent was approaching Tehran, and sent a party to Shāhābād, a short distance from Tehran, in the middle of the night, to see what they were up to. It is significant to note that two representatives of the British Legation accompanied this party. The cat was finally let out of the bag, twenty years later, in the Second World War, when the British Information Services issued the statement that "it was the British who made possible Reza Shah's rise to power." [18]

To say that Seyyed Ziya or Reza Khan were aided by Great Britain is not to conclude, as unfortunately many Persians do conclude, that they were traitors to the best interests of Iran. In the twentieth century no country, even the superpowers, have complete independence of action. Most certainly Iran in the chaotic years after the First World War was not in a position to act independently. No one could have done anything without the aid of Great Britain or Russia or some other power. Seyyed Ziya, in his life-long pro-British attitude, was not any less of a nationalist than Bahār who, without being a Communist, thought that cooperation with the Soviet Union was vital to Iran's interests.

We have become somewhat familiar with Seyyed Ziya. The other main actor in the coup d'état was Colonel Reza Khan, a man diametrically opposite to Ziya in background, education, temperament, and life style. He was a man with little education who at the age of fifteen had joined the Cossack brigade and through his courage and initiative had risen to a position of command. His long association with Russian officers had turned him against them, and perhaps against all Russians. When the October Revolution left the Russian officers of the Persian Cossacks stranded, it was Reza Khan who wrested power from them. He was a nationalist but unlike Seyyed Ziya, his life-long military experience led him to think of the salvation of Iran in military terms. Because of his harsh experience under Russian commanders, he was generally antiforeign and especially anti-Russian and certainly anti-Bolshevik.

Reza Khan in command of the Cossack forces fighting against Kuchek Khan in Gilān had come in close proximity with the chaotic situation in the government and had been convinced that something must be done about it. It was evident that he needed a partner who knew his way around in politics, who could make speeches, and do many other things for which he himself was not as yet prepared. On the other hand Seyyed Ziya was rightly convinced that he would not be able to stage a coup without military support. Inasmuch as they did not know each other, it is not at all surprising that the British Legation,

18. Avery, *Modern Iran*, p. 20.

who knew them both, put them in touch with each other and let them work out their plans. So far as we know Seyyed Ziya went to Reza's headquarters in Qazvin twice, which was not enough for them to get to know each other, let alone plan a coup d'état. This lack of planning became evident after they came to power.

The entrance of Ziya and Reza at the head of some 2,500 Cossacks into Tehran at the early hours of Sunday, February 21, 1921, was rather uneventful. A few machine gun and rifle shots were perhaps more for effect than necessity. Since there was no planning, the cabinet was not formed until the end of the week, with Ziya as Prime Minister. Reza was given a new title, *Sardār-e Sepah*, Comander-in-Chief of the Armed Forces, but no cabinet post. The main activity during that week was the indiscriminate arresting of people from the ages of 14 to 80 and from known reactionaries to famous radicals. Even in this, there was no previous planning. Sometimes Reza would free a person whom Ziya had ordered arrested and vise versa. For example on Thursday of that week Ziya called the poet Bahār and asked him to be editor of the *Iran* newspaper. That same evening Reza arrested him, most likely because he was a known liberal.[19]

In any case the government of Seyyed Ziya did not last more than three months. On April 25, 1921 Reza Khan became Minister of War in the cabinet while holding his command of the armed forces, and on May 24, Ziya was forced to leave the country. The immediate issues were the taking over of gendarmes by the Minister of War and dismissing the British military advisor in the Cossack brigade, both of which were opposed by Ziya. The difference between the two was wider than this. Reza Khan, to use a modern cliché, was a fascist who had the temperament and the power to carry out his purpose. On the other hand Seyyed Ziya wanted to be a fascist but did not have the temperament and did not know how to gain power when he had the opportunity. In the words of Bahār, Ziya "was not enough of a communist to kill everyone, not enough of a fascist to cooperate with the nobility, not decisive enough to silence the communists. He did not have a political party so that he could give positions of responsibility to fellow members and dismiss the rest. Neither was he a member of a tribe to be able to subdue others with its help. According to his own statement, he had not even planned ahead and did not have a hundred friends to count on to prevent Sardār-e Sepah from pulling the rug from under his feet in three months." [20]

The question as to who was the leader of the coup d'état will probably never be answered. In later years, Seyyed Ziya gave an interview in his residence in Palestine stating that he was the leader and even told

19. Bahār, *Political Parties*, p. 90.
20. Ibid., p. 94. The Persian expression for "to pull the rug . . ." is "to sweep under his feet."

anecdotes about the evening of the coup d'état trying to show Reza Khan's lack of courage and decisiveness. These are so obviously out of line with Reza Khan's character as to be entirely spurious. On the other hand Reza Khan also issued a long statement in which he claimed to be the leader. Among other things he said, "With me around, isn't it ridiculous to search for the planner of the coup d'état?" [21] Very likely both initiated it separately and each thought that he would use the other. It was Reza Khan who was the winner.

As soon as Seyyed Ziya was ousted, the prisoners were released and Qavām al-Saltaneh, the brother of Vosuq, became Prime Minister, and it seemed that the old order was back again. But there was a significant difference and that was the person and power of Reza Khan. In many ways he was to the Persian Revolution what Napoleon was to the French Revolution. As a person who was definitely anti-Bolshevik and anti other radical ideas, he was the darling of the landed gentry until he began to liquidate some of them. As a leader who carried out some of the goals of the Revolution and limited the power of the clergy, he was acceptable to the liberals even though he was not using democratic methods. To the masses he was the god-sent deliverer because he used the reorganized army (no more called Cossacks) to subdue rebellion, to disarm the tribes, and to bring every corner of the country under the authority of the central government. His methods were ruthless, but the villages and roads were safe from brigands; and, for the first time in a century, well-laden caravans could travel in all parts of the country without fear of molestation. All of this needed money, and thanks to oil and a reorganization of the country's finances, money was available. During Qavām's premiership, Iran employed Dr. Arthur Millspaugh of the United States to be financial advisor. He and his party arrived in 1922 and served Iran well for five years.[22] He, unlike Morgan Shuster, did not consider himself an employee of the Majles. He realized where the center of real power was and cooperated with him.

THE RISE OF REZA KHAN

In October, 1923, Reza Khan became Prime Minister. For the first time since the revolution, not only a military man was a Prime Minister, but all the provinces had military governors or men under the influence of the commanders of the area. The Fifth Majles was elected in a military dominated atmosphere. It proved to be a very important session and also the last Majles until 1942 in which deputies dared to speak their minds. Soon after Reza Khan became Prime Minister,

21. Ramazani, *Foreign Policy of Iran*, p. 176. For the full text of these see Bahār, *Political Parties*, pp. 112–15 and 185–88.
22. For a detailed account of Millspaugh's mission see his *The American Task in Persia* (New York: The Century Company, 1925).

Ahmad Shah, contrary to all advice, decided to go on another trip to Europe, a practice which had become endemic in the Qājār family. Reza Khan faced the Fifth Majles in which there were three factions. There were reformers who approved of Reza Khan; socialists who approved of him but hoped to influence him in line with democracy; and the "minority," headed by the cleric Modarres, who opposed Reza Khan. The rest were "independent."

Reza Khan, however, had prepared his strategy well. In a very short time, he had organized a strong army, had created a central authority, and had appeased the clergy, had gained control of the cabinet, and had manipulated the Majles.[23] The climax of Reza Khan's popularity came when he established the central government's authority over the oil-producing province of Khuzestan. Sheykh Khaz'al was the semi-autonomous ruler of that province with special agreements with Great Britain. Reza Khan moved against him in spite of Great Britain's opposition. Sheykh Khaz'al surrendered unconditionally and Reza Khan had a triumphal entry back into Tehran.

It was after the triumphal entry that the talk of a republic got started. The newspapers began to criticize the Shah and the whole Qājār dynasty. On the whole, the supporters of a republic were liberals, moderates, and the military. The clerics and their followers were against it. This was the time when Turkey had proclaimed a republic and had abolished the caliphate. Certainly this influenced both the opponents and proponents of the idea for opposite reasons. The *Iranshahr*, a magazine which was published in Germany and was safe from censorship, in its February 15, 1924, issue, discussed the idea and was all for it; but at the same time it doubted whether Iran was ready to "do anything with a republican form of government when we have not benefited from a constitutional monarchy." The movement for a republic had progressed so fast that the same magazine in its March 22, 1924, issue thanked Reza Khan for bringing about a republic and devoted a good many pages to it and expressed the wish in a poem that "As today Iran has been freed from having a king, tomorrow she may escape the evils of the clergy."

It was not only the clergy and the merchants of the bazaars who were against a republic, but the ultra liberals were also against it, mainly because it was led by a "dictator Cossack." The talented poet and dramatist, Eshqi, used to lampoon Reza Khan and his "synthetic republic" in his paper, *Twentieth Century*. He was assassinated and the people blamed Reza Khan for it. Reza Khan was shrewd enough to see the handwriting on the wall. He had a hasty conference with the chief clergy in Qom and issued a statement saying that he and the clergy had decided to ask the people "to stop mention of the republic and

23. For a detailed description of these points see Ramazani, *Foreign Policy of Iran*, pp. 177–86.

instead spend their energies helping me to . . . strengthen the foundations of Islam and the independence of the country."

The talk of a republic died down but not the criticism of Ahmad Shah. Even though the Shah dismissed Reza Khan as Prime Minister, the Majles did not pay any attention to his request to nominate another person. On October 31, 1925, the Majles deposed the Qājār dynasty and called for a constituent assembly to choose a new king. Only four deputies had the courage to oppose the resolution. Not one of them defended the Qājārs, but they felt that such a move was against the Constitution. In the light of future events, it is interesting to note that Dr. Mosaddeq argued that it was a shame to promote an active prime minister like Reza Khan to the inactive position of a shah. If, as shah, he became active then he would be a dictator and if not, then the country would have lost an active prime minister. Of the four, Dr. Mosaddeq was under arrest and banishment until he was pardoned at the intercession of the new crown prince. The second one, Mirza Yahya Dolatābādi left public life, and Taqizadeh and Alā served the new Shah in important posts. The constituent assembly met and amended the Constitution on December 12, 1925, and proclaimed Reza as Reza Shah Pahlavi.

The Pahlavi Reforms

Very much like Shah Abbās, Reza Shah was popular among the masses, mainly because they had security. His ruthlessness was directed against the leaders of the tribes and nobles rather than the peasants. He was a nationalist reformer, who, unlike Kemal Ataturk, did not have a philosophy or a party to back it up and make it a continuous process. His lack of education made him impatient with philosophy and ideology and his personal temperament as a loner precluded any discussion of issues in a political party. On the whole, he was more interested in the glitter of Western civilization than in its substance; more in industrialization for the power of the state than for the good of the people; more in independence from foreign rule than for freedom of thought and initiative on the part of the people. He sent scores of students to Europe for study but would not allow them to express themselves when they returned. He was an indefatigable worker, and like Peter the Great of Russia, did not think that any one could do anything as well as he. Even if he did not start that way, the constant nauseating flattery of newspapers, members of the Majles, and others made him think he was a paragon of knowledge and wisdom. Perhaps it was this rationalization that made him acquire so much land on the ground that he would develop the land for the good of the state. Either by instinct or by osmosis he had grasped the central message of Western nationalism, namely that whatever is good for the state is good for the people, rather than the other way around.

There were great improvements, however, during the rule of Reza Shah. He built roads, constructed wireless service and took over the operation of the telegraph company from the British. In communication, his greatest achievement was the construction of the railroad from the Caspian to the Persian Gulf. He was rightly proud of the fact that it had been financed by a special tax on sugar and tea with no foreign loans. He abolished extraterritoriality, established a national bank, and took over from the British the privilege of issuing bank notes. He curbed the power of the clergy and took away the control of religious endowments from their hands. Islamic laws were partially set aside and Islamic education was abandoned in public schools. The Islamic lunar calendar was replaced by the old Persian Zoroastrian solar calendar with Persian names for the months of the year. He discouraged religious processions and passion plays in the month of Moharram, frowned upon the giving of the call to prayer and made it difficult for the faithful to go to Mecca.

He opened schools for men and women and inaugurated adult education. He abolished all titles and required that everyone should choose a family name. Like Ataturk, he forced Persian men to abandon their Persian hats and attire in favor of European ones and he made women abandon the veil. He established a Persian academy whose task it was to rid the Persian language of Arabic words. He built cement, sugar, and textile factories; he built state monopolies, and subjected all commerce to strict state control.

In the opinion of all nationalists, liberals or moderates, all of the above reforms were considered to be the *sine qua non* of westernization. These had to be done in order for Iran to be a nation among nations. At the same time it was evident that none of these would have been done, certainly not in this century, if force had not been used. This has been the greatest dilemma for all developing nations. In order to silence the critics of reform all criticism was banned and newspapers, one by one, went out of business and the handpicked members of the Majles eulogized the Shah.

The creative enthusiasm that had been ignited during the revolutionary period died down under extreme censorship. Political criticism gave way to moralizing, and social reform was concentrated on the position of women, which was the vogue of the day. Poets chose the conventional subjects of the bygone past and prose writers experimented with European-style novels. Representative examples of the latter are *Tehran-e Makhuf* (*Dreadful Tehran*), by Morteza Kāzemi in 1922; *Jenāyāt-e Bashar* (*Man's Crimes*), by Rabi' Ansāri in 1930; and *Man Ham Geryeh Kardeh-am* (*I Have Also Wept*), by Jahāngir Jalili in 1933. These and others mostly deal with prostitution, temporary marriage, and the low status of women in society. The most prolific novelist and short-story writer who began in this period and continued into the 1960s is Mohammad Hejazi. But "both as a stylist and thinker he is weak because he fails to evince any definite principles or take up a position." [24]

The writer who has truly influenced contemporary Persian literature not only in style but also in subject matter is Mohammad Ali Jamālzādeh. He established his reputation with the publication in 1921 of the delightful satire *Yeki Bud Yeki Nabud* (*Once Upon a Time*). Though most of his works were written after the Second World War (he is still active), it is believed that they did not equal the "conciseness, novelty of form, originality of ideas, a biting sense of humour . . ." of his earlier works.[25]

This was the period of the founding of the University of Tehran, the first in modern times, and the importation of western music, architecture, and cinema. It was also the time when the increasing number of students returning home from abroad experienced that phenomenon that later came to be known as "culture shock." A play by the late Hasan Moqaddam, *Ja'far Khan az Farang Amadeh* (*Ja'far Khan Has Returned from Europe*), began the discussion of the problem that is still part of the social scene.

PERSIAN OIL

No history of Iran is complete without an account of oil, and the story of oil in Iran is replete with crises. By 1933 Reza Shah had virtually wiped out almost all the remnants of the old economic imperialism save the oil concession. He decided to challenge it for both nationalistic and economic reasons. This was the period of world economic depression and oil royalties had depreciated.

The presence of oil in the Middle East was long known. Noah's ark was prepared for sailing by the use of pitch, and the Zoroastrians of Iran built their fire temples around ignited natural gas. In the infamous concession given to Baron de Reuter in 1872, oil was one of the items mentioned. William Knox D'Arcy, whose name has been immortalized in connection with Persian oil, was an Australian oil prospector. He heard about the possible presence of oil in Iran through his friend Sir Henry Drummond Wolff, the former British Minister in Iran, who had heard it from a Persian customs official by the name of Ketābchi Khan, who had read an article on the subject by a French archeologist in Iran.

D'Arcy sent his representatives to Iran in 1901 and after receiving a favorable report applied for a concession from Mozaffar al-Din Shah. The Shah would not do anything without permission from the Russians. With proper inducement, the grand vazir, Amin al-Soltan, told the British Minister to write him a letter in Persian and describe the terms of the concession and he would then send the letter to the Russian

24. For a detailed discussion of Hejazi see *Modern Persian Prose*, pp. 73–84.
25. Ibid., pp. 91–112.

Legation for comment. He then explained to the British Minister, no doubt with a wink, that he knew that the Persian interpreter of the Russian Legation was going to be away on vacation and the letter would not be read until his return. In the meantime he would tell the Shah that no objection had been received from the Russian Legation. All this happened and the Shah signed the concession.[26]

The term of the concession was for sixty years, after which all machinery, buildings, and installations would revert to Iran without compensation. The area of the concession was all of Iran except the five northern provinces. The Persian government was to receive £20,000 in paid-up shares plus an annual royalty of 16 percent of the net profits. The exploration for oil continued for seven long years without result. When they were about to abandon the whole project, oil was discovered near Masjed-e Soleymān on May 26, 1908. A year later the Anglo-Persian Oil Company was formed with a capital of £2,000,000. At this time the Persian Revolution was two years old. The members of the First Majles discussed the oil concession, but it is evident that the deputies were not aware of its importance.

In the same way that the British Legation had helped D'Arcy get the concession, it also helped the company to arrange with the Bakhtyāri chieftains for the lease of the land and with Sheykh Khaz'al, who claimed jurisdiction over the area. At the beginning of the First World War, the British Navy started to use oil. In order to obtain it at a low price and to prevent other countries from having a share in the rich deposits, in May 1914 the British Admiralty bought enough shares in the company to become its controlling partner. Later the House of Commons approved the project, and the British government became the concessionaire instead of the Anglo-Persian Oil Company. From that date until the nationalization of Persian Oil in 1951, the British Navy bought oil from the company at a special price. It was never revealed what this price was nor whether the navy paid anything at all. Inasmuch as the Persians were never allowed to examine the books, it has remained a well-kept secret.

In keeping with the rivalry that existed between Great Britain and Russia over concessions, it was inevitable that Russia would clamor for a concession in the north. The Russo-Japanese war, followed by the Russian Revolution of 1905 and the fact that it had a good deal of oil in Baku, prevented Russia from seeking a concession. In 1916 a Russian entrepreneur, A. M. Khoshtaria, got a concession from Vosuq al-Doleh for oil in the north. The terms of the agreement were similar to D'Arcy's except that it was for seventy years. A most significant difference was the fact that the concession to be valid had to be ratified

26. Mostafa Fāteh, *Panjāh Sāl Naft (Fifty Years of Oil)* (Tehran: Chehr Press, 1956).

by the Majles.[27] The Majles never ratified it and the Persians thought the matter closed.

It has already been intimated that during the long period of Anglo-Russian rivalry a group of Persians had considered Persian salvation to depend upon the introduction of a third power into the scene. Qavām, the successor of Sayyed Ziya as Prime Minister, belonged to this school. He was instrumental in bringing the American financial Mission and he was also instrumental in trying to give a concession for the northern oil to the Americans. The Americans, of course, were very eager to have the concession.

An agreement was signed between the Persian government and the Standard Oil Company on November 22, 1921. Both the Russians and the British protested. The Russians protested on the basis of Article Thirteen of the recently signed treaty which stated that Iran should not cede a concession which they had given up. The British, however, objected on the ground that they had bought the concession from Khoshtaria and had organized the North Persia Oil Company. Iran's answer to both was the same, namely that Khoshtaria's concession was null and void because it had never been ratified by the Majles.

Great Britain had the upper hand not in logic but in the right of way. The APOC had exclusive rights of oil transportation in the Persian Gulf Area and would not allow anyone to pipe oil to any port on the Persian Gulf. Consequently, the Americans and the British formed a partnership for the northern oil with the Americans having the controlling vote. The Persians, however, did not agree to have the British in the north and the case was dropped.

The Majles, however, was adamant about keeping the British out of the north and passed a law permitting the government to negotiate with "any independent and responsible American company." In 1923 the Sinclair Oil Company became interested in the project. Sinclair had the advantage over Standard in that it had extensive arrangements with the Soviet Union for the marketing of Baku oil and had the Russians' blessing in the Iran project. In March, 1924, the Majles ratified the Sinclair concession and the company's representative came to Tehran to sign the agreement. From then on the story is stranger than fiction. A wing of the Majles was burned, reportedly by arsonists. One of the numerous water fountains in Tehran was said to have performed a miracle and throngs of people, encouraged by the clergy, went there to see the place or be cured or both. In the midst of all this, Major Imbrie, the swashbuckling Vice Consul of the United States, decided to go and photograph the miracle-performing fountain. This he did at the instigation, and in the company of, an American employee of the Anglo-Persian Oil Company and against the advice of American and

27. See Avery, *Modern Iran*, p. 257, for the exactly opposite statement.

Persian friends. He was murdered by the mob, but his companion was not harmed. At about the same time, thousands of miles away in the United States Sinclair was involved in the Teapot Dome Scandal. Somehow the news wires of the world and imaginative reporters put all these events together and made a very exciting international intrigue out of it.

The Persian government executed three of the ringleaders of the murder, paid $60,000 to Imbrie's widow, and $110,000 to the United States government for the expense of sending a battleship to take the body of the slain vice consul home. The American government promised to set aside this sum to be used as scholarships for Persian students studying in the United States.

It will be remembered that 1924 was also the year of moves and countermoves that culminated in the change of dynasty. Reza Khan had many enemies, especially among the clergy, who wanted to embarrass him and get the populace on their side. These events can be explained better in connection with the internal affairs of Iran than as means employed by the British to stop the Americans from having the oil in the north. Nevertheless, the Imbrie incident smacked of oil. I have examined the voluminous Imbrie Papers in the Archives of the United States. More than half of this collection has to do with the successful attempt of Mrs. Imbrie, through her Congressional Representative and Senators, to stop the setting up of a scholarship fund for Persian students. This in itself is an interesting study of the mysterious workings of the Congress of the United States. It is evident from the rest of the papers that the miracle of the fountain and the murder of Imbrie did not have anything to do with the Sinclair Concession. There are, however, repeated complaints by the members of the American Legation that the British Legation had almost taken the Imbrie case out of their hands. The Americans thought that the British were using the Imbrie incident to their own advantage. In any case what is important in our story is that the question of the northern oil did not come up again until after the Second World War.

In the meantime the profits of the Anglo-Persian Oil Company were increasing in meteoric proportions. By 1933, the company was producing upwards of seventy million tons of crude oil and the large refinery in Abadan had a capacity of more than five million tons annually. In the course of years there were problems between the Persian government and the company, some of which were solved and the rest swept under the rug. Up until 1930 most of the administrative staff of the company were recruited from among the Englishmen who were in the service of their government in India. They brought with them their paternalistic and superior attitudes and dealt with the Persians as they had dealt with the Indians. Indeed, a good number of unskilled and semiskilled laborers were from India. The accounts of the company were in Indian rupees and the laborers were paid in that currency. The administration of the company was in the hands of people like "Sir Charles Greenway whose purpose was the exploitation of the Persians and their oil and who tried, in every way possible, to make the maximum profit while giving only a minimum to Iran." [28]

With the rise of a nationalistic government in Iran under Reza Shah, it could not be expected that the old order would be allowed to continue. In 1928 the Shah and a large number of Persian officials went to Khuzestan for the opening of the main highway which had been constructed. The company invited him to visit the oil installations. He refused to go but sent a message to the president of the company through Mostafa Fateh in which he repeated more than once that "Iran cannot anymore endure that the huge profits of oil should go into the pocket of foreigners and Iran be deprived of it." [29]

The warning was given and negotiations dragged on until 1931 when, because of the depression, the royalties decreased by a little over three million pounds. Iran refused to receive the royalty and members of the Majles talked about revision of the D'Arcy agreement. On November 27, 1933, Taqizādeh, the Minister of Finance, informed the company that the Persian government considered the D'Arcy agreement null and void because it was signed prior to the establishment of a constitutional government. It also said that Iran was willing to negotiate a new agreement. Great Britain appealed to the League of Nations and World Court, but the matter was settled by the intervention of the Shah himself.

The impatience of the Shah and the idea that only he could get things done made him take the matter out of the hands of four able Persians who were negotiating with the company. In 1949, Taqizādeh, one of the four members, in a long speech to the Majles, explained the situation and how the all-powerful Shah had silenced them and had brought the matter to a close by signing a new concession.[30] The new agreement contained two advantages for Iran which proved to be superficial. One was the reduction of the area of the concession to only 100,000 square miles. The company had already gathered considerable geological data and knew in which areas oil could be found and saw to it that these were within the area left to it. Secondly, the royalty was arranged in such a way as to guarantee a fixed income for Iran. This was good for times of depression but in times of prosperity all that Iran got was 20 percent of dividends distributed to ordinary stockholders. On the other hand, the company gained tremendously by being exempt from paying taxes and by prolonging the duration of the concession to sixty years from 1933. These were tremendous losses for Iran.

28. Fāteh, *Fifty Years of Oil*, pp. 279–80.
29. Ibid., p. 286. Mr. Fateh was for a long time the senior Persian officer in the APOC.
30. For the full text of this important speech see ibid., p. 289.

RELATIONS WITH NEIGHBORS

In his struggle for independence from Russia and Great Britain, Reza Shah had to be friendly to Iran's neighbors, a number of whom were involved in a similar struggle. The closest neighbors of Iran, other than the Soviet Union and the British government in India, were Afghanistan, Iraq, and Turkey. The problems with Afghanistan centered around the waters of the Helmand River and some minor border disputes. Both governments agreed in 1934 to accept the arbitration of a neutral power. The fact that this power was Turkey showed that a new era had dawned and Iran would not use the good offices of a European power. The arbitration was accepted even though Iran was not too pleased. The Helmand River problem was solved by the signature of an agreement in 1938 which made it possible for both countries to use the waters for irrigation purposes.[31]

The problems with Iraq were more serious partly because of the proximity of oil lands and mostly because Iraq's treaty with Great Britain did not give her complete independence of action. Inasmuch as these same problems have reasserted themselves in the contemporary Irano-Iraqi relations, it is useful to mention them here. These were, first, the problem of the Kurdish tribesmen, second, the status of Persian citizens in Iraq, and third, the Shatt al-Arab River. Due to fortunes of wars, the region which has been traditionally the home of the Kurdish tribes is divided among three countries, Iran, Iraq, and Turkey. The Kurds, perhaps because of their cultural and linguistic affinity with Iran, have had more difficulty with Iraq and Turkey than with Iran. More than once Iraq has accused Iran of helping the Kurdish rebels against Iraq. The problem of the status of Persians in Iraq is directly related to religion. The most important Shi'i shrine as well as some of the lesser ones are in Iraq. Consequently, there are quite a number of Persian nationals who have permanent residence in that country and the Persian government has always taken an interest not only in the upkeep of the shrines but also in the welfare of its citizens.

The most important problem, however, between the two countries is the Shatt al-Arab. It has been the cause of the eruption of the other two problems. The river forms the boundary between the two countries. Iran claimed that the boundary should be the main channel, *thalweg*, of the river while Iraq wanted its boundary to include the whole width of the river to the bank on the Persian side. The dispute in the end was "solved" by a compromise in 1937.[32]

Both Turkey and Iran had changed enough to see the futility of the Perso-Ottoman wars. These two antagonists, who had fought each

31. Ramazani, *Foreign Policy of Iran*, pp. 207–9.
32. For the text of the treaty see League of Nations Series, CXC, 267–68.

other as equals, had respect for each other in peace. The first conclusive boundary treaty was signed on January 23, 1932 and ended centuries of dispute. At the same time a treaty of friendship was signed. Reza Shah paid a state visit to Turkey in 1934 and laid the foundation for expansion of economic ties.

The crowning achievement of Reza Shah in Iran's policy with its neighbors was the Sa'dābād Pact on July 8, 1937. It was a nonaggression agreement among Afghanistan, Iran, Iraq, and Turkey. For the first time in modern times these countries arrived at a pact without European tutelage. It was a sign of growth, and the fact that the only rift in recent years has been between Iran and Iraq bodes well for the future.

Reza Shah and Germany

The life of Reza Shah is an excellent example of leaders in the long history of Iran who have done a great deal of good, but at the same time, because they have taken all powers in their own hands, have done the country a great deal of harm. Furthermore, concentration of power in one man's hands suffocated initiative and creativity. The dictatorship of Reza Shah was not very efficient, but nevertheless it affected every person in the country. Censorship became so strong that every mailbox had a person sitting beside it to inspect letters. These stringent measures forced the thoughtful, and especially scores of students who had returned from Europe, to go underground for their discussions. It opened the way for the spread of communism, the very thing Reza Shah wanted to avoid.

In the 1930s, the Comintern shifted its emphasis and tried to reach the intellectuals. Returned students, such as Dr. Erāni, were not activists like the separatist leaders of Gilān and Āzarbāyjān but were intellectuals who had come under the influence of Marxist-Leninist ideology in western Europe rather than the Russian context. Dr. Erāni edited the journal *Donya* and formed underground circles in Tehran. Fifty-three members of the group, including Dr. Erāni, were arrested, tried, and most of them were imprisoned for violating the anti-Communist Act of 1931. Dr. Erāni died in prison, but the rest were freed in 1941 and formed the nucleus of the Tudeh Party in Iran.[33]

The rise of Hitler and his anticommunism appealed to Reza Shah. In Germany, he saw an effective third power to free Iran from the Anglo-Russian domination. Commercially and culturally relations with the Third Reich increased by the month. To make his dictatorship more effective, Reza Shah brought advisors from Germany. A council for the "Nurture of Thought," *Parvaresh-e Afkār*, was formed, and

33. See Zabih, *Communist Movement*, pp. 60–70.

when the students were not marching or singing martial songs, they were listening to speeches on 'God, Shah, and Country.'

When the Second World War started, Iran declared its neutrality, but the declaration was no more effective then than it had been during the First World War. When Germany attacked Russia, Iran became the only route through which lend-lease material could be sent to the Soviet Union. Furthermore, there were scores of Germans in Iran in the vast commercial and cultural activities which had been going on for some time. It was assumed that a large number, if not all, of these were political agents. The Allies demanded that Iran expel the Germans. Reza Shah procrastinated. Many theories have been advanced as to why Reza Shah did not acquiesce to the demands. Some blame the Shah himself; others accuse his counselors; still others blame the Germans; and Mohammad Reza Shah Pahlavi blames the Allies.[34]

Even though there is truth in all of these views, it seems that the Allies should bear a good part of the responsibility for harping only on the expulsion of the Germans and saying nothing about lend-lease material or other strategic considerations. They well knew that Reza Shah was a proud man as well as a proud nationalist. Expelling the Germans would have been an admission that he was not able to keep them in check. Furthermore, one must add to the above theories the fact that Reza Shah was anti-Russian; and there were few men in 1941 who did not think that the Germans were going to win. A man in Reza Shah's position would procrastinate or await the results. It is also likely that the Russians and the British did not want him around because they knew they could not work with him.

Be that as it may, the British and the Russians attacked Iran simultaneously at dawn on August 25, 1941. By August 27, the Persian military strength had been dissipated. The Prime Minister resigned and the new Premier, the veteran Mohammad Ali Foroughi, accepted the Allied terms. Reza Shah abdicated in favor of his son Mohammad Reza, and was taken under British custody to the Island of Mauritius. Later he was transferred to Johannesburg, where he died on July 26, 1944.

34. For details on each theory see Ramazani, *Foreign Policy of Iran*, p. 290 ff.

9

Struggle for Power

Reza Shah's abdication and his departure from Iran let loose the pent up feelings of the whole nation. People in all walks of life started doing what they were not supposed to and gave up doing what they had been doing, just because they were tired of acting or not acting at the command of one person. For twenty years, the whole nation had been gradually forced to think, to speak, and to wear that which had been decreed. Now that the source of power had disintegrated, the people reacted and went all the way back to what had been. Some women wore their discarded veils, and men their abandoned old-style hats; the sound of the call to prayer was heard from the minarets, and some of the unlicensed clerics donned their turbans and were seen walking in the streets mumbling their prayers. Even when the butcher was asked why he did not have his regulation white apron he replied, "Haven't you heard, the Shah has left the country." [1]

Newspapers that had been suppressed started publishing as though nothing had happened. The members of the Majles, the same hand-picked eulogists of his ex-majesty, started abusing him and putting all the blame on him. They started wrangling among themselves and acted as though they had been elected by the people. Even the Allies were not immune from this. The Russians occupied the north and the British the south as they had done before the First World War, and they both rushed their troops to Tehran. To ease the sting of "occupation," Great Britain and Russia concluded a Tripartite Treaty with Iran on January 29, 1942, stating that the presence of their troops in the country did not constitute occupation. They also agreed to evacuate

---

1. A personal experience of the author.

their troops from Iran within six months after the end of hostilities. The Persians, who were rightly afraid of the resumption of the old Anglo-Russian rivalry in Iran, rejoiced when American service troops came to Iran in great numbers to facilitate the transportation of lend-lease material. The constant interference of Great Britain and Russia in the internal affairs of Iran reminded the Persians of the old days.[2] The Persians, therefore, were happy for a third power to come in, and proposed an agreement with the United States along the lines of the Tripartite Treaty. Unfortunately, the Americans refused and preferred to come into Iran on the coattails, so to speak, of Great Britain. Later events proved this to be a mistake, for the Persians came to identify the Americans with the British, which, justifiably or not, was not meant to be a compliment. Throughout the war one could read in the newspapers and hear in conversation the statement "The Allies and Russia," always lumping the United States and Great Britain and separating the two from Russia. In a short time all the real and imaginary sins of Great Britain were transferred to the United States. In a few years, however, the Americans accumulated a few sins of their own.

Great Britain and Russia, who were fighting the war for democracy and freedom, missed their opportunity to help the Persians create such a government. They could not very well suppress the mushrooming press and the feverish activity in the formation of political parties. The affairs of government remained in old hands, for the Allies were more interested in winning the war than in establishing democracy and preferred to do business with the known and tried older men than with the hotheaded young nationalists who were clamoring to be heeded.

Once again Ahmad Qavām became Prime Minister. He, it will be remembered, was a believer in the concept of introducing a third power in the affairs of Iran. It was he who, as Prime Minister twenty years earlier, had arranged for employing an American financial mission headed by Dr. Millspaugh. So he started where he had left off and asked the same Dr. Millspaugh to come again in 1943 and resume his old position. Millspaugh, also, acted as though nothing had happened in Iran during the sixteen years that he had been absent and got himself into all sorts of difficulties. He was forced to resign in 1945 and came home to write his memoirs.[3]

The younger men, however, would not be denied. During the twenty years of the Pahlavi era, a new generation of Persians had gone through a significant social change. Education at home and abroad, construction of railroads, and industrialization under Reza Shah had created a middle class that had provided the entrepreneurs and contractors of the new era. They were slowly replacing the bazaar in trade and were represented in the army and in many new institutions created

2. *Mission for My Country*, p. 76.
3. *Americans in Persia* (Washington, D.C., 1946).

by Reza Shah. The industrialization, limited though it was, had created a new labor force which had reached the unprecedented figure of over half a million in 1942.[4] The old titles had been abolished and a number of the title holders had left public office. Some of their sons and a larger number of the sons of people who did not belong to the nobility, A'yān, came back from Europe with the new titles of Doctor and *Mohandes*, 'Engineer', and expected to determine the destiny of the country.

THE TUDEH PARTY

All of these were involved in feverish political activity. They organized political parties and received permits to publish two or three newspapers so that if one was suppressed they could publish another one. Most of these political parties did not have a national base but represented either interest groups or personal ambition. The one glaring exception was the Tudeh Party, which was organized by some of the fifty-three young men who had been tried on the charge of communist activity. Their leader, Dr. Erāni, had died in prison and the rest were freed after the abdication of Reza Shah. They formed the *Tudeh*, 'Masses', which became, by far, the best organized political party in the country.

The Tudeh was admittedly Marxist, but either because of the presence of a number of nationalists in their group or because of the realities of Soviet diplomacy, they claimed that they were not communists, thereby minimizing their dependence upon the Soviet Union.[5] They were organized along communist lines with a central executive committee, a platform of labor legislation, social insurance, trade unionism, free education, distribution of land, rights of minorities, disarmament of tribes, and the like. At no time did they ask for the nationalization of property.[6] They had cells, *hozeh*, among workers, women, peasants, and students and a branch in every section of the country. They were strongest in the north which was occupied by the Soviet forces. They edited a number of newspapers, held conferences, mass meetings, and were able to organize the workers in the textile mills of Esfahān, and in the oil fields in the south. Their slogan was "Bread, Health, and Education for All."

Meanwhile, the presence of thousands of foreign troops handling war supplies to Russia necessitated more currency than the country had. According to His Majesty the Shah, the Allies forced the Persian govern-

4. Zabih, *Communist Movement*, p. 72.
5. In the discussion of the Tudeh Party, unless otherwise noted, I am indebted to the splendid book of Sepehr Zabih to which I have already referred.
6. *Hezb-e Tudeh-ye Iran Che Miguyad va Che Mikhāhad* (*What Does the Tudeh Party Say and What Does It Wish*).

ment to print large amounts of currency.[7] This coupled with the fact that there was very little import, created a rocketing inflation. Contractors and entrepreneurs supplying the Allies with their needs became wealthy. Land prices and house rentals went up, and it got so that shopkeepers and grocers would hoard their goods to sell them to foreigners at prices which the Persians could not afford. Furthermore, the Persian Army, following the attack by Great Britain and Russia, had become so disorganized that when thousands of soldiers were discharged no one apparently thought of collecting the weapons. These were either sold to the tribes, who rose against the central government, or were used by the ex-soldiers to pillage the countryside. Added to all this, the poor crops caused near famine and Persians, even in Tehran, had to stand in long lines to buy bread. It is quite evident that under such circumstances the program of change and reform as put forward by the Tudeh Party would have great appeal. In the election of 1943 they won eight seats from the north.

THE NATIONAL WILL PARTY

The British, who were alarmed at the rapid growth of the pro-Soviet Tudeh Party, countered with moves of their own. In addition to the landed gentry, one of the most conservative groups was the clergy, whom Reza Shah had pushed to the background and who were becoming prominent after his abdication. Based on the naive belief that religion, especially organized, will stop communism the British encouraged the Shi'i clergy. Travel abroad, which was hard to come by in war times, was opened to thousands of Persian pilgrims to Mecca. Āyatollah Qomi, who had been exiled by Reza Shah, came back and was welcomed by Premier Soheyli. The theological school connected with Sepahsālār Mosque became a faculty of the Tehran University, and the government radio started its daily broadcasts with recitations from the Koran. The clergy were against communism, but they were also against westernization, which meant that they were against most of the reforms approved by the majority of the noncommunist educated class.[8] The Society for the Propagation of Islam was formed with branches in different cities of the country, and through the publication of magazines and books it tried to inculcate the tenets of Islam. This group continued its work until 1953 and then gradually went out of the picture. It is revealing of the nature of their emphasis to note that of all their publications only one dealt with the problem of science and religion.[9]

7. *Mission for My Country*, p. 76.
8. George Lenczowski, *Russia and the West in Iran, 1918–1948* (Ithaca: Cornell University Press, 1948), pp. 239–42.
9. For detail see my "Islamic Literature in Postwar Iran," in R. B. Winder and James Kritzeck, eds., *The World of Islam* (New York: St. Martin's Press, 1960).

Another important anticommunist activity was built around the person of Seyyed Ziya Tabātabā'i, the coleader of the coup d'état of 1921. He came back from his exile in Palestine wearing a hat which was similar to the one which he had worn when he left Iran. He was elected to the Majles in 1943 and a year later he organized a right-wing, pro-British, and anticommunist party called the *Erādeh-ye Melli*, 'National Will.'

It is interesting to note that the National Will had an organization similar to the Tudeh. Its cells were called *halqeh*, circle, and were composed of nine men and a chief. Every nine circles formed a "Little Parliament," which sent its representatives to the National meeting, which was called the "Great Parliament." Its executive committee was headed by Ziyā himself and the magnificence of the Party headquarters seemed to indicate that money was not one of its problems. The platform of the party dealt with justice, health, division of state domains, industrialization, and so forth. The special policies advocated by the party were "stronger defenses of the political and economic independence of Iran; friendly treatment of the tribes; defense of Islam; introduction of religious teaching into the school programs; and a foreign policy of eternal neutrality for Iran, following the Swiss pattern." [10]

While it is true that the Soviet Union and Great Britain supported the Tudeh and the National Will parties respectively, it would be grossly misleading to think that these parties existed because of outside support. Each one represented the needs, ambitions, and interests of certain segments of the population within the country. The National Will had the support of elements from the clergy, bazaar merchants, landlords, and the tribes, while the Tudeh had the support of elements from labor, intelligentsia, white-collar workers, professionals, and students. Of course, there were people from every one of the above segments who were independent nationalists and afraid of domination by the Soviet Union or Great Britain. The young Shah was against the Tudeh Party, but it cannot be said that he was altogether with the National Will or they with him. The bulk of the army was loyal to the Shah. On the whole, it can be said that most of the political parties considered the Shah's position above political wranglings and did not take him into account.

Great Britain and the Soviet Union were certainly involved in the internal affairs of Iran but their attitude had also changed. During the constitutional period it was Great Britain that sided with the liberals and revolutionaries who demanded change, while Russia was on the side of reaction and status quo. During the Second World War when the two rivals entered Iran again, their positions had changed. The Soviet Union was on the side of revolution and change while Great Britain preferred the status quo. We have also seen that the British

10. Lenczowski, *Russia and the West*, p. 244.

who supported revolution in the earlier years did so out of self-interest and not for any commitment to democracy or freedom for the Persians. They did not hesiate to betray the revolution of 1907 when their self-interest demanded it, or to acquiesce in the Russian ultimatum in the case of Shuster, which ended the first phase of the revolution. Similarly the interest of the Soviet Union in revolution and change during the period after the Second World War was prompted by self-interest and not by any commitment to socialist revolution for Iran. As we shall see, they also betrayed their comrades in 1946 for the sake of the oil concession, which is reputed to be a capitalistic disease, and abandoned them altogether in 1953.

THE NORTHERN OIL

By 1945 the two parties were at each other with hammer and tongs. At one time or another the Tudeh party had an aggregate of thirty-nine newspapers disseminating its message while the National Will had over twenty-seven. The rivalry between these two parties had all the earmarks of developing into a genuine two-party system divided along ideological, social, and economic lines. But 1945 was also the year in which the war ended; and the Soviet Union refused to evacuate Iran on March 2, 1946, the date set by the Allies. It was also in 1945 that a group of communists launched a separatist movement in Āzarbāyjān and the Kurds demanded autonomy. All of these events are related to each other and to the fact that the Soviet Union wanted a concession for the exploitation of oil in the northern provinces. So did the United States, but in all the confusion that ensued the American desire was forgotten and the attention of the world together with the anxiety of the Persians were directed to the Irano-Soviet relations of 1946.

While the war was still raging in 1944 some British but principally American companies had been talking with the Persian government about oil concessions in the north. When Premier Sā'ed reported this to the Majles in August 1944 there were expressions of caution and opposition on the part of some deputies. In September, however, Sergei Kavtaradze, the Assistant People's Commissar for Foreign Affairs of the Soviet Union, came to Iran at the head of a large delegation and asked for concession of northern oil. The result of the negotiation was the announcement of the Persian government to the effect that no oil concessions will be given to any country until after the war. This brought a direct attack on the government by the Soviet representative. The Tudeh party, which had opposed the giving of concessions to anyone, came out in favor of a concession to the Soviet Union. It organized demonstrations in Tehran and some northern cities and caused Sā'ed to resign. It was during this tense period that Dr. Mohammad Mosaddeq, a leading independent deputy, offered a bill which made it a criminal act on the part of any government or minister to negotiate or grant oil concessions to any foreign government without the previous permission of the Majles. The Soviet official went home with another harsh statement but the matter was closed for the time being.

THE ĀZARBĀYJĀN AFFAIR

When World War II was over and the British and American troops prepared to withdraw from Iran by March 2, 1946, it became increasingly clear that the Soviet Union did not have any intention of doing so. Iran, like many countries of the world, has and does still have its regional problems. The problem facing Iran is somewhat more acute, partly because in some of these regions people speak in a different dialect and partly because the central government has not usually been attentive to their needs. This regional interest began to cause a rift in the ranks of the Tudeh party toward the end of the summer of 1945.

More of an activist than a theoretician, and more of a provincial than a Persian nationalist, Ja'far Pishevari started agitating for a separate Āzarbāyjān. He had been active in the establishment of the Gilān Autonomous Republic of 1920, and had lived in exile during Reza Shah's period. He asked that the people of Āzarbāyjān live within the constitutional democracy of Iran but with the right of self-government. He also demanded that the Azari-Turkish be the official language of the province in order "to develop our national culture and education." By December 1945 the Tudeh party of Āzarbāyjān had been replaced by a new party, called "Demokrat," which deposed the governor of Āzarbāyjān and took matters into its own hands.

When a contingent of the Persian Army was sent to Āzarbāyjān to deal with the insurrection, it was stopped by the Red Army from advancing into the province. In February 1946, Qāzi Mohammad was declared the President of the Peoples Republic of Kurdestan. Soon the two autonomous regions signed a treaty of alliance and mutual defense. All of this shook the Central Committee of the Tudeh party as well as the rest of the nation. Khalil Maleki, the brilliant theoretician of the party proposed a resolution refusing to recognize the new party. The Soviet embassy, however, intervened and the Tudeh was made to congratulate the leaders of the Demokrat Party.[11] Later on, Maleki repudiated Tudeh's subservience to Moscow and formed a socialist party called the Third Force.

For a while there was the unusual phenomenon of two communist parties in Iran, the Tudeh and the Demokrat, not counting the "Peoples Republic of Kurdestan." In a penetrating article Mr. Ābrāhāmiān describes that these two parties "were separated from each other by

11. Ervand Abrahamian, "Communism and Communalism in Iran," *International Journal of Middle East Studies*, 1, no. 4, p. 311.

contrasting social bases, conflicting interests, and, at times, clashing interests." [12] The leaders of the Tudeh were intellectuals believing in class struggle while the organizers of the Demokrat were activists believing in communalism. The fact remains, however, that both of these parties were manipulated by the Soviet Union for its own ends. In 1946 the Red Army was the only foreign force in Iran. It was effectively protecting the two insurrectionist provinces, and it had another party with members in the Majles to do its bidding. The Soviet Union felt that Iran did not have any other recourse but to comply with its demands.

In January 1946 the Cabinet had changed and, once more, Qavām was the Prime Minister. A week before his appointment on January 19, Iran had formally requested the Security Council of the United Nations to stop the Soviet Union's interference in the internal affairs of Iran. This was the first important case presented to the fledgling organization and all it did was to ask the opposing parties to negotiate and report the result. It was evident that the United Nations could not do very much in a dispute where a strong power was involved. Nevertheless, Iran's case got world publicity and in the early days after the war the Soviet Union was more sensitive to world opinion.

The new Prime Minister went to Moscow in March and in his talks with Stalin he realized the Soviet Union was after oil. He told the Russians that he could not do anything as long as the Red Army was in Iran. He came home empty-handed, but negotiations dragged on both in Tehran and in the Security Council. On April 4, 1946, a draft agreement was signed between Iran and the Soviet Union. According to this the Red Army agreed to evacuate Iran by May 9, and in return Iran agreed to the formation of an Irano-Soviet Oil Company for the exploitation of oil in the northern provinces of Iran. The term was to be for twenty-five years and Iran was to receive 51 percent of the profit.[13] It also recognized the Āzarbāyjān incident to be an internal affair, and Iran promised to solve it peacefully "with due consideration for the legitimate grievances of the people." [14] The Oil Concession, however, to be legal had to be ratified by the Fifteenth Majles, which was yet to be elected.

Qavām instructed Ambassador Hoseyn Alā in Washington to withdraw Iran's case from the Security Council. This able and sincere nationalist, fearing that Qavām had perhaps sold out to the Russians, refused to comply and kept Iran's case on the agenda. This brought upon his head the wrath of the Tudeh and Āzarbāyjān Demokrat parties, who were rejoicing at the success of their cause. Both were at the peak of their power. The Tudeh party was basing its argument on what was later called "positive neutrality"; that is, since Iran had given the oil concession to the British in the south, it should give

12. Ibid., p. 316.
13. Lenczowski, *Russia and the West*, p. 300.
14. Zabih, *Communist Movement*, p. 108.

one to the Russians in the north. Indeed, the Tudeh Party went a step farther and claimed that all of the northern region of Iran was essential to the security of the Soviet Union. This sounded very much like the proletarian version of the old capitalistic "sphere of influence." To this the Tudeh deputy in the Majles had the oft repeated answer: "The Soviet government cannot and will not advocate colonialism, for Russia is a classless society where no exploitation of many by man or by state takes place. Such a society is incapable of pursuing colonial policies. We should know our neighbor better in order to formulate a correct policy towards its government." [15] In a few months he had occasion to know the neighbor better and would find out that a kick in the back does not hurt any less when it was delivered by a worker rather than by a capitalist.

The Qavām government recognized the Āzarbāyjān regime, and on June 13, 1946, signed an agreement to this effect accepting a number of items on their platform.[16] In May the Red Army evacuated Iran and later Qavām formed a coalition Cabinet in which he invited three Tudeh members to participate. Then, in preparation for the election, he formed a new political party called *Iran-e Demokrat*, which turned out to be a coalition of all political parties including the Tudeh. It had an extensive organization and a uniformed "Guard of National Salvation." For good measure, he arrested the anticommunist Seyyed Ziya and disbanded the National Will Party. In December 1946 the Persian Army took possession of Āzarbāyjān and Kurdestan and severely punished the Communist rebels. Pishevari and some of the leaders of the movement escaped to Russia. The Soviet Union, whose declared policy was to help all "national liberation movements" in all parts of the world, betrayed the one which it had helped organize and abandoned the movement for the sake of the oil concession.

The Fifteenth Majles was opened in August 1947. Qavām was still Premier and his party had the majority. He presented the Irano-Soviet Oil Agreement for ratification, and on October 22, 1947, the Majles defeated it with only two dissenting votes. Qavām resigned, his Party was disbanded, and the Tudeh Party was discredited. In the absence of further evidence it is difficult to evaluate the role of Qavām in this affair. It is possible to say that he was clever enough to beat Stalin at his own game and save the province of Āzarbāyjān from becoming part of the Soviet Republic of Āzarbāyjān. It is also possible to think that Qavām did not believe that the oil concession in the north would be detrimental to the interests of Iran and that it would be a cheap price to pay for saving Āzarbāyjān. An Irano-Soviet Fisheries Company had been in operation for some time, and it had not threatened the independence of Iran.

15. Ibid., p. 93.
16. Ibid., p. 110.

World opinion as expressed throughout the debate in the United Nations helped Iran. Also important was the pressure the United States brought to bear on the Soviet Union. The members of the Majles were certainly reassured shortly before voting on the concession when they heard the American Ambassador, George Allen, say that the "American people will support fully their [the Persians'] freedom to make their own choice." The role of His Majesty the Shah was that of a constitutional monarch. He showed determination in refusing to go along with compromise plans in dealing with the Āzarbāyjān problems. He accompanied the army into Āzarbāyjān and received the plaudits of the inhabitants.

IRAN AFTER THE WAR

The solution of the Āzarbāyjān problem saved Iran from dismemberment but did not open the door for reform. The oligarchy and the tribal chiefs, who had been pushed aside by Reza Shah, bounced back to regain their lost prestige and power. They were helped by the clergy and supported by old army officers, and they ruled without regard to the Constitution and the democracy it envisaged. Just as the presence of foreign troops had been an important cause of inflation, their departure brought in its wake economic depression and unemployment. This unemployment was especially acute among the educated, who in their frustration joined radical groups of both right and left.

On the right were the religiously oriented groups which became important factors in the political scene of postwar Iran. One of these was the *Fedā'iyān-e Islam*, 'Devotees of Islam,' under the leadership of a young cleric named Navvāb Safavi. He had been greatly influenced by the methods and organization of the Moslem Brotherhood of Egypt and was in touch with them. Another group was the *Mojāhedin-e Islam*, 'Warriors of Islam,' which was led by the well-known Āyatollah Abol-Qāsem Kāshāni, who later became a member of the Majles and eventually its president. On the right also was an important nonreligious group called the Pan-Iranist Party. They had the reputation of being fascist in their orientation and espoused the extreme radical and nationalistic views.

On the left there was the Tudeh Party, which, even though bruised in the Āzarbāyjān incident and discredited in the defeat of the Soviet Oil Concession, was still strong and active. A splinter group from the Tudeh was the Third Force Party led by Khalil Maleki. This group was Marxist-oriented but it became increasingly anti-Stalinist. Slightly to the left of the center was the Toiler's Party led by Dr. Mozaffar Baqā'i. He was an intellectual deputy in the Majles and non-Marxist in his approach, who vacillated between the left and the center during the oil nationalization crisis. In the center and slightly to the right was the Iran Party, made up of progressive nationalists among the young intellectuals, businessmen, lawyers, doctors, and teachers. Their titular leader was Allāhyār Sāleh, a former minister of finance and member of the Majles.

The position of the Shah, as has been mentioned, was that of a constitutional monarch. It was difficult, however, for the monarch to remain constitutional when practically nothing else was. Having gained experience in the Āzarbāyjān incident, he began to take a more active role in affairs. On February 4, 1949, he went to visit the University of Tehran where a man in the guise of a photographer fired five shots at him at close range. Fortunately the shots only grazed him and he was able to address the nation from the hospital. The would-be assassin was killed, but a search of his room revealed that he had had connections with both the communist party and the extreme Moslem groups. The Tudeh party was outlawed. His Majesty took advantage of this occasion and took steps to make it constitutionally possible for him to be more active in government. One of these steps was to establish the Senate which the constitution had provided for but which had not been implemented. This meant that the throne would appoint half of the members and exert a great influence through them. The second was even more important, namely that the constitution was amended to give the Shah the power to dissolve the Majles and order new elections.

The economic disorganization and the terrific inflation could not be solved by political reorganization alone. Economic measures were necessary. As early as 1946 a study was started by Persian initiative to prepare a development plan for the country. Later they were aided by the American Overseas Consultants. The result was that in 1949 the Majles approved of a Seven-Year Plan for development. It was to cost about $58 million a year. Forty million dollars of this was to come from oil royalties and the rest from other sources.

OIL NATIONALIZATION

The nationalization of oil, which drained the Persians economically and emotionally and revealed the best and the worst in them, must be understood in the context of the time in which it occurred. The vast expansion of the oil industry after the war had made a revision of the Anglo-Iranian Oil Agreement necessary. Furthermore, the success of the Seven-Year Plan depended upon oil royalties. Added to these was the emotional involvement of the Persians in the recent Āzarbāyjān crisis and the defeat of the Irano-Soviet Oil Concession. Lack of sensitivity on the part of the British to the changing situation in Iran contributed to the intensity of the crisis. It was hard for Great Britain to accept its reduced position in the world scene. Sir Winston Churchill, who was not willing to preside over the dissolution of the

British empire, had been ousted from office and a new Labour government had wisely consented to give up India and eventually the rest of the empire. Certainly in Iran Great Britain was losing its grip. In 1948 the second most powerful British economic concern in Iran, namely the Imperial Bank of Iran, had been ended. Its name was changed to the "British Bank of Iran and the Middle East," and it was brought under the jurisdiction of the Persian government. Also the predominant place of Great Britain in Iran was taken by the United States, which had announced the Point Four Program. Great Britain was getting a bad press in Iran, so much so that "a British agreement to indemnify Iran with over £5 million for use of the railways during the war and the gift in July 1949 of two frigates to the Persian navy did not have the effect of reducing anti-British feeling." [17]

The picture will not be complete without mentioning that in the new Majles, which convened in 1950, eight of its members had formed a coalition by the name of the National Front. It was basically a union of the liberal nationalists and the clergy. What appeared to be the common denominator was their goal to uproot the last vestige of economic imperialism, namely the Anglo-Iranian Oil Company. Imperialism to the liberal nationalists meant specifically Russian or British. In their minds the United States and other foreign countries had not been contaminated with the evils of imperialism so far as Iran was concerned. Imperialism, however, to the Shi'i clergy meant all foreign influence and domination. As Āyatollah Kāshāni, the clerical member of the National Front said, "Islam warns its adherents not to submit to foreign yoke." [18] This yoke embodied not only political and economic exploitation but all types of westernization dear to the heart of the liberal nationalists. It was precisely the same goal that had brought the two groups together in 1905 and precisely the same disagreement in interpretation which had pulled them apart. The National Front did disintegrate within two years, but at the moment they were joined together under the leadership of Dr. Mohammad Mosaddeq, a distinguished lawyer and a man who had a reputation for honesty and patriotism.

The story of the nationalization of oil is too long, complicated, and controversial to be related here. It seems that throughout the controversy solutions were advanced always a little too late, with the results that the provisions of the solutions were not considered to be enough. In any case while oil negotiation was in progress, His Majesty the Shah went to the United States in November 1949. Although he made a very good impression across the country, he was not successful in getting any help for the Seven-Year Plan and went home empty-handed.

17. Avery, *Modern Iran*, p. 413.
18. Quoted by R. W. Cottam, *Nationalism in Iran* (Pittsburgh University Press, 1964), p. 152.

The oil negotiation, which had resulted in a tentative agreement called the Supplemental Oil Agreement (also referred to as "Gass-Golshāyān") was not in time for the Fifteenth Majles. The Sixteenth Majles, which after some difficulties came into being, was dominated by the small band of the National Front. The Supplemental Oil Agreement was sent to a committee headed by Mosaddeq for study and recommendation. In the meantime, the Shah, in continuation of his reform policies, appointed the enlightened young General Razmārā as Prime Minister in June 1950. Throughout the rest of that year Razmārā reorganized the administration by replacing officials who were either inept or had a reputation for corruption with younger men. The Soviet Union arranged a $20 million trade agreement with Iran, but the response of the United States was a $25 million loan from the Export-Import Bank. In the light of the fact that Iran had prepared a comprehensive Seven-Year Plan for development which met all the requirements of the Point Four Program, and in the light of the generous aids which the United States was giving to the former Axis countries, this small sum infuriated the Persians.

The National Front members in the Majles began to talk of the nationalization of the oil industry, a concept which had been popularized in those days by the programs of nationalization carried out in Great Britain. Lack of sensitivity on the part of the British and lack of response on the part of the United States led the National Front to say that it was beneath the dignity of the nation to send its king begging when it had all the required money for the Seven-Year Plan in oil revenues. This fell on receptive ears in the Majles and outside. The Oil Committee headed by Mosaddeq rejected the Supplementary Oil Agreement and espoused the principle of "negative neutralism." This was in belated response to the Tudeh Party's "positive neutralism," which argued that since Iran had given an oil concession to Great Britain, it should give one to the Soviet Union. The National Front's "negative neutralism" reasoned that since Iran had refused to give an oil concession to the Soviet Union, it should take it away from Great Britain.

After the rejection of the Supplementary Oil Agreement, negotiation had started again but was not getting anywhere. It was announced in January that the Arabian American Oil Company had offered the Saudi Arabian government a 50-50 profit-sharing plan. The news strengthened the hands of the National Front. By the time the AIOC consented to do as the Americans had done, it was too late. Prime Minister Razmārā, who had expressed himself against the practicality of nationalization, was assassinated in the Sepahsālār Mosque by a member of the Devotees of Islam. It was reported that the murderer, Khalil Tahmāsebi, was encouraged in the act by a religious *fatva*, issued by Kāshāni. The assassin stated, "If I have rendered a humble service, it was for the Almighty in order to deliver the deprived Moslem people of Iran from foreign serfdom. My only desire is to follow the doctrine of the Koran." The fact that the Majles voted to exonerate the assassin gives credence to the involvement of Kāshāni in the affair.[19]

On March 15, 1951, a week after the murder of Razmārā, the Majles passed a nine-point enabling law nationalizing the oil industry. Hoseyn Alā, who was in charge of the government after the assassination, supported nationalization and replied to the protest of Great Britain that this was an internal matter and that the British government had no right to interfere. Events occurred swiftly from then on. On April 15 the British closed the Abadan oil refinery and on April 28, Mosaddeq became Prime Minister. There was wild enthusiasm in Iran, consternation in England, and disbelief in the rest of the world. There were charges and countercharges. From the British point of view Iran did not have the right to act unilaterally, while the Persians felt that the principle of nationalization superseded any prior agreement. The British accepted the principle of nationalization but felt that the appropriation of the company was against the 1933 agreement. The Persians, on the other hand, said that since they had provided in the nine-point law the payment of compensation to the company, the question of appropriation was not involved. They had done to the oil company what the British government had done to the steel industry in Great Britain. Perhaps the most important question was Iran's contention that this was an internal affair between the Persian government and a company and not the business of the British government to interfere.

The case was taken to the United Nations by Great Britain and Dr. Mosaddeq went to New York to present Iran's case. The Security Council referred the question to the World Court and the Court decided in favor of Iran, stating that the problem was an internal question and outside the jurisdiction of the World Court or of the United Nations.

This, however, did not solve the problem. Several alternative proposals were advanced and even though all of them accepted the principle of nationalization, they failed to bring about a solution. Great Britain overreacted and, for a time, forgot that this was not the nineteenth century. Neither they nor the other Western countries understood the depth of the feelings of the population in this matter. The Persians had an opportunity to show their support in the tobacco protest of 1890, the constitutional movement of 1905, the crisis of the dismissal of Morgan Shuster in 1911, the change of dynasty in 1924, and the oil nationalization of 1951. Without doubt the popular support for nationalization was broader and deeper than any of the rest. The British reaction was gunboat diplomacy when they sent the cruiser

19. Ibid., p. 150 ff.

Mauritius to the Persian Gulf, when they froze Persian assets, when they seized a few tankers taking Persian oil, and when they persuaded the United States to withhold aid to Iran. Furthermore, Great Britain looked at the company as a purely business venture. In all the plans that they submitted, they not only wanted compensation for the assets of the company, which the Persians acknowledged, but they wanted payment for all the profits they would have made until 1993. Also the British sincerely felt that they had done the Persians a great service by developing the oil industry and did not understand why the Persians were not appreciative. The fact that their huge profits in some years reached 150 percent did not matter. What was important in their minds was that the Persians would not have had any oil income at all were it not for the British effort.

On the other hand the Persians could not forget that they were refused the inspection of the company books; that the company was not replacing foreign technicians with Persians fast enough; and that the company was not willing to give them a larger share of the profits. But what made the reaching of any solution difficult was the fact that Dr. Mosaddeq and his advisors looked at the nationalization of oil with romantic nationalism mixed with a great deal of naivete. He apparently felt that all he had to do was to nationalize the oil and customers would flock to buy the Persian oil. The fact that Iran did not have a single oil tanker did not bother him. He should have known that the European countries who were buying Persian oil would tap the vast oil resources of Kuwait and Saudi Arabia. He was too much of a romanticist to think that the Arab countries would refuse to help a brother Moslem nation against the Christians of the West. Egypt gave Dr. Mosaddeq a rousing welcome when he stopped there on his return from the United Nations, but Egypt had no oil. An excellent description of the oil industry in the world was prepared for Dr. Mosaddeq and he was shown several charts explaining the interrelatedness of the large oil companies of Europe and the United States and the control they exercised on shipping and marketing.[20] Even if Great Britain had not challenged nationalization, Iran had to depend upon the major companies to market the oil.

At the base of Dr. Mosaddeq's inability or unwillingness to reach an agreement were at least two factors. The first was his personal hatred of the British, which he allowed to cloud his judgment. Among all the proposals made, perhaps the plan presented by the World Bank was the best. It adhered to all the points of the nationalization law but Mosaddeq rejected it because the World Bank, as a neutral world organization, wanted the freedom to employ British personnel in its operations.

20. This writer has seen the special study prepared for Dr. Mosaddeq and has examined the charts.

The other factor was the fact that Dr. Mosaddeq was not a revolutionary. To him the nationalization of the oil industry was an end and not just the means to carry on reforms. He was reluctant to inaugurate internal reforms for fear of offending the other members of the coalition. Professor Cottam believes that the great mistake of Mosaddeq was that he did not comprehend "that the immensity of his popular support gave him a freedom of action that no Iranian statesman had ever enjoyed." [21] Nevertheless, Dr. Mosaddeq's name will go down in history as the charismatic leader who, in spite of the fact that he did not offer a constructive program, moved the Persians to the depth. During the two years of Mosaddeq's regime, the Persians were cooperative, their officials were less corrupt, and they took more interest in the affairs of the nation because they believed a new day had dawned.

As the crisis dragged on, the internal situation worsened, and disagreement developed among the members of the National Front. The election of the Seventeenth Majles was freer than many an election held before, and therein lay Mosaddeq's difficulty. The members refused to go along with him. He demanded more power and as more and more of his friends left him he had to rely upon the underground Tudeh Party for support. His communication with the Shah, which was none too good, broke altogether. On August 13, 1953 the Shah dismissed Mosaddeq and appointed General Fazlollah Zāhedi, but Mosaddeq arrested the officer who had brought the message. Three days later the Shah and the Empress left Iran. For three days Tehran was in the hands of the mob whom Mosaddeq could not control. The Tudeh Party came into the open breaking the statues of the Shah and his father. It is probable that the Tudeh could have taken control of the city, but perhaps they did not receive promise of support from the Soviet Union, which had its own leadership crisis. In any case, by August 19 the tide had changed. General Zāhedi's soldiers arrested Mosaddeq. He was later tried for treason and convicted, but his sentence was commuted on the request of the Shah. On August 22, His Majesty returned to Tehran and Prime Minister Zāhedi and a large crowd were there to welcome him.

It has been alleged that the American Central Intelligence Agency helped engineer the downfall of Mosaddeq with planning and money.[22] His Majesty the Shah also tacitly admits such a possibility when he writes, "I do not deny that payments could in some cases conceivably have been made. . . . But . . . it takes much more than money to impel people to do what Iran's loyal citizens did during those days." [23] The fact that almost immediately President Eisenhower put $25 mil-

21. Cottam, *Nationalism in Iran*, p. 270.

22. For a detailed account see David Wise and Thomas Ross, *The Invisible Government* (New York: Random House, 1964), pp. 110–14.

23. *Mission for My Country*, p. 106.

lion at the disposal of the penniless government, an aid he had refused
to Mosaddeq, shows that the United States was pleased at the latter's
fall.

The Shah returned to Tehran with a new resolve. For twelve years
he had reigned; now he wanted to rule. From that time on the political,
economic, social, educational, and cultural life of Iran have been
closely connected with the person of the Shah. Iran faced grave problems. One of them was economic, the other was international; but the
most important of them was the alienation of the educated youth.

Economic Recovery

One of the most important steps for the economic recovery was
the solution of the oil controversy. Agreement was reached and passed
by the Majles on October 21, 1954. The agreement is long and complex.
In brief it accepted the principle of nationalization and recognized the
National Iranian Oil Company. A consortium was formed to operate
the oil fields and the refinery in Abadan. There were eight companies
in the consortium. The Anglo-Iranian Oil Company, whose name was
changed to British Petroleum, held 40 percent of the shares; five major
American companies held 35 percent while nine minor American companies held 5 percent; the Dutch Bataafse Petroleum Maatschappij
N.V. held 14 percent; and the Compagnie Française des Petroles held
the remaining 6 percent. The consortium was incorporated in the
Netherlands but its permanent headquarters were in Iran. The President of the consortium was Dutch.

It was arranged that Iran pay the former AIOC the sum of $25
million in ten years without interest. In addition, the other members
of the consortium agreed to pay the British company 10 percent per
barrel of crude oil and other products exported from Iran until $510
million had been paid. The British company did not lose much, but
for the Persians the agreement was not as good as some of the plans
Dr. Mosaddeq had rejected. Under the circumstances, however, it
was the best possible. In later years the National Iranian Oil Company
made separate arrangements with other companies; it has discovered
oil in central Iran and has become a well-organized economic institution.

The second means of economic recovery was planning. The first
Seven-Year Plan was a complete failure, mostly because of the oil
crisis. A second Seven-Year Plan was started in September 1955.
As part of the plan, an economic bureau was formed made up of
well-trained Persians supported by foreign advisors. Its job was to
study the program of the plan organization and make recommenda-
tions.

The plan organization has had its problems. According to Mr.
George Baldwin, "At present there is no solution that will make plan-

ning work. The only solution. . . is for people to adjust downward their expectations of tidiness, rationality, and efficiency and to hope that the spending of the oil revenues will somehow produce a more effective use of less abundant resources." [24] The economic planning has also had its successes during the past fifteen years. The success has been due to the growth of a class of industrial entrepreneurs, a modern banking system, encounter with the West, and the government.[25] The Second and Third Seven-Year Programs have come to an end and the country is now in 1972 in the Fourth and preparing for the Fifth. The objective of the planning has become comprehensive and includes all aspects of the economy, including the private sector. The fact that the oil revenue is there to enable the Planning Organization to experiment is, in the long run, beneficial. Without doubt, the program which in 1963 became known as the White Revolution would not have been possible without the work and accomplishments of the plan organization.[26]

A third means of economic recovery was the Point Four Program which was first mentioned in President Truman's inaugural address on January 20, 1949, and implemented in Iran in 1952. Iran has received more aid than any country in Africa or the Middle East except Turkey. It has also been the largest in size. From 1952 to 1962 the United States had between 200 and 300 technical personnel each year in Iran and the United Nations had an additional 100 to 150.[27] This program has been praised and criticized most emphatically by experts in the field. In going over Dr. Jahāngir Āmuzegār's excellent study on this subject,[28] it would seem that both views are true. Considering the vast expenditures of money and manpower, Iran should have benefited more than it has.

Unfortunately Point Four coincided with the period of the Cold War in which military and strategic considerations outweighed the economic and social ones. Furthermore, due perhaps to the peculiar practices of the United States Congress, only annual appropriations were made and these "were not compatible with long-range planning. Putting too many resources in too many projects in too short a time not only resulted in a good deal of waste and inefficiency but also damaged the chance of a steady and gradual assimilation of the project." [29]

On the Persian side the idea of Point Four was not understood

24. George Baldwin, *Planning and Development in Iran* (Baltimore: Johns Hopkins Press, 1967), p. 52.
25. Ibid., p. 195.
26. For this particular study I am indebted to the honors paper prepared by my former student Gholam Vatandoust from Macalester College.
27. Baldwin, *Planning and Development*, p. 201.
28. *Technical Assistance in Theory and Practice, The Case of Iran* (New York: Praeger, 1966).
29. Ibid., p. 254.

and the "host officials were not compelled to coordinate their thinking and actions with that philosophy or in that direction." [30] Nevertheless, the Point Four Program benefited the government of Iran in meeting its exchange needs; the farmers in the improvement of seeds, poultry, and livestocks; the students who were able to study abroad; landlords in the improvement of their holdings; a variety of professional and skilled Persians who found employment; and the private industrialists who were able to receive technical guidance.[31]

IRAN AND THE WORLD

From 1953 to 1970 the international attitude of Iran has gone full circle from a form of neutralism to partisanship and back to neutralism. The important difference was that the early quiescent neutralism had given way to a more active and creative one. In the Anglo-Russian rivalry, Iran was mostly passive. It either gave to Russia what had been given to Great Britain or withheld from Great Britain what had been withheld from Russia. About the boldest concept up to 1953 was a search for a third power to neutralize the two rival powers and, hopefully, set Iran free.

The policies of search for a third power and quiescent neutralism were abandoned after 1953. The reasons were the impracticality of the former policies, the demands of internal security, and the aggressive initiative taken by the United States.[32] In 1955 Iran became a member of the Baghdad Pact and, for the first time, joined the "Western Bloc" in the polarization that had developed in the Cold War. There was already a NATO in which Turkey was a member and a SEATO where Pakistan was a member. The Baghdad Pact included both Turkey and Pakistan plus Iran, Iraq, and Great Britain. In the beginning the pact was not popular in Iran partly because Great Britain was in it, whose membership is still an enigma; partly because the United States was not included, a factor which weighed heavily with third-power enthusiasts in Iran; and also because there was fear that such a pact would bring down the wrath of the Soviet Union upon Iran. It did, but no more than in radio broadcasts. Indeed, the Shah and the Empress paid a state visit to the Soviet Union in 1956 and the relations were very correct and cordial. With the demise of the Iraqi kingdom in 1958, the pact was named CENTO and, reacting to the international situation, its activities have become less military defense and more economic and social cooperation.

The Persian government went a step farther in alignment with the

30. Ibid., p. 121.
31. Ibid., p. 21–22.
32. A very useful study on this subject is the article by Sepehr Zabih, "Iran's International Posture: De Facto Nonalignment Within a Pro-Western Alliance," *Middle East Journal* (Summer, 1970), Vol. 24, no. 3, pp. 302–18.

West by concluding a bilateral military agreement with the United States. This alarmed the Soviet Union and it threatened to invoke Articles Five and Six of the 1921 treaty, which provided for the entry of Russian troops in Iran if the latter was used as a base of operation against the Soviet Union. In the long negotiation on this subject nothing was changed. Nevertheless, Iran has won the ability of independent action without regard to the particular interpretation of the 1921 treaty by the Soviet Union. There was a great deal of resentment on the part of the Soviet Union; by 1965 they were willing to have extensive commercial relations with Iran without insisting that it give up its pro-Western alignment.[33]

The relation between Iran and the Arab countries remains fluid. The problems are the Irano-Iraqi border dispute on the Shatt al-Arab River, the defense of the Persian Gulf, and relation with Israel. The border dispute with Iraq has been discussed before,[34] and the present dispute is in essence the same, except that it is aggravated by the problem of security in the Persian Gulf. The announcement of British withdrawal from the Gulf in 1971 has raised the problem of security in the area. Iran, which is the strongest state on the Persian Gulf, stated its preference for a regional defense plan comprising all the Gulf states. Since Iran claimed jurisdiction over Bahreyn, it would not attend a meeting of the Persian Gulf states in which Bahreyn was present. The problem of Bahreyn has been on the agenda of Iran's foreign policy for years. Very wisely the Shah declared that the future of the island should be decided by its inhabitants and accepted, in advance, the decision of a United Nations' team of inquiry. In May 1970 the United Nations' team reported that the majority of the people of Bahreyn preferred to be independent.[35]

Apparently the way is clear for some sort of a regional defense plan, but the larger question of the Persian Gulf is not settled. In recent years the Arab countries have been referring to the Persian Gulf as the "Arabian Gulf" and Iraq has claimed jurisdiction over Khuzestan and a good deal of the coastline north of the Persian Gulf. Iran, quite understandably, is apprehensive that if the Arab countries ever get united, such claims will pose difficulties. Since the only other state in the area that is threatened by any show of a united Arab strength is Israel, it is quite natural that Iran and Israel should have a close relationship.[36] At the same time, however, both Iran and Turkey are apprehensive lest Israel's policy of possession through conquest become fashionable—hence their insistence that Israel evacuate the territory won in the 1967 war.

33. See above, p. 135.
34. See above, pp. 148–49.
35. For the full text of the report see *Middle East Journal* (Summer, 1970), Vol. 24, no. 3, pp. 373–80.
36. Bayne, *Persian Kingship*, p. 212.

The White Revolution

With the fall of Mosaddeq, his followers were pushed underground but were not subdued. They held demonstrations, published clandestine literature, and carried on strikes in colleges and high schools. It was soon discovered that a large number of young army officers had been influenced by the Tudeh Party. These were symptoms of a basic alienation that the educated youth felt toward the established authority of their country. There was practically no communication between the Shah and these people, some of whom belonged to the Tudeh and some to the National Front. Most of them, however, did not belong to any organized group. They had simply lost their confidence in their own government.

Without the cooperation and participation of the bulk of these talented young individuals any forward movement was extremely difficult. The only way the Shah could enlist their allegiance was to show that his program of reform included all that they had been clamoring for. He felt that there was a difference between those who were alienated and those who were consciously subversive. To uproot the subversives and also to protect the government from problems arising from the Cold War, he sought the assistance of a retired captain of the Chicago police and with the cooperation of the C.I.A. established SAVAK in 1957. This organization combines characteristics and functions of the American C.I.A. and the F.B.I.[37]

The SAVAK of Iran proved no better in separating the subversive from the alienated than similar institutions have done in any other country in the world. To the security police everyone is a suspect, and as far as they are concerned there is not much difference between the concerned patriot, the alienated, and the actively subversive. Consequently, to quote a Persian saying, "the wet and dry burned together"— many suffered and a few were permanently alienated.

In the meantime, however, the Shah started his program of reform among the peasants, who were in the majority and who were willing to listen. Not only were the bulk of the efforts of the Seven-Year Plans and the Point Four Program directed toward agriculture, but the Shah started the distribution of his lands which had been halted by Mosaddeq. By 1961 he had become a popular figure among the peasants and had attracted enough of the National Front and some of the Tudeh to his side to send a bill to the Majles limiting the amount of land a person could own and distributing the rest. The Majles, which was made up of landlords, attached so many amendments to it as to make it meaningless. On May 6, 1961, His Majesty dissolved the Majles and,

---

37. For a detailed discussion of SAVAK, see Bayne, *Persian Kingship*, pp. 179–84.

in effect, suspended the constitution by not calling for an election. Under the leadership of Dr. Ali Amini, a new liberal cabinet was formed in which there were a few with leftist tendencies. The man of the hour, however, was the able Dr. Hasan Arsanjāni, who, as Minister of Agriculture, carried out the land distribution program in a systematic way.

The Shah had virtually become the leader of a peasant revolution. In January 1963 on the occasion of the opening of a conference on rural cooperatives, he announced a six-point program of reform which became known as the "White Revolution." These points, to which others were added later, were: distribution of land, abolition of share-cropping, nationalization of forests, a uniform profit-sharing plan for factory workers, revised electoral laws, a massive rural literacy program, formation of health corps, creation of extension and developmental corps, enfranchisement of women, and the establishment of houses of equity for the rural areas. Not only are most of these points new in Iran and revolutionary, but—significantly—ever since 1963 the whole activity of the nation has been directed at the implementation of one or the other of these programs.

There are still many problems in Iran, and one can safely say that new ones are being created. In a country as old as Iran and burdened with centuries of relevant and obsolete traditions, no one person can reform a nation. If the long history of Iran teaches anything at all, it teaches that only when the Persians have been free from repression have their genius, ability, and imagination taken wings and flown to great heights.

Suggested Readings

Anyone who wishes to study the history and culture of Iran would do well to consult L. P. Elwell-Sutton, *A Guide to Iranian Area Study* (Ann Arbor: J. W. Edwards, 1952). It has an annotated bibliography with historical and topical introductions. The quarterly magazines *The Middle East Journal* (Washington, D.C.) and *International Journal of Middle East Studies* (Cambridge, England) carry occasional scholarly articles on Iran. The former especially is useful in that it has a chronology of recent events in all of the countries of the Middle East. A very important quarterly for those interested in Iran is *Iranian Studies,* Journal of The Society for Iranian Studies (New York: Box 89 Village Station), which publishes more articles on Iran than the above two put together.

Unfortunately, there is only one book that deals with the history of Iran from ancient beginnings to the present. Sir Percy Sykes, *A History of Persia,* 2 vols. (London: Macmillan & Co. Ltd.), first appeared in 1915 and was reprinted in 1951. It is rather old but it is the only one. There are several small volumes of introductions to Iran, all written after the Second World War. Two of these are especially useful. William S. Haas, *Iran* (New York: Columbia University Press, 1946), is good in describing the nature of the Persians and their culture. Donald Wilber, *Iran: Past and Present,* 6th ed. (Princeton: Princeton University Press, 1967), has one of the best abridgments of Persian history, plus a more up-to-date account of Persian institutions.

Works on pre-Islamic Iran are numerous. The three general accounts mentioned here are not only by distinguished authorities, but they are available in paperback. In order of their publication they are: R. Ghirshman, *Iran* (Baltimore: Penguin Books, Inc., 1954) is based on the author's archeological findings; A. T. Olmstead, *History of the Persian Empire* (Chicago: University of Chicago Press, 1960) deals only with the Achaemenid Empire; Richard N. Frye, *The Heritage of Persia* (New York: New American Library, Mentor Books, 1963) is an able interpretation of Persian pre-Islamic history and culture. On Zoroastrianism, the religion of ancient Iran, one of the best is A. V. Williams Jackson, *Zoroaster, the Prophet of Ancient Iran* (New York: The Macmillan Company, 1899). A fuller and more up-to-date account is by Ernst E. Herzfeld, *Zoroaster and His World*, 2 vols. (Princeton: Princeton University Press, 1947). Jacques Duchesne-Guillemin, *The Hymns of Zoroaster* (Boston: Beacon Press, 1963) is a good translation and should prove profitable.

Those who wish more specialized archeological accounts, replete with excellent illustrations, are advised to look into William Culican, *The Medes and Persians* (New York: Praeger Publishers, Inc., 1965); Jean-Louis Huot, *Persia I* (New York: World Publishing Company, 1965), translated from the French; and Vladimir G. Lukonin, *Persia II* (New York: World Publishing Company, 1967), translated from the Russian. Those who are interested in the latest scholarly work on Persepolis may read Donald Wilber, *Persepolis, the Archeology of Parsa, Seat of the Persian Kings* (New York: Thomas Corvell, 1969). Also of great value is *The Legacy of Persia*, edited by A. J. Arberry (London: Oxford University Press, 1953), which is one of the best sources for the contributions of Persian civilization to the world. What promises to be a most valuable work on Iran is *The Cambridge History of Iran*, projected in eight volumes. Judging by the two that have been published, each volume is a compilation of essays written by specialists on the subject. The two volumes published so far are Volume I, W. B. Fisher, ed., *Land of Iran* (Cambridge: Cambridge University Press, 1968) and Volume V, J. A. Boyle, ed., *The Saljuq and Mongol Periods* (Cambridge: Cambridge University Press, 1968).

Coming to the early Islamic period we find that there are no books on Iran alone. Usually Iran is dealt with as part of Islamic history and, unfortunately, more often than not as an appendage to Arab or even to Ottoman history. The two exceptions, which give an account of Iran in the context of Middle East history, are Carl Brockelmann, *History of the Islamic Peoples* (New York: G. P. Putnam's Sons, Capricorn Books, 1960), and Yahya Armajani, *Middle East Past and Present* (Englewood Cliffs, N.J.: Prentice-Hall, Inc., 1970). There are useful books, however, that describe different aspects of Islam necessary for the understanding of Iran. Among these the following may be mentioned: Gustave E. von Grunebaum, ed., *Unity and Variety in Muslim Civilization* (Chicago: University of Chicago Press, 1955), E. I. J. Rosenthal, *Islam in the Modern National State* (Cambridge: Cambridge University Press, 1965), and J. J. Saunders, *A History of Medieval Islam* (London: Routledge and Kegan Paul, 1965). These deal with subjects in Islam that are applicable to the situation in Iran. Inasmuch as the majority of the Persians are Shi'is, D. M. Donaldson, *The Shi'ite Re-*

ligion (London: Luzac, 1933) is very good even though it is rather old. For a more recent but much shorter account of the subject one may consult Mahmood Shehabi, "Shi'a," in Kenneth W. Morgan, *Islam—The Straight Path* (New York: The Ronald Press Company, 1958). Seyyed Hossein Nasr, *Ideals and Realities of Islam* (New York: Praeger Publishers, Inc., 1967) discusses the subject from a Shi'i point of view. By the same author is the succinct essay on "Ithna 'Ashari Shi'ism and Iranian Islam," in A. J. Arberry, ed., *Religion in the Middle East*, Vol. 2 (Cambridge: Cambridge University Press, 1969). The reading of Cyprian Rice, O.P., *The Persian Sufis* (London: George Allen and Unwin Ltd., 1964) should prove useful for an understanding of a good deal of Persian mystic poetry. The whole issue of *Iranian Studies*, Vol. 2, Nos. 3 and 4 (New York: Box 89, Village Station), is devoted to "Persian Sufism in Its Historical Perspective," by A. H. Zarrinkoob. It is probably the best treatment of the subject in English.

Not much has been written in recent years on the post-Mongol period of Iran. Guy Le Strange, *The Lands of the Eastern Caliphate, Mesopotamia and Persia and Central Asia from the Muslim Conquest to the Time of Timur* (Cambridge: Cambridge University Press, 1930) is still useful. Ahmad Ibn-Arabshah, *Timur the Great Amir*, translated by J. H. Saunders (London: Routledge and Sons, 1938) is very good on Tamerlane. Laurence Lockhart, *Nadir Shah* (London: Luzac, 1938) gives the contemporary account of the interesting and resourceful general. By the same author is *The Fall of the Safavi Dynasty and the Afghan Occupation of Persia* (Cambridge: Cambridge University Press, 1958). Perhaps it should be mentioned here that a student of history would do well to consult *Islamic Dynasties*, by C. E. Bosworth (Edinburg: Edinburg University Press, 1967). This is No. 5 in the *Islamic Surveys* and has chronological tables of all Islamic dynasties, including Persian, up to the twentieth century, with a short introduction on the origins of each.

Much more has been written on the culture of Iran. The best on the subject and available only in libraries are the six large volumes by Arthur Upham Pope, *A Survey of Persian Art from Prehistoric Times to the Present* (London: Oxford University Press, 1939). More recent studies and also more readily obtainable are Basil Gray, *Persian Painting* (London: B. T. Batsford, 1947), and B. W. Robinson, *Persian Miniatures* (New York: Citadel Press, Inc., n.d.). On Persian literature, E. G. Browne, *A Literary History of Persia*, 4 vols. (Cambridge: Cambridge University Press, 1902–1924 and reprinted in 1964) is still unsurpassed. A shorter and more recent work on the subject is A. J. Arberry, *Classical Persian Literature* (London: George Allen and Unwin Ltd., 1958) is highly recommended. Lovers of Hāfez and Sa'di will enjoy reading A. J. Arberry, *Hāfiz, Fifty Poems* (Cambridge: Cambridge University Press, 1962), and Edward Rehatzek, *The Gulistan or Rose Garden of Sa'di* (New York: G. P. Putnam's Sons, Capricorn Books, 1964). Many good translations from Persian literature are found in James Kritzeck, ed., *Anthology of Islamic Literature* (New York: Holt, Rinehart & Winston, Inc., 1964). For a brief survey of modern and contemporary Persian literature, see H. Kamshad, *Modern Persian Prose Litera-ture* (Cambridge: Cambridge University Press, 1966). A. J. Arberry, *Aspects of Islamic Civilization* (Ann Arbor: University of Michigan Press, Ann Arbor Books, 1967) deals with the Moslem world depicted through its liter-ature and contains much that is Persian. There are four volumes that de-scribe aspects of Persian culture other than art and literature: Laurence Lockhart, *Persian Cities* (London: Luzac, 1960); A. J. Arberry, *Shiraz, Per-sian City of Saints and Poets* (Norman: University of Oklahoma Press, 1960); Hans E. Wulff, *The Traditional Crafts of Persia, Their Develop-ment, Technology and Influence on Eastern and Western Civilization* (Cam-bridge, Mass.: The M.I.T. Press, 1966); and G. Griffin Lewis, *The Practical Book of Oriental Rugs,* 5th ed. (Philadelphia: J. B. Lippincott Co., 1920).

An increasing number of books are being written on modern Iran. A classic on nineteenth-century British imperialism in Iran is George Curzon, *Persia and the Persian Question,* 2 vols., first published in 1892 and re-printed by Frank Cass, London, 1966. To see why Iran held such an impor-tant place in British diplomacy, see R. L. Greaves, *Persia and the Defense of India* (London: The Athlone Press, 1959). For a general survey of the diplomatic history of Iran, Rouhollah K. Ramazani, *The Foreign Policy of Iran, 1500–1941* (Charlottesville: The University Press of Virginia, 1966) is very useful. Both Russian and British imperialism are described in a scholarly volume by Firuz Kazemzadeh in *Russia and Britain in Persia, 1864–1914* (New Haven: Yale University Press, 1968). Professor Nikkie Keddie has two small volumes that shed light on the period of imperialism. One of them is *Religion and Rebellion in Iran (Tobacco Protest of 1891–1892)* (London: Frank Cass, 1966), which describes a successful rank-and-file protest, aided by the Shi'a clergy, against the policy of the Shah. The other is *An Islamic Response to Imperialism (Political and Religious Writ-ings of Sayyid Jamal al-Din al-Afghani)* (Berkeley: University of California Press, 1968), which is a forerunner of a more detailed work on the very in-teresting and important pan-Islamic political thinker. A very important work on the religious situation of nineteenth-century Iran is by Hamid Algar, *Re-ligion and State in Iran, 1785–1906: The Role of the Ulama in the Qajar Period* (Berkeley: University of California Press, 1969). For a survey of eco-nomic problems, the latest book is by Charles Issawi, *The Economic History of Iran, 1800–1914* (Chicago: University of Chicago Press, 1971).

Coming to twentieth-century Iran, two volumes are important. One is E. G. Browne, *The Persian Revolution, 1905–1909,* which was published in 1910 and reprinted by Frank Cass, London, in 1966. In the absence of any other volume on the Revolution, this is essential and will always be a good source material. The other one is *The Strangling of Persia,* by Morgan Shuster (New York: Century House, Inc., 1912), which is an excellent and exciting account of the experiences of the first American financial adviser to Iran and the Anglo-Russian machination that ousted him. Just to show that Russia and Great Britain were not the only European countries interested in Iran during the first decades of the twentieth century, you may read the very engaging account of the German intelligence agent in the First World War, *Wassmuss*, by Christopher Sykes (New York: Longmans, 1936). For a history of modern Iran there are two volumes that bridge the nineteenth and the twentieth centuries and pre- and post-revolutionary Iran. One is a well-written small volume by Joseph M. Upton, *The History of Modern Iran, an Interpretation* (Cambridge: Harvard University Press, 1961). The other volume, by Peter Avery, *Modern Iran* (New York: Praeger Publishers, Inc., 1965), is a detailed history of modern Iran written for the general public, with a good deal of understandable and sometimes exaggerated British nationalism.

Those interested in the diplomatic accounts of special periods are referred to Nasrollah Saifpur Fatemi, *Diplomatic History of Persia, 1917–23* (New York: Russell Moore, 1952); and George Lenczowski, *Russia and the West in Iran, 1919–1948* (Ithaca: Cornell University Press, 1949). The former uses a good many Persian sources, while the latter uses Russian.

There are a number of well written books that deal with specific subjects in modern Iran. Richard Cottam, *Nationalism in Iran* (Pittsburgh: Pittsburgh University Press, 1964), and Leonard Binder, *Iran: Political Development in a Changing Society* (Berkeley: University of California Press, 1962) deal with much the same subject during the same period. Though both show great insight, they should be read with caution, for it is difficult to write about the deep feelings of a people after a short visit. A. Reza Arasteh, *Man and Society in Iran*, second edition (Leiden: Brill, 1970), is about the only one on the subject in English. For a very interesting description of life and customs among contemporary Persian tribes, read Vincent Cronin, *The Last Migration* (New York: E. P. Dutton & Co., Inc., 1957). Sepehr Zabih, *The Communist Movement in Iran* (Berkeley: University of California Press, 1966) is also the only volume on the subject and a good one. On the important topic of development, technical and otherwise, there are at least four useful volumes. Jahangir Amuzegar, *Technical Assistance in Theory and Practice* (New York: Praeger Publishers, Inc., 1966) deals exclusively with the American Point Four Program in Iran. George B. Baldwin, *Planning and Development in Iran* (Baltimore: The Johns Hopkins Press, 1967) is an excellent appraisal of the subject, while Paul W. English, *City and Village in Iran* (Madison: University of Wisconsin Press, 1966), specifically deals with settlement and economy in the Kerman region. Norman Jacobs, *The Sociology of Development, Iran as an Asian Case Study* (New York: Praeger Publishers, Inc., 1967) is quite provocative, but there are those who question his application of specific theories to Iran. On the important question of agriculture and land reform, the two volumes by A. K. S. Lambton are absolutely essential. *Landlord and Peasant in Persia* (London: Oxford University Press, 1953) describes the historical foundation of the relationship, and *The Persian Land Reform* (London: Oxford University Press, 1969) is an authoritative account of the results of the recent distribution of land in Iran. Another very important special subject related to Iran is oil. There are several volumes available. Benjamin Shwadran, *The Middle*

East Oil and the Great Powers (New York: Council for Middle Eastern Affairs, 1959) gives the historical background. George Lenczowski, *Oil and State in the Middle East* (Ithaca: Cornell University Press, 1960) deals with the legal and economic aspects of the relations between the oil-producing countries and the oil companies. L. P. Elwell-Sutton, *Persian Oil: A Study in Power Politics* (London: Lawrence and Wishart, 1955) gives the account of the controversial oil nationalization as objectively as is possible. Norman Kemp, *Abadan* (London: Allan Wingate, 1953) is a first-hand account of the Persian oil crisis by an Englishman.

Inasmuch as the defense of the Persian Gulf might become an important issue in the near future, *The Persian Gulf*, by Sir Arnold T. Wilson (London: Oxford University Press, 1928), provides a good background. A more recent publication is by Sir Rupert Hay, *The Persian Gulf States* (Washington: The Middle East Institute, 1959).

Unfortunately, there is no biography of Reza Shah for a study of recent and contemporary Iran. Arthur C. Millspaugh, *The American Task in Persia* (New York: Century House, Inc., 1925) is the account of the second American financial adviser, which gives insight into the life of Reza Shah before he ascended the throne. L. P. Elwell-Sutton, *Modern Iran* (London: Routledge and Sons, 1941) is a general account of Iran during Reza Shah's period; while Amin Banani, *Modernization of Iran* (Stanford: Stanford University Press, 1961) is an able interpretation of the rule of Reza Shah by a Persian historian. No study of contemporary Iran will be complete without the reading of *My Mission for My Country*, by H.I.M. Mohammad Reza Shah Pahlavi (New York: McGraw-Hill Book Company, 1961), and E. A. Bayne, *Persian Kingship in Transition* (New York: American Universities Field Staff, 1968). Both of these give insight into the thoughts of the man who guides the destiny of Iran. The latter is an account of the recorded conversation between the Shah and the author. For a behavioral study of modern Iran you may consult Marvin Zonis, *The Political Elite of Iran* (Princeton: Princeton University Press, 1971).

There are so many travel books on Iran that the listing of them would fill pages. Almost any one of them will provide useful reading. *The Travels of Marco Polo* (London: Routledge, 1931), with an introduction by the eminent Iranologist Sir Denison Ross, is always interesting. The Hakluyt Society Series has at least two travel accounts of great interest to the student of Iran. One is *Narrative of the Embassy of Ruy Gonzalez De Clavijo to the Court of Timour at Samarcand, A.D. 1403–06* (New York: Burt Franklin) no. 26. This not only gives an insight into the character of the great conqueror but also describes the life and mores of the people of Iran. The other one, from the seventeenth century, is by Anthony Jenkinson, *Early Voyages and Travels to Russia and Persia*, 2 vols., nos. 72 and 73 (New York: Burt Franklin). This is the account of the first British attempt to establish trade with Iran, at the time of Shah Tahmasp, the second Safavid king. Coming to more recent times, E. G. Browne, *A Year Amongst the Persians, 1887–1888* (Cambridge: Cambridge University Press, 1896; reprinted 1966), is a delightful account by the eminent Iranologist. A. V. Williams Jackson, *Persia Past and Present* (New York: The Macmillan Company, 1906) is a scholarly account of the travels of the American historian who was interested in pre-Islamic Iran. Henry Filmer, *The Pageant of Persia* (London: Kegan Paul, 1937) is a popularly written account of history and travel. The most modern and also informative travel book on Iran is *Strange Lands and Friendly People* (New York: Harper & Row, Publishers, 1951) by the American Justice of the Supreme Court, William O. Douglas.

There are a number of very interesting and informative historical novels on Iran. The prolific writer on the Middle East, Harold Lamb, is the author of three of them. *Cyrus the Great* (New York: Doubleday & Company, Inc., 1960) is a historical novel about the founder of the Persian empire. *Genghiz Khan* (New York: McBride, 1927) and *Tamerlane* (New York: McBride, 1928) depict two different periods of Persian history. He has written a fourth book, on *Omar Khayyam* (New York: Doubleday & Company, Inc., 1934), for those who are interested. Another historical novel, *The Carmelite*, by Elgin Groseclose (New York: The Macmillan Company, 1955), is based on the times of Shah Abbās the Great. The same author has written another novel, *The Persian Journey of the Rev. Ashley Wishard and His Servant Fathi* (New York: The Bobbs-Merrill Co., Inc., 1937), which describes life in Iran in the 1920s. There are also two other novels written by two talented missionary ladies, and both discuss family life and the freedom of women in Iran. One is *The Iranian*, by Elizabeth Patton Moss (Philadelphia: Muhlenbuerge Press, 1952), and the other is *The Unveiling*, by Grace Visher Payne (Duarte, California, Westminster Gardens, 1957).

On the lighter side, *The Travels of Hajji Baba of Ispahan*, by James Morier, is always delightful. There are so many editions of this classic in print that it is not necessary to pick a particular one. Alice G. Kelsey, *Once a Mullah* (New York: Longmans, Green and Co., 1954) is a collection of humorous stories and satire on life in Iran. There is also a very intimate and well-written account of the experiences of the English wife of a Persian university professor. Olive Suratgar, *I Sing in the Wilderness* (London: Edward Stanford, 1951).

Pictorial accounts of Iran have appeared from time to time. Two of the most recent ones are A. Costa, *Persia*, with 105 pictures with notes by L. Lockhart (New York: Praeger Publishers, Inc., 1958), and *Iran* (Tehran: Mebso, 1969). The 141 photographs are by Roger Wood, the introduction is by James Morris, and notes on the plates are by Sir Denis Wright, the British Ambassador in Iran. An increasing number of publications, pictorial and otherwise, are issued by the Iranian Tourist Organization in Tehran, Iran.

Index